Illustrating the Gospel of John

Illustrating the Gospel of John

Donald Grey Barnhouse

Fleming H. Revell
A Division of Baker Book House Co
Grand Rapids, Michigan 49516

Published by Fleming H. Revell
a division of Baker Book House Company
P.O. Box 6287, Grand Rapids, MI 49516-6287

New trade paperback edition published 1998

Previously published under the title *The Love Life* by Regal Books

Printed in the United States of America

Library of Congress Cataloging-in-Publication Data

Barnhouse, Donald Grey, 1895–1960.
    [Love life]
    Illustrating the Gospel of John / Donald Grey Barnhouse.—
New trade pbk. ed.
      p.   cm.
    Originally published: The love life. Glendale, Calif. : Regal
Books, 1973.
      ISBN 0-8007-5662-2 (pbk.)
      1. Bible. N.T. John—Commentaries. I. Title.
BS2615.3.B29   1998
226.5'07—dc21   97-38744

Scripture quotations are taken from the following versions:

The King James Version of the Bible.

The Living Bible © 1971. Used by permission of Tyndale House Publishers, Inc., Wheaton, IL 60189. All rights reserved.

NEW AMERICAN STANDARD BIBLE ®. Copyright © The Lockman Foundation 1960, 1962, 1963, 1968, 1971, 1972, 1973. Used by permission.

The New English Bible. Copyright © 1961, 1970, 1989 by The Delegates of Oxford University Press and The Syndics of the Cambridge University Press. Reprinted by permission.

The New Testament in Modern English, copyright J. B. Phillips 1958. Used by permission of the Macmillan Company.

Revised Standard Version of the Bible, copyright 1946, 1952, 1971 by the Division of Christian Education of the National Council of the Churches of Christ in the USA. Used by permission.

For current information about all releases from Baker Book House, visit our web site:
    http://www.bakerbooks.com

Contents

Preface

Donald Grey Barnhouse was one of the most gifted and colorful Bible expositors of the twentieth century. He was also unpredictable, and at times his spur-of-the-moment exegesis brought insight that no amount of library research could have provided.

As editor in chief of *Eternity* magazine, he analyzed the world at large and the Word in depth, which made his magazine a publication that Christian leaders watched and respected.

As the speaker on the *Bible Study Hour* radio broadcast, he surprised the experts by taking twelve years to go verse by verse through Paul's Epistle to the Romans and building an audience rather than losing one over the course of the hundreds of broadcasts.

Six months each year he preached in Philadelphia's historic Tenth Presbyterian Church, which he served for thirty years. Three months were devoted to missionary travel, ministering to faithful workers overseas, and three months were given to itinerant Bible teaching in some of the largest churches in the country. Besides that, he held regular Bible classes midweek in places closer to Philadelphia, such as New York City, Lancaster, and Pittsburgh.

If you wanted to hear Barnhouse at his best, you had to hear him live, unedited, and unexpurgated. That's why this pastoral commentary on the Gospel of John is so unique. It was put together after his death from his Bible teachings at Tenth Presbyterian Church.

Some editing has been done, but unlike his more carefully crafted commentaries, it is "Barnhouse live."

There was always a vivid informality about Dr. Barnhouse's unusual expository ministry. Few men in the English-speaking world have possessed the ability to use illustrations as did this gifted servant of Christ. Anyone who heard a message by Dr. Barnhouse could not forget the thrust of what he was talking about. At times his directness and forceful style irritated some in his audiences, but they never forgot what he said. Literally thousands of Christians were established in the biblical faith by this salty warrior. Ministers, missionaries, and mature lay leaders have gone around the world because of this man's prolific trenchant ministry.

When you connect Barnhouse's illustrative style with the beloved Gospel of John, you have something special. The Gospel of John is different from the other three Gospels. Only in this Gospel do we find the account of the marriage at Cana, Christ's night meeting with Nicodemus, the conversation with the Samaritan woman, the raising of Lazarus, and the washing of the disciples' feet by the Lord himself. Only in John's Gospel do we have some of the longer discourses of Jesus as the Light of the world, the Bread of life, and the Way, the Truth, and the Life.

The purpose of reissuing this delightful commentary on John's Gospel is the same as it has always been: that it be used to help others "believe that Jesus is the Christ, the Son of God" and "in believing . . . they might have life through his name."

William J. Petersen

The Marks of Sonship

The fact that we can call ourselves sons of God is a miracle of God's great love to us. Love that goes upward, from the heart of man to God, is adoration. Love that goes outward, from one heart to another, is affection. But love that stoops is grace, and God stooped to us. This is the most stupendous fact of the universe. It reveals to us that our God is love.

You cannot find love in the forces of nature. There may be plan and determination, order and intelligence, but nothing in the movements of the millions of suns that fleck the universe, nothing that can come within the vision of telescope or microscope, will indicate love. You cannot put love in a test tube. You cannot measure it with a micrometer. You cannot synthesize it or analyze it. Love is not to be found in nature.

Perhaps you think you see love in a calm scene of natural beauty. You stand in the pine forest and listen to the softness of the wind in the branches, a sound broken only by the whir of a bird's wing. Or the smell of the sea comes up on the breeze to swell your heart. But then the wind changes. Clouds drive forward. The thunder roars. Lightning strikes the trees. Hail beats down the flowers. The roaring waves of the sea beat against the shore again and again. Where is the love?

Or maybe you pass down the street and your eye catches the warm light coming from a window. You glance into the room. What a scene of comfort! A father sits in a big chair reading. Children play on the rug before the fire. The mother sits nearby sewing. What a scene of love! Then suddenly the mother rises and touches the cheek of one of the little ones. She glances quickly at the father and speaks to him, with a tone of urgency in her voice. He looks at the child, puts his hand on the feverish forehead and then telephones for a doctor. The doctor comes. . . , and then the undertaker. Where is the love in the forces with which we must contend in the world?

If the universe around us were our only source or hope of love, we would never know that God is love. Even if God altered the stars in their courses, so that instead of forming Orion or the Big Dipper, they spelled out the words "God Loves You" in fiery letters across the sky, still we would have a right to conclude that we were the unfortunate playthings of some fortuitous hazard, the victims of grim impersonal chance.

But God has demonstrated His love. When we were dead in trespasses and sins, He came. "The Word was made flesh, and dwelt among us" (John 1:14).

The word *dwelt* literally suggests putting up a tent, indicative of temporary residence. He "tented" with us for a while. In the Old Testament, God "tented" with man in the temporary Tabernacle in the wilderness. Later, He took up a more permanent residence in the Temple until it was destroyed.

God came in Jesus Christ and "tented" for thirty-three years. When we were dead in our trespasses and sins, He came, taking the form of a servant, being made in the likeness of man. And that was not all. "Being found in fashion as a man, he humbled himself, and became obedient unto death, even the death of the cross" (Phil. 2:8). By this we can know that God is not some far distant, impersonal force. By this I know that God loves me.

What does this loving God expect from those to whom He came? Upon those who believe, God puts two marks of sonship.

The first mark is the right to become a son of God. Many who speak of the Fatherhood of God are either stealing a privilege they know is not theirs, or they have been deceived into believing that they have a privilege which has never been granted to them. We read in John 1:12, "But as many as received him, to them gave he the power to become the sons of God, even to them that believe on his name."

What does it mean—to "receive Him"? The same thing that it means to receive a gift someone offers us—we put out our hand and take the proffered gift. So, when we "receive Christ," we acknowledge that God has given us eternal life. Therefore, acting on this conviction, we take God at His word. We have "power" to become sons of God.

Our word *power* is the English translation of several different Greek words. One of these is *dunamis*, from which we get dynamo, dynamite, dynamic. This word describes that power which manifests itself in mighty works. It is a divinely provided energy that changes lives. The gospel of Jesus Christ is the dynamic power of God unto salvation to everyone that believes. (See Rom. 1:16.) Another word is *kratos*, from which we get autocrat, plutocrat, aristocrat, democrat. This is power which manifests itself in dominion and rule. Neither of these words is used in John 1:12. The word there is *exousia*, meaning authority, or right, or permission. When Jesus overturned the tables of the money-changers, the leaders said, "By what *authority* doest thou these things?" (Mark 11:28). It is the same word. To as many as receive Christ, God has given the *right* and *authority* to become the sons of God.

A schoolteacher in a small Central American village challenged a missionary, "Since God created the race, are we not all His children?"

Looking about the schoolroom the missionary answered, "Who made those benches?"

The teacher replied, "José made them."

"Do you believe that these benches are José's children since he made them?"

"Oh, no!"

"But why don't you?"

"They don't have the life of José in them."

Looking straight at the teacher, the missionary asked, "Do you have the life of God in you?"

It is not true that all men are sons of God. Only those who believe on the Lord Jesus Christ and receive His life become the sons of God. This mark of sonship, the right or authority to be sons of God is the theme of the Gospel of John.

The second mark of sonship is the right to call Him Father. It was not always so. You do not find any suggestions of this privilege in the whole of the Old Testament. Our relationship to God as sons depends upon the work which Christ accomplished at the cross of Calvary.

How different our manner of approach to God from that of believers who lived before Christ came! This fact is not always understood, even by Christians. In 1918, just after the Armistice which ended World War I, a great Bible conference was held in Carnegie Hall in New York City. The minister who opened the session with prayer addressed God in this manner: "O Thou great and terrible God, great is Thy majesty, great is the distance that separates us from Thee! From the abyss of our helpless and lost condition we cry after Thee, guilty sinners that we are! Have mercy upon us, oh, God and . . ." There was much more in the same vein, but about that moment in prayer, one of the Bible teachers on the platform, a dear old man of God, whispered softly to the man next to him, "Why doesn't someone give that man a New Testament?"

We do not need to stand away from God, afraid to approach Him because of the majesty of His holiness. He has preached peace to us who were far off so that we might draw near to Him with full assurance in the righteousness of Jesus Christ. He has told us that we may come boldly to the throne of grace to find strength for help in time of need. (See Heb. 4:16.)

When Christ hung upon the cross, dying in the darkness, there was a great earthquake and the veil of the Temple was torn in two from top to bottom. This act disclosed the holy of holies to the public eye. Till that moment no man, except the high priest, had ever gone behind that veil. He went only once a year on the Day of Atonement and never without having offered a sacrifice for his own sins, and then for the sins of the people. Taking the blood of this second sacrifice he entered the holy of holies behind the veil and sprinkled the blood on the mercy seat. God Himself had ordered this form of worship to teach that He is holy and cannot be approached at will or whim by anyone who desires to approach, or by whatever means the approaching person cares to use.

There is but one way to God, the way that recognizes His holiness and justice. It is the way of sacrifice. It is the way of Jesus Christ, who said, "I am the way, the truth and the life" (John 14:6). Christ made one sacrifice for sins forever. (See Heb. 10:12.) Nothing now stands between the soul and God—no priesthood, no altar, no sacrifice. All have been swept aside for Christ has died. The way is open for us to come boldly to God. No longer need we cry, "O Thou great and terrible God! Great is the distance that separates us from Thee!" Rather we come tenderly as a child comes to his father and cry "Abba, Father!"

What does the word *abba* mean? I once spent a summer in a small city in Greece. In the cool of the evening I sat out in the courtyard of the house and listened to the language of the people, trying to catch a word here and there. A woman called one of the children playing nearby, and as he ran toward her, I heard him say, "Mama." That was the first word of modern Greek that I learned. Then a man came down the street and a little girl ran to him crying, "Abba, Abba!" At that moment I learned my second word in modern Greek. *Abba* is the Greek equivalent of our *Papa* or *Daddy*, the intimate names we give to our own fathers. These terms suggest closeness, familiarity, and informality. And this is the meaning of Romans 8:15,16 where it says, "Ye have received the Spirit of adoption whereby we cry, Abba, Father. The Spirit itself beareth witness with our spirit, that we are the children of God." There, you see, are the two marks of sonship tied together in the same passage.

If *abba* is a Greek word, how then did it get into our English Bible? The translators who produced the King James Version were the best scholars of the seventeenth century. When they read Romans 8:15, "For ye have not received the spirit of bondage again to fear; but ye have received the Spirit of adoption, whereby we cry—" they must have stopped to think about what really belonged there. Everyone of them probably knew the English equivalent of *abba* should be translated Daddy or Papa, but no one dared translate this intimate term. Instead, they created a monstrosity by transliterating *abba*, thereby creating a phrase that is just the opposite of what God desired to convey to His children. When we read that we have received the spirit of adoption, whereby we cry "Abba, Father," the mind trails off, unaccustomed to the very word which is supposed to suggest intimacy with God, and God is removed from us one degree.

But God was seeking to break down barriers between the soul and Himself. The "Word became flesh" in order that enmity might be slain at the cross. When we receive Him, we are reconciled to God by the death of His son. He then puts on us the new robe of spotless righteousness. Eternal life is now begotten in us because of the life of the risen Lord Jesus. As His children, God longs for us to come to Him in the intimacy that exists between fathers and children.

When a father comes home from a day's work and the children run to meet him, he takes them in his arms and carries them the last short distance to the house. The baby toddles ecstatically across the garden walk to meet him. All together they are in one joyous embrace. All this is in the word *abba*.

A child moans restlessly in bed, burning with fever. The father lovingly places his hand upon the forehead and the child faintly whispers, "Daddy!" All this is in the word *abba*.

A teen-ager comes home in shame and humiliation over misconduct. "I didn't mean to do it, Daddy!" The father says, "That's all right, I forgive you." With arms open they embrace each other and their tears are mingled together. All that is found in these words, "Abba, Father."

This implies, of course, none of the flippancy which exists in too many homes today; none of that disrespect which some children show towards their parents. There is none of that know-it-all spirit that leads to lawlessness. When God tells us to address Him as Abba, Father, His Holy Spirit within moves us to speak thus. Such words do not rise from the human heart. The Holy Spirit alone can call us to such grandeur. When we "receive" Jesus Christ, He gives us the authority to be called sons of God and the privilege of addressing God Almighty as Daddy.

He First Found His Brother

The moment a man becomes aware that he has been made alive in Christ, there is the urge to let someone else know about it. That urge is as natural as the cry of the newborn infant. When no such desire to witness occurs, there may be a serious question as to whether a stillbirth has taken place instead of the birth of a living healthy babe in Christ.

One of the most poignant stories of the New Testament is hidden in the simple words which tell how Simon Peter came to Christ. John the Baptist had been preaching in the Jordan Valley. As he stood standing with two of his disciples, Jesus Christ walked by. John said, "Behold the Lamb of God" (John 1:36). "The two disciples heard him say this, and they followed Jesus. Jesus turned and saw them following, and said to them, 'What do you seek?' And they said to Him, 'Rabbi' (which means Teacher), 'where are you staying?' He said to them, 'Come and see.' They came and saw where he was staying; and they stayed with him that day, for it was about the tenth hour.'" (See John 1:37-39.)

One of those who came to Jesus Christ that afternoon was Andrew, Simon Peter's brother. After he had spent time with Jesus, John records that he first found his brother, Simon, and said to him, "We have found the Messiah!" (See John 1:41,42.)

Here we see Andrew witnessing to his brother, landing the big fisherman, even before the Lord Jesus told His disciples that if they would follow Him, He would make them fishers of men. (See Mark 1:16-18.) The Lord has given us this story as an indication of a field of witness that is often overlooked. Many who think they can be used in far fields have never begun where the Lord Jesus meant them to begin—right at home.

It is true that the first generations of believers in many tribes often come straight out of heathenism, generally by the witness of some outsider who has brought the gospel specifically to them. Much of church history is the story of some alien who entered a certain area with little knowledge of the local language and who preached Christ in the power of the Holy Spirit so that people were saved. Paul, the Jew, took the gospel to the people of Asia Minor, to Macedonia and to Greece. Irenaeus, a Greek, was the first to take the good news to Gaul, which is now France. A Latin from Rome was the first missionary to England, while an Englishman, Boniface, first carried the gospel to Germany.

In recent times the list of similar instances covers the world. Henry Martyn took the gospel to Hindustan and Persia, Adoniram Judson went to Burma, Hudson Taylor to China, Mary Slessor to Calabar, Livingstone to Central Africa. And the list goes on today, as we see many organizations all over the world dedicated to proclaiming the gospel to "every creature."

However, these pioneers win but a small portion. The vast majority of those who come to Christ is not won by foreign missionaries, but by home missionaries. The informant who teaches his language to the missionary usually ends up by coming to know the missionary's Saviour. Then he goes and finds his own brother. This is the pattern in countless situations. The God of Abraham becomes the God of Sarah, Abraham's wife. The God of Naomi becomes the God of Ruth. The God of Isaac becomes the God of Jacob.

Household salvation is a precious truth. Charles Spurgeon said, "Though grace does not run in the blood, and regeneration is not of blood nor of birth, yet doth it very frequently"—I was about to say almost always—"happen that God, by means of one of a household draws the rest to Himself. He calls an individual, and then uses him to be a sort of spiritual decoy to bring the rest of the family into the gospel net. Paul said, "Believe on the Lord Jesus, and you will be saved, you and your household"[1] (Acts 16:31).

To witness successfully in the circle where we are best known demands certain conditions. If we meet a stranger and talk with him concerning matters of faith, he has no way of knowing whether or not we are living in conformity with what we are saying. He does not know whether we leave others to do tasks that we should do ourselves. He does not know whether we take overly large portions when others might be hungry. He does not know whether we dawdle in the bathroom while others are waiting. He does not know whether we are quick to defend our proud sensibilities. In short, he has no idea whether or not our life is centered in self or in the Christ of whom we are speaking.

But a brother knows. A brother knows all about our personal habits and idiosyncrasies. He knows when we are being real and when we are not. He knows what upsets us. He knows where we are weak. And if he hears us talk in flowery language about new life and accepting Jesus, but sees no changes in the way we act at home, he will erect defensive barriers against us and our witness of Jesus Christ.

In order to have an effective witness, to those in our own household, therefore, we must allow Christ to become Lord of the inmost self. They will be attracted to Christ when they cannot miss the transformation, the obvious presence of new life.

In the first epistle of John, the beloved disciple explains the nature of true Christian witness. We read in 1 John 1: "That which was from the beginning, which we have heard, which we have seen with our eyes, which we have looked upon and touched with our hands, concerning the word of life—the life was made manifest, and we saw it, and testify to it, and proclaim to you the eternal life which was with the Father and was made manifest to us—that which we have seen and heard we proclaim also to you . . ."¹ (1 John 1:1-3).

This is what we must do if we are to be true witnesses. When Andrew and the other disciple met Jesus at the tenth hour—four o'clock in the afternoon—they spent the night at His place. What did they talk about until suppertime? What were their thoughts as they saw, for the first time, Christ lifting His eyes to heaven and thanking the Father for the bread which He broke for them? How did they spend the evening? What Scripture did He bring to their minds as they talked together? How late did they stay up talking of spiritual things?

It is not astonishing to me that there is no record of what happened that night. Such things cannot be set down in human language. The nearest thing to it in the Word of God is that spoken by the disciples on the road to Emmaus, after the Lord vanished from their supper table: "Did not our hearts burn within us while he talked to us on the road, while he opened to us the scriptures?"¹ (Luke 24:32). Such experiences must be the prelude to spiritual power. If you pass through such unspeakable glories you will be able to go out and find your brother.

Have you ever talked with Jesus Christ for a whole evening? Oh, I tell you the truth—I know what it is to sit at my typewriter with my Bible beside me and my books around me, and to listen for His voice and hear the tones of love and to feel my heart swelling until I didn't think I could contain any more. A thousand times I have known it thus, and only when the body becomes cramped or cold does my eye turn to the clock and I realize, with a start, that the night is long gone toward morning. And after such a night, one is constrained to go out and find his brother. Notice that when Andrew first went to Simon he did not begin with a theological exhortation or with an apologetic argument. He did not invite Simon to a religious ceremony. He testified of a fact that he had seen, and he invited his brother to participate in the experience that he himself had been through. He just simply said, "We've found the Messiah." Then he brought him to Jesus.

Throughout his Gospel, John also conveys the direct reality of his own experience with Christ by repeatedly using verbs to reveal his inmost heart: "We have heard Him"; "We have seen Him with our eyes"; "We have looked upon Him"; "We touched Him with our hands"; "We saw that life"; "We have seen Him"; "We have heard Him." He uses seven different verbs, showing the involvement of three of the five senses, to describe his personal involvement with Christ.

In addition to one of the common Greek verbs for seeing, there is a second verb that describes a close and meditative scrutiny. This is the verb used in the first chapter of John 1:14 when he writes, "We beheld his glory. . . ." Christ used the same verb when He said, "Lift up your eyes, and see how the fields are already white for harvest"[1] (John 4:35). We cannot touch Jesus as He bade Thomas and the other disciples to do. But we can see Him—we can see Him with the eyes of the Spirit, and we can hear His voice in the Word, and in the tones and longings that the Spirit brings to the ears of our hearts. And with all our heart and soul and mind we can contemplate Him, meditating on the wonder of His being, thinking of who He is, remembering what He has done for us, realizing the nature of the spiritual blessings which He has promised us.

When I was a student I had to fill out a report sheet of work done, of hours studied, of the number of Gospels or Testaments distributed, the number of people witnessed to and, God forgive us, the number of decisions brought about. I once met a fellow student rushing out late one Saturday evening. When I asked him where he was going, he replied that he was going over to the park nearby, to do some "personal work" so he could get the quota he had set for himself.

Looking back on that now, I can understand why many of those converts soon became victims of backsliding. There had been no true contact between the worker and Christ. Nor was there any true contact between the heart of the worker and the one to whom the so-called witness was given. Consequently, there was no contact between the needy one and the Lord Himself. In fact, the student preparing for Christian work was more needy than the vagrant in the park. For at least the vagrant knew he was needy, while the student thought he had arrived at a level of spiritual maturity.

When you have spent time with Jesus Christ, and when you have been to your brother, then you can think seriously of going farther afield. If you are not able to bring men to Christ from your own environment, you will not be able to reach them in Africa or South America. Crossing the ocean has never made a missionary out of anyone. Christ defined the term *neighbor* by telling the story of the Good Samaritan. I believe He would define the term *brother* by pointing to the man who lives nearest to us. Our fellowman is to be the recipient of the love of Christ through our hearts and the touch of Christ through our hands.

It is not selfish, however, for someone to seek most earnestly the salvation of his own loved ones. If charity begins at home, so, most certainly, must the love of souls. Those who live under our roof have special claims upon us. Spurgeon said of this, "God has not reversed the laws of nature, but He has sanctified them by the rules of grace; it augurs nothing of selfishness that a man should first seek to have his own kindred saved. I'll give nothing for your love for the wide world, if you have not a special love for those of your own household. The rule of Paul may, with a little variation, be applied here; we are to 'do good to all men, but especially to such as be of the household of faith.' And so we are to seek the good of all mankind, but especially of those who are of our own near kindred. Let Abraham's prayer be for Ishmael, let Hannah pray for Samuel, let David plead for Absalom and Solomon, let Andrew first find his own brother Simon, and Eunice train her son Timothy. Oh, they will be nonetheless large and prevalent in their pleadings for others, because they were mindful of those allied to them by ties of blood."

The Life of the Party

The event covered by this chapter centers about a wedding, a festive occasion in the city of Cana of Galilee. Cana was a small village about ten miles west of the Sea of Galilee where two of Jesus' miracles were performed—the healing of the nobleman's son (see John 4:46-54) and the turning of water into wine. (See John 2:1-11.) Cana was also the home of Nathanael. (See John 21:2.)

Two suggested sites may be identified with Cana of biblical times. One is *Khirbet Kana*, about eight miles north of Nazareth. (The word *Khirbet* means ruins.) The other possible site of ancient Cana is *Kefr Kenna*, much nearer Nazareth among the fertile hills on the main highway. This latter place is probably the true Cana. It has an ample water supply of springs, as well as shady fig trees, such as the one where Jesus first saw Nathanael. (See John 1:48.)

One of the important things we learn from this story is that our Lord was no recluse nor killjoy. We sometimes think of Him as only "the man of sorrows." He was that in the light of the incalculable burden He bore as the world's Redeemer. Yet, our Lord must also have been a popular dinner guest, who loved to mingle with people and enjoy their fellowship. That He was so often invited into homes, that young children seemed to love to be near Him, indicates His pleasant personality. He was no gloomy, morose person.

His presence at this wedding at Cana points to His warm, friendly humanity. For, although Jesus Christ was God, He was also man. Here we see Him as Lord of relaxation as well as Lord of work. John the Baptist and his disciples fasted, but Christ was accused of being "a man gluttonous, and a winebibber." (See Matt. 11:19.) It is but another example of the Word being made flesh and dwelling among us.

Writing about this very idea, someone has said, "Selfishness, bad in nature, is worse in religion. The dream of every religion but the Christian was monasticism. Even Christianity has relapsed into it literally, and also morally in the selfishness which marks out certain persons, phrases, recreations as signs of a world lying in wickedness. Far less difficult would Christian duty be if we might quit the world and have done with it, but we cannot and we dare not. This parable of our Master's life shows us this.

"Let the disciples now take the Master with them (into their social life, their business life, etc.). For some this may be irksome. They either go without Christ, or else stay away. The former is sinful, the latter faithless."

Jewish marriage customs in Jesus' day called for a betrothal or "engagement" period of not more than a year prior to the marriage consummation. The prospective bridegroom would present—either in person or by messenger—a letter to the bride-to-be, signifying his intention of marriage. The letter might also be accompanied by a monetary gift.

From the moment of betrothal, both parties were considered as married, although they did not live together till the actual ceremony. But any infidelity on the part of either partner would be looked upon as adultery. The betrothal, and the marriage, could only be dissolved by formal divorce proceedings.

Before the marriage ceremony, the pious would often fast, confessing their sins. Entrance into the married state was considered almost a sacrament, and the symbolism suggesting the relationship of husband and bride, God and His people, was not overlooked.

On the eve of the marriage, lavish preparations were made by friends of the couple. A great wedding feast was held—as much as could be afforded —prepared by the women of the community. The bride, surrounded by her friends and the "friends of the bridegroom," was led from her house, to that of her husband. When she stood before her husband, a sacred formula was read: "take her according to the Law of Moses." A formal document—the *Kethubah* —was then signed and the marriage ceremony was over.

After a ritual washing of hands the supper was begun. Such a feast might last one day or more—

depending upon how long the food lasted and interest was sustained.

Such was the wedding to which Jesus was invited with His disciples: Andrew, Peter, Philip, Nathanael, James and John. Mary, Jesus' mother, living in nearby Nazareth, probably was present as a friend of the bridal couple and a helper in preparing the feast.

We may wonder why the wine supply gave out so quickly. Apparently, this had not been anticipated, for the anxiety in Mary's statement can be sensed: "They have no wine." Why did she come to Jesus? It was the responsibility of the steward of the feast to see to it that the supplies did not run out.

Jesus fully intended to take action, but He wanted it clearly understood by Mary that she was not to assume the role of mediatrix or intercessor with Him.

That is why He said to her, "Woman, what have I to do with thee? mine hour is not yet come." Now this phrase in English sounds difficult, almost as though it were a degrading term, but it was not so in that day. It was the equivalent to the French *Madam*, and he spoke to her with respect, but simply meant, "What have we in common? I am the God-man; you are but human." In other words, "You are never to presume upon your earthly relationship." From this moment forward, Mary was to bear in mind her new role as completely subservient to Jesus Christ.

The idea that anyone can go to the Virgin Mary and get something from Christ, that they could not get by going to Him directly, is the equivalent of saying, "Dear tender-hearted Virgin Mary, I tried to get something from your hardhearted son and couldn't make the grade and I'd like you to use a little pull for me." This is totally alien from the Bible. It comes from mother-son ideas prevalent in pagan religions. By accepting His rebuke and directing the servants to do whatever Jesus told them, Mary showed her understanding of what Jesus had said.

A word is in order about the wine used at the wedding feast. Was it fermented? Many believe it was! The process of keeping grape juice from fermenting dates from Louis Pasteur. In the warm climate of Palestine the juice would have fermented very quickly.

Of course, this does not mean that our Lord condones drunkenness. Wine was a staple drink in oriental lands where the water supply was contaminated. Everyone drank it, usually diluted to make it last longer.

The writer of the book of Proverbs said: "Look not thou upon the wine when it is red . . ." (Prov. 23:31). This was undiluted wine—red, not pink as when mixed with water—and dangerous for prolonged imbibing.

What, exactly, was the nature of the wine Jesus provided? We do not know. But that it was real wine, and not just "grape juice," there can be no doubt. The "steward of the feast" (v. 9)—a skilled wine-taster—sampled it, and pronounced it the best wine served thus far.

The Jewish religion had become more and more

external by the time Christ had come, but this miracle symbolizes what Christ came to do—transform the old externalism into a new vitality of the spirit.

The water pots were used for outward cleansing. In fact, they were probably large massive stone basins holding twenty to sixty gallons of water each, which stood in most houses for foot-washing after guests came in from the dusty roads. But Jesus transformed the water that stood for outward cleansing into wine for inward assimilation. Christ came to clean up the inside of a man.

We may not know just when the miracle of water into wine took place. Was it in the pouring of the water into the stone jars? Or, at the drawing out of the water was it made wine? It is not important! The simple fact was that the miracle was performed which saved the day for the host and hostess—and helped to spread the fame of Jesus far and wide.

Note that the governor of the feast did not know where the wine came from. You know, I'd rather be a servant and know where the wine came from than be governor and not know where it came from. A Christian has a better idea of what could happen in the next hundred years than anyone in Congress or the United Nations. Neither the average man-in-the-street nor the prominent political leader knows the plan of God. He doesn't know about the second coming of Christ. He doesn't know the prophecies. Amos 3:7 says, "Surely the Lord God will do nothing, but he revealeth his secret unto his servants the prophets." I'd rather be a servant and know the plan of God than be governor and not know the plan of God.

In verse 11, we find a significant phrase, "This beginning of miracles Jesus did in Cana of Galilee." This is important because it simply rules out numerous traditions about Jesus' early life. Back in the early centuries, many people wrote pseudo-gospels telling fantastic stories about the boyhood of Jesus. In one story, the boy Jesus is playing with some companions. One of them throws a stone and hits a playmate in the neck, accidentally killing him. Jesus stops the game, goes over and raises him from the dead, and then they all go on playing. In one of the other gospels, the Jordan River catches on fire when Jesus was baptized.

"Well," someone says, "how do we know these things didn't happen?" "This beginning of miracles . . ." God had safeguarded the reputation of His Son by telling the time and the place of the first miracle of Jesus' public ministry.

Water could not take the place of wine at the wedding feast. When touched by the power of God, the six pots, symbols of human inadequacy, were changed from the ordinary to the extraordinary. The result of this miracle was that the disciples "believed in Him." And that is the response that John would have us take too. Today, He waits for us to share our needs with Him. He waits to provide His strength in our areas of weakness. He waits to bring joy and abundance to our lackluster, humdrum lives.

One of the biggest hindrances in our prayer life is our unwillingness to let God do things His way. Mary's desires were first rebuffed, but after she told the servants, "Whatsoever He saith unto you, do it," there was divine action.

"Yes, I believe in prayer," a rough old sailor admitted at the mission. "But my old mother once heard me praying and told me: 'Son, don't bother to give God instructions; just report for duty.'"

In those simple words lies the secret to real power in prayer—and lasting change in lives.

Understanding New Birth

By any man's list, John 3 and John 4, put side by side, are two of the great passages of the Bible. Chapter 3 is about a man, chapter 4 is about a woman. Chapter 3 took place at night, chapter 4 took place at noon. Chapter 3 has to do with a ruler, chapter 4 with a prostitute. The ruler is a Jew, the prostitute is a Samaritan. She believed in Jesus. We have no knowledge whether Nicodemus is in heaven or not. He heard great preaching, but there is no word at all of his immediate reaction to it. It is a tremendous story.

How happy Christ must have been in the conversation with Nicodemus to realize that Nicodemus had real understanding of some spiritual truths. We all like to be understood. No one likes to give thought and effort to an explanation only to hear a question that shows our hearer has totally misunderstood us.

Nicodemus, a ruler of the Jews, had come to Jesus by night with a question. He was aware of the work that Jesus was doing. As a thinking man he had verified the reports that were going around concerning the works of the Lord Jesus, he had become convinced intellectually of the supernatural reality of these works. "Rabbi," he addressed the Lord Jesus, "we know that thou art a teacher come from God, for no man can do these miracles that thou doest, except God be with him" (John 3:2).

But in saying, "We know you are a teacher come from God," Nicodemus betrayed one basic misunderstanding. You see, Jesus was not a "teacher come from God," but God come to teach. There have been thousands of teachers come from God—Moses, Isaiah, Paul, the disciples, Luther, Calvin, Augustine. Many men today are teachers come from God. But only once did God come to teach. It is not enough to believe that Jesus was the best of mankind, that He was a "good teacher," but to believe that He is God manifest in the flesh.

There are times when the longest way round is the quickest way home and Jesus took that way. He did not start to discuss the question of His deity. He went to the heart of the matter and said to Nicodemus, "Verily, verily, I say unto thee, Except a man be born again, he cannot see the kingdom of God" (John 3:3).

Here is the place where Nicodemus showed that a flash of spiritual truth had reached his heart, and that he was being awakened by the Spirit of God to true understanding. Thousands of people today, if they were told that they must be born again, would answer, "Well, *why* must I be born again? What is wrong with me as I am? Did I not come into this world without my consent, and have I not made a pretty good job of my life? Why should God require anything supernatural of me? I have lived a good life. I pay my debts. I am faithful to the duties imposed upon me by family, society and state. Why should a man have to be born again?"

But Nicodemus was not so thickheaded. There was a flash of real spiritual vision that shows the presence of the enlightening Spirit of God. The answer of Nicodemus was *"How* can a man be born when he is old? Can he enter the second time into his mother's womb and be born?" Nicodemus would certainly have challenged the Lord's statement unless he had understood the necessity of the new birth. The fact that he asked as to the method carries with it a belief in the need for such a work.

A great many leaders in the religious world would answer Christ differently, if they had an opportunity to speak with Him. Many theological professors would attempt to argue the matter out with God and would seek to convince Him that He was quite mistaken. The retired president of one of the most influential theological seminaries of the country wrote about the need for new birth. He said, "the doctrine of divine imminence, which is now generally accepted among liberals, ascribes divinity to man, since it is supposed that man's nature is one with God's and he needs simply to awake to that fact. This means, of course," this theologian concluded, "a revolution in the old conception of salvation. What a man requires is not regeneration in the old sense, or a change of nature, but simply an awakening to what he really is."

Many denials of Christ's claim that man must be regenerated, do not alter the facts. Man is today, what he always has been. If man does not understand the necessity of the new birth, it is because he has failed to understand the holiness of God and the real nature of man in his sinful condition.

We read in the book of Job, "How then can man be justified with God? or how can he be clean that is born of a woman? Behold even to the moon, and it shineth not; yea, the stars are not pure in his sight. How much less man, that is a worm?" (Job 25:4-6).

Man must be brought to realize the truth of the statement of the Lord Jesus, "That which is born of the flesh is flesh." (See John 3:6.) What the individual heart needs today is to realize the vast distance that separates us from God and to know that that distance has been bridged only in one place, at the cross of Calvary where the Lord Jesus Christ took our place and paid the price of our redemption that we might have eternal life through His blood.

It does not suffice merely that a man should say that God is his Father. There is no more dangerous lie in existence today than that which is being so widely circulated under the phrase "the universal fatherhood of God." There is not one verse in the Bible that could teach for a moment that God is the Father of all men. The sheer presumption of those who claim sonship with God without any regard for His permission, or His holy claims, is unparalleled in the history of man's rebellion against God.

The man who lies about his social position or his financial connections in order to gain money is sent away to prison or obtaining money under false pretenses. He is not half so guilty as the one who would stand before men and say that all men are brothers and that God is the Father of all.

If you were walking down some important street in the midst of great crowds, and should see a dirty beggar child holding out his hand toward you, your heart would be moved to pity. But if the child kept running after you and called out to you, "Mother," or "Father," when you had never seen the child before, you would be stirred to a righteous indignation.

What right would that child have to attract attention to you and turn the gaze of all the passers-by from the child's filth to you? The desire of a child can not create a parental relationship. The choice of the parents must bring this relationship.

If you go to the child in the street and lead him to your home, give him new cleanliness and new clothing, and adopt him into your family, then he has the right to call you father, and the law will recognize that right. But the right and authority must be given by you.

In the divine relationship God has made full provision for sonship. If we are to become sons of God, the first step is realizing that we are not sons of God, and cannot be except through the channel which He Himself has opened up to us through Christ. We must not forget what He said to those who claimed, "We have one father, even God." That was a false claim. His answer to it was, "I speak that which I have seen with my Father: and ye do that which ye have seen with your father. . . . If God were your Father, ye would love me" (John 8:38,42).

The touchstone of sonship is the love of the individual heart for the Lord Jesus Christ. Men must not claim that they love Him unless they accept His claims. How can a man claim that he loves Christ and at the same time seek to pull Him down to the level of a common humanity, attempting to prove Him a liar as to His claims to deity?

In *A Guide to the Study of the Christian Religion,* a late professor in the University of Chicago wrote this about the need for new birth: "One may say that not supernatural regeneration but natural growth, not divine sanctification but human education, not supernatural grace but natural morality, not the divine expiation of the cross, but the human heroism—or accident?—of the cross . . . not Christ the Lord, but the man Jesus who was a child of His time; not God and His providence, but evolution and its process without an absolute goal—that all this, and such as this, is the new turn in the affairs of religion at the tick of the clock."

Now with this in mind, listen to the Lord Jesus Christ, "If God were your Father, ye would love Me." The man who talks about the fatherhood of God and then speaks of Jesus as being a child of His time shows clearly that he himself comes under the stigma of the Lord, when He says, "Why do ye not understand my speech? Even because ye cannot hear my Word. Ye are of your father the devil, and the lusts of your father ye will do: he was a murderer from the beginning, and abode not in the truth, because there is no truth in him. When he speaketh a lie, he speaketh of his own: for he is a liar, and the father of it" (John 8:43,44).

We read in His Word that we are "born again, not of corruptible seed, but of incorruptible, by the word of God, which liveth and abideth forever" (1 Pet. 1:23). If we are to have the proper understanding of all that God means we must hold in our minds that the new birth is given to us as an analogy with physical birth. We are familiar with the biological processes by which we exist in the world today. We know precisely that we are alive physically as the result of the union of two life seeds—which union caused the beginning of the growth of our bodies. God takes this wonderful mystery of life and parallels it very closely in His story of regeneration. You have received your body from your father and your mother; you have inherited characteristics that are the marks of that union.

God says that we are born again with a different kind of life seed. The first was corruptible and we have inherited the decay that is in our being and which ultimately carries man to the grave. Now, says God, the new birth is indeed a new life, but it comes from an incorruptible seed. This is the Word of God. This Word goes into the womb of the heart where faith lays hold upon it. By this contact of faith and the Word there comes forth a new life. It is as real as physical life. It is entirely different from physical life. It is eternal life. It is spiritual life. It is abundant life. By this union of the Word and faith within our hearts we have become sons of God.

That is what Jesus was pointing out to Nicodemus when He said, "Truly, truly, I say to you, unless one is born of water and the Spirit *(hudatos kai pneumatos)*, he cannot enter the Kingdom of God." Now, the wording, "of water and the Spirit," is a very unfortunate translation in most Bible versions. In the Greek there are two words here. One is a form of *hudor*, the common Greek word for water. You see it in *hydromatic, hydroelectric, hydrophobia*, all of which are Greek words combining forms that have to do with water. The other is *pneuma*, the Greek word for wind, which you know in *pneumonia* and *pneumatic*. Now literally, it reads, "Except a man be born of water and wind. . . ." The translators took the Greek word for water and translated it into the English word *water*, but they took the Greek word for wind, interpreted it, and translated it *Spirit*.

This is one of several illustrations in the Gospel of John where Jesus used physical illustrations to show spiritual truths. In John 2, He said, "Destroy this temple and in three days I will raise it." He was talking about resurrection and they were talking about masonry and brick. Here in John 3 He talks about supernatural life, and Nicodemus' mind is in the delivery room. In John 4, Jesus talks about the water of life, and the woman thinks of H_2O and the depth of the well.

So when He mentions water to Nicodemus, He means the Word of God. The likeness is given because of the cleansing power of the Word. (See Psalm 119:9; John 15:3; Eph. 5:26.) Actually, no one is ever born again apart from some contact with the Word of God—spoken or written. We are thus born into God's kingdom by the Word of God. (See James 1:18; 1 Peter 1:23.)

And when He refers to wind, He means Spirit, as we see in John 4:24, "God is Spirit, and those who worship him must worship in spirit and truth."¹ With this interpretation in mind, the verse reads, "Except a man be born of the Word of God and the Spirit of God, he cannot enter the Kingdom of God."

The Holy Spirit's part in this new birth process was covered by Jesus' illustration in John 3. He said, "When you hear the sound of the wind blowing, when you see the branches of trees stirring as the wind blows do you know where the wind comes from? Where is it going? You see its effect, but can not tell its source. So is every one who is born of the Holy Spirit." (See John 3:8.)

The Holy Spirit effects the new birth—regenerates the individual. We may see the effect of the Holy Spirit's ministry, but we may not understand the method or source of the new birth.

Nicodemus did not seem to understand this. It was strange and new to him. Groping for words to express himself, he said: "How can this be?" And Jesus answered: "Art thou a master of Israel, and knowest not these things? . . . If I have told you earthly things, and ye believe not, how shall ye believe, if I tell you of heavenly things?" (John 3:10,12).

In simple language, Jesus told this religious leader that if he did not appropriate or apply the simple truths Jesus gave him, it was useless for Him to offer more advanced truth. It would be just as fool-

43

ish to put a child who has not mastered first-grade arithmetic in an advanced algebra class.

God does not force more light on those who are not interested in advancing. But He *does* make available all the depths of Christian truth to the hungry, eager heart.

The core of teaching on the new birth is found in the account of Jesus Christ and His death for sinners. Jesus used, as His closing illustration before Nicodemus, the Old Testament story of the bronze serpent raised up on a pole in the camp of Israel, and likened it to His own elevation on the cross.

The Old Testament story (found in Numbers 21:4-9) tells of the complaints and impatience of the Israelites. God tired of their constant murmuring, and sent serpents into the camp to bite the people and many of the people became ill and died.

The survivors cried out for mercy and God offered His remedy. "Make thee a fiery serpent, and set it upon a pole: . . . every one that is bitten, when he looketh upon it, shall live" (Num. 21:8). Moses fashioned a serpent out of bronze and did as God said. And, as the ailing populace looked in faith to the elevated serpent, they were healed.

However silly this might have seemed to them, these were the directions of God. So, man the sinner, bitten and infected with the venom of sin, is not to concoct spiritual lotions for sin. He is not to find relief from sin by humanitarian gestures. He will gain no help by seeking to fight sin in the energy of the flesh. He cannot pay God for redemption or "reconsecrate himself to God." He will pray ever so fervently—in vain, if he prays in his own wisdom. And if he looks at religious leaders or engages in self-examination, he will be no nearer salvation. For God has established only one way of redemption. Look to the cross on which Christ died. See Him there as substitute, Saviour and friend.

Many Bible scholars believe that the rest of this chapter contains John's commentary on Jesus' remarks. The well-known and much-loved John 3:16 is found in our text. Frequently, we misinterpret this text. This text is not speaking of the magnitude of quantity of God's love, but of its special *quality*. Literally, "in such a way, God loved the world, that He gave . . ."

Not all "love" is *giving* love. There is much that goes by the title of "love" which is desire, lust or passion. But God's love had an intelligent, giving quality that was willing to share heaven's finest with sinful man in order to provide redemption.

We give so much attention to John 3:16 that we sometimes forget that a few verses further on the clear statement of the condition of the unbeliever is found. "He that believeth on him is not condemned: but he that believeth not is condemned already."

This shows the fallacy of those who say, "If you don't believe in Jesus, you *will be* lost." Nonsense! If you don't believe in Jesus, you are *already lost*. And you will stay lost until you put your faith in Jesus Christ as Lord and Saviour.

The basis of God's judgment is found in verse 19. We have already referred to this in part in an earlier lesson. God sent light into the world, and "men loved darkness rather than light, because their deeds were evil" (v. 19).

Everyone must face this basis of judgment. Light has come in Jesus Christ. God's searching light on our lives is not always pleasant, but it is for our correction. Let us not become offended at a lesson or at a sermon that speaks to us, but rather let us ask the Holy Spirit of God to rearrange our lives accordingly.

When a housewife was scolded because of the untidiness of her house, she responded, "I am sure the rooms would be clean enough if it were not for the nasty sun; it's always showing the dirty corners." Similarly we often get irritated with God's Word because it shows us our sin.

Ahab had 400 false prophets in whom he delighted, but the true prophet Micaiah (1 Kings 22:8) he hated: "for he doth not prophesy good concerning me, but evil."

Men love the state of darkness. Their works are malicious. They practice worthless living. They hate the light. They refuse to come to the light. They fear exposure. This is a terrible indictment of the unregenerate heart of man. (See Jer. 17:9.) Yet, this is exactly what God sees in the life of the sinner who repudiates the grace of God.

It was such a world that God loved. And you and I are a part of that world. His grace sent Jesus Christ into the world, not to condemn, but to redeem. The price was incalculable for the Son of God. But the offer of free salvation is ours, because "Jesus paid it all!"

"Come See a Man . . . !"

One is almost overwhelmed these days with the sense of the need of the human race. Round about us we find men and women whose hearts are failing them for fear. One of the leading surgeons of the country has pointed out in an address before the convention of the American College of Surgeons that more than half of all hospital beds are now occupied by mental cases. Great numbers who are not mentally sick enough to be in institutions are passing through nervous breakdowns. Myriads of others are haunted with fear and despair.

A greater burden of responsibility rests upon the true Christian today than at any time within our generation. While there has been no change in the cause of world conditions, there is an ever increasing number of people who are willing to admit that they have need. We who have passed out of darkness into light and from death unto life know we have the remedy that can meet the need of men and women today. A most solemn obligation is upon us to speak to those round about us words which will bring the light of God to focus upon the need of those we meet.

There is a wonderful story in the Gospel of John which teaches us lessons that are most fitting for our time. It is the story of the Lord Jesus Christ and the woman who came to Jacob's well to draw water. In this story there is something for the Christian and something for the non-Christian. There is that which can give release from worry and that which can set on fire for service of others. Above all, it pictures the entrance of eternal life into the human being so that we can be possessed, here and now, by a power and a presence more wonderful than any thrill which life can give.

The Lord Jesus Christ is the center of the picture. Though other characters come upon the scene they shine with no light except that which is reflected from Him. The woman herself would never have been known to another generation had it not been for this passing conversation, but because of this contact with Him she enters that class of which Daniel the prophet spoke, "They that be wise shall shine as the brightness of the firmament; and they that turn many to righteousness, as the stars for ever and ever" (Dan. 12:3).

Our Lord was on a trip from Jerusalem to Galilee. John 4:4 tells us He had to pass through Samaria. Actually, He didn't have to do anything of the kind, geographically speaking, because there were two other routes from Judea to Galilee. Most often He took the other routes, but this time He had to pass through Samaria. That's like saying that a G.I. from Korea landed in San Francisco on his way to Philadelphia, but he "had to" go through Miami, Florida. There are shorter routes, but you see, his fiancee was there. Then we understand why he "had to" go through Miami. Now in exactly the same way, Jesus had to go through Samaria because before the foundation of the world, God knew there were people in that town who would be saved. That's why Jesus had to pass that way.

He came, with His disciples, to a little village named Sychar. The road they were traveling on ran down through the valley. The village itself was up on the hill where the inhabitants could find better protection from the dangers of those days. Since there was no water in the village, every day the inhabitants took the 45-minute walk down the rocky path to the age-old well that still flows today, and from which men still drink.

There is, just here in the story, one of those little touches which shows the real humanity of our Lord. He was tired. He sat down by the well to rest from His weariness while the disciples climbed the steep path to the village in order to procure provisions for the noon meal.

At this moment there came to the well a woman of the village, bearing a waterpot upon her shoulder. Proceeding to draw water from the well, she was surprised by the voice of Jesus, asking her to give Him a drink. She was surprised because the Jews looked down upon the Samaritans and had no dealings with them at all. She was also surprised because very probably no man had spoken to her like a gentleman for a long, long, time. She was the village harlot. She was used to wisecracks and dirty digs.

So when the woman expressed her amazement that He, being a Jew, should ask a drink of her, an outcast Samaritan, Jesus answered that it was because of who He was. "If thou knewest the gift of God, and who it is that saith unto thee, Give me to drink; thou wouldst have asked of him, and he would have given thee living water" (John 4:10).

Are there any words more poignant than those of the Saviour as He speaks to this woman? "If thou knewest . . ." These are words that came to us in our day with unparalleled force. "If thou knewest . . ." There are some who have read the accounts of suicides and wished that they might have courage to take the step which they thought might be the end of present misery. "If thou knewest . . ." Christ speaks this word to you today.

You may have lost everything you had so that you must take a small place in a community where. you were once a leader. You may have used your last savings and not know where money will come from to buy tomorrow's bread. The Lord Jesus meets you now, just where you are, and says to you, "If you only knew the gift of God. If you only knew all that I am willing to do for you and in you, if you will give Me the chance! I will give you living water that shall be all life to you."

When the Bible says "water," in nine verses out

of ten, it does not mean H_2O. What a terrible thing to try to make "water" mean H_2O when it means the Word of God or salvation. The woman said to him, "Sir, you've nothing to draw with." You see, her mind was on H_2O and the well was deep. She did not yet understand.

This shows the heart of humanity. God comes offering a great gift and we begin to measure God by our methods of doing things. If people would stop trying to limit God, much greater blessing would come upon them. She saw merely the deepness of the well, the lack of a container, and asked, almost sarcastically, if Jesus were greater than Jacob, who had dug the well.

Do not expect to be rebuffed by the Lord if you come to Him with a doubt. If you are honest He will meet your need. What He will not tolerate is that you should use doubts as a cloak for sin. But where there is an honest doubt He will meet it. The woman had wondered about the water that He offered and had expressed the difficulties as she saw them. Then He made the promise stronger. Jesus said to her, "Everyone who drinks of this H_2O will thirst again, but whosoever drinks of the supernatural water (the Word of God, the divine salvation) that I shall give him will never thirst. The water that I shall give him will become in him a spring of water welling up to eternal life." (See vv. 13,14.)

We have been going to all the springs of earth and have drunk deep, but always we have thirsted again. Some men have drained a cup at the well of riches, others have drawn water from fame, honor, pleasure. Some have even sought satisfaction at the

51

wells of lust, or have drunk the exciting waters of crime, but no man has ever been fully satisfied with the products of earth's streams. But what a promise is this from the lips of the Lord Jesus! The believer shall have a new life. This new life shall be a continuing spring and it shall never run dry.

The woman still has her mind on earthly things and she thinks, "I've just walked downhill and it took me forty-five minutes and I'm going to take an hour to walk back uphill and this round trip every day is two hours. Now if I had running water in the house this would save me a lot of steps. Plumbing is the answer." She was not ready to receive this living spring. Her idea of it was still on the plane of selfishness, and there was no thought of the cost to the giver. So she said to Him, "Sir, give me this water, that I may not thirst nor come here to draw" (v. 15). Now when a person is stupid like that, what are you going to do? You've got to put your finger on the fact that they're sinners. "Woman," He said, "Go call thy husband." Now this was her sin. If he was talking to some men, He'd say, "Go and get your income tax form and let me see it." Or He might say something else that covers your particular sin and relationship to the Lord.

What will be her answer to this question? For He is revealing His deity and showing her that He knows the thoughts of her heart and the actions of her life. She is forced to respond that she has no husband. Forced, I say, for immediately the Lord shows her the extent of His knowledge. "Thou hast well said, I have no husband: For thou hast had five husbands; and he whom thou now hast is not thy husband: in that saidst thou truly." (See vv. 17,18.)

So to you today the Lord speaks, offering living water, springing up within you. But if your heart is to receive the gift of this eternal spring you must first admit your sinfulness before the Lord. There are some who may be low in sin as men count their standards. There are some who may be high. But pride is as bad in the sight of a holy God as adultery, and murder can be forgiven where God will not receive the one who rejects the atoning value in the death of Jesus Christ.

The woman is confused. Here a stranger surprised her by engaging her in conversation and has kept the talk on a level which she had never known before. He had made wonderful promises and then, suddenly, had told her the secret thoughts and actions of her life.

She knows already that this is no ordinary man. So she takes the first step saying, "Sir, I perceive that Thou art a prophet."

This is what is known as a red herring across the trail to try to get the subject changed as fast as possible. Brother, he has just made it hot for her and she is taking recourse in theology. Theology is very, very frequently the first recourse of the person who is convicted of sin. You talk to people about their souls and they say, "Oh, tell me, what do you believe about evolution." They will twist away like a game trout and will do all they can to avoid the definite approach to their own need. Men are quite willing to listen to talk about the sins of the social order or about men of old; but if you come down to the penetrating "Thou art the man," they seek to avoid the implications of that declaration which is intended only to bring them over into the place where God can bless them.

But the Lord used even the theological argument to bring out further truth for her. She had said, that since He must be a prophet, she would like to know His opinion about the age-long controversy between Jew and Samaritan concerning the place of worship. Was it in reality at Jerusalem as the Jews claimed, or upon the nearby mountain as the Samaritans contended? He was very true to the Scriptures in His answer, and yet He found it possible to bring the subject back from the by-path of a theological discussion.

He pointed out that the time was soon coming when men would no longer be required to worship God with any geographical restrictions. Worship was to be taken away from temples made with hands into the inner sanctuaries of men's hearts. Her fathers had indeed been wrong and she was worshiping in ignorance, for salvation was indeed of the Jews. "But the hour cometh, ard now is when the true worshipers shall worship the Father in spirit and in truth." (See vv. 23,24.)

What conviction is in this explanation! God does not desire external form, but a heart that understands the sin of the old nature and realizes that the unchanging holiness of God demands a sacrifice no less than the blood of Jesus Christ. To such a heart God makes Himself known. To such a heart God brings life.

Once again Jesus brought the conversation down

to her personal need and the woman once more sought to escape. She broke in with an attempt to stop the conversation entirely. "Messiah who is called Christ will come," she argued. "When He comes He will be able to bring a fulness of teaching, answering all questions." This was a polite hint that the question could now be dropped for good. Messiah is greater than any prophet and she was willing to wait for Messiah. How astounded she must have been at the breath-taking answer of the Lord Jesus. For in words that could not be misunderstood He announced simply that He was the Messiah.

To any one familiar with the Old Testament such an answer classifies the speaker at once. Jesus claims to be the Messiah. This claim is true or false. If it is true, then He is the Saviour. If it be false then He is of the spirit of the antichrist. There can be no middle ground. Jesus is Jehovah or He was an hallucinated being with religious megalomania. No one can truly stop with mere praise of Christ. The Lord Jesus Christ must be cursed or worshiped if one is to retain the least semblance of proper thinking.

He claims to be Jehovah. If He is not what He claims to be reason leaves no other response; He would be a deceiver or deranged. But we accept His claim and worship Him as the eternal God. At this moment the disciples returned.

The woman, in amazement at the revelation of the Person of Jehovah the Messiah, left her waterpot and started up the hill in haste to the village. Forgotten was her errand at the well. She arrived in the village and came to a group of men probably seated in the shade by the village gate, looking down over the valley. They knew her. A woman cannot live in a village and have had five husbands and be living with another man without her name and fame being bandied about among the men.

When I was a boy from fifteen to seventeen years of age in my little hometown in California, I had a job after school hours that took me up and down the business streets collecting money for an agency. Among the places I visited were about forty saloons. Some of the first lessons I learned about the sordid side of life were from the conversations of hangers-on of these places as they freely spoke of the women of the town.

Here on the hillside of Samaria some two thousand years ago human nature was no different. As the woman had come up the path toward the group, they had talked about her and her escapades. Into this group she came with the wonderful words of witness, "Come and see a man which told me all things that ever I did!"

The minute she said that, a lot of those men were convicted of sin. They started down the hill, the younger men going straight down and the older men going down the zig-zagging path. Someone went back into the town and called the other people who were there. Then the younger girls began to come, followed by the older women. Pretty soon the whole hillside was alive with town people coming down to see Jesus.

Meanwhile, the disciples besought Him saying,

"Rabbi, eat." But He said to them, "I have food to eat that you know not of."

"Hmm!" said the disciples, "Did anyone bring Him food? Who brought Him lunch?"

Jesus said to them, "My food is to do the will of Him who sent me and to accomplish His work. Do not say that there are yet four months and then comes the harvest. I tell you, lift up your eyes and see how the fields are already white for the harvest." (See vv. 31-35.)

One day I was at the very spot where this conversation took place. I was sitting by a small tree and had this passage open in front of me and was reading it. I could not understand why Jesus had chosen this setting to say these significant words about the "fields being white unto harvest." So I started reconstructing the sequence of events that took place that afternoon.

John 4:6 says that Jesus arrived at the well at about the sixth hour, that is, noon. While He waited at the well, His disciples started up the hill to the village. If it took them at least 45 minutes to get there, they were in the village about 12:45. Give them 15 minutes to find and buy food and they are starting back down the hill at 1:00. At 1:45 they get back to the well just in time to see the woman leave Jesus. That's when they wondered about His talking with a woman. Between 1:45 and 2:30, while the disciples were eating, the woman was climbing up the hill. At about 2:30, she reached the village and proclaimed her good news. Then the whole town started pouring down the hillside to find out if what she said was true.

If Jesus was sitting looking up at the hill, the disciples probably had their backs to His view. When He noticed the moving mass of people coming out of the village, He said, "Don't say there are four months to the harvest." (Now seasonally speaking, there were four more months until the harvest.) "Lift up your eyes and look at the fields." They turned around and looking up, saw the townspeople coming down the hill. This was the harvest.

Then the Lord said this tremendous thing. "He who reaps receives wages and gathers fruit for eternal life"—that is to say, the man who witnesses for Christ—"so that the sower and the reaper may rejoice together. For here the saying holds true, 'One sows and another reaps.' I sent you to reap." (See vv. 36-38.) Jesus is telling His disciples, "You just went up there because I had chosen this town before the foundation of the world." God sent the disciples up and all they did was bring back lunch. So Jesus saved the harlot and sent her up and she brought back the town.

I am glad we have the record of the woman's testimony and of the men that believed because of it. If you should go into a hospital at the moment when a new baby is entering this world you would see that all the attention of the doctors and the nurses is normally concentrated upon the baby until they can hear him cry. At times it is necessary for the nurse to give the infant a sharp slap to bring that cry which lets all know that the baby is alive.

So when I hear this woman's testimony concerning Christ I know she is alive. There are thousands of church members that have never opened their lips for Christ. We have no outward means of knowing whether or not they have been born again. If you are a believer in the Lord Jesus Christ as your own Saviour, go to others with that cry, "Come and see a man who revealed my inner nature and who revealed His own power and love. This is the Saviour."

You will find a new joy that you have never known before as a Christian. The flow of the living spring from within you will bring life to thirsty souls in the desert through which we travel.

Lessons in Worship

Many Christians know little about true worship. Oh, I know the newspapers announce that "morning worship" will be held in certain places at certain times every Sunday. But very frequently, morning worship is "morning service" or "morning liturgy" or "morning pass-an-hour-and-a-half at religious exercises." How much of that is real worship? Just as God seeks the lost to be saved, so He seeks believers to worship Him. John 4:23 says, "The hour cometh, and now is, when the true worshippers shall worship the Father in spirit and in truth."

How would you define worship? Undoubtedly many people in the world think of worship in terms of attending service or watching a priest going through the formularies of the Mass. To others, worship is simply thanking God for His goodness to them. There can be worship in all of these, but none of them in and of itself is true worship. Mere thanksgiving is not worship. When we thank God for something we have experienced, we are displaying an element of selfishness. Our thanksgiving can rise out of gratitude that something happened to us. There is nothing wrong with that, but it is not worship.

Someone has defined worship as "the adoring contemplation of God revealed in the Lord Jesus Christ." "Adoring contemplation" is acknowledging God and just being happy and glad about who He is. We have all seen a mother watching her child. The look in her eyes tells you she loves that child. You can see written all over her face that she is just as proud as can be to have that child. Well, that same emotion, when turned upward, is worship. Love that stoops down is grace. Love that reaches out on our level from one person to another is affection. Love that rises up to God is worship.

There are many examples of worship in the Book of Revelation. Revelation 4:8-11 says: "The four (living creatures) had each of them six wings about him; and they were full of eyes within: and they rest not day and night, saying, Holy, holy, holy, Lord God Almighty, which was, and is, and is to come. And when those (living creatures) give glory and honor and thanks to him that sat on the throne, who liveth forever and ever, the four and twenty elders fall down before him that sat on the throne, and worship him that liveth forever and ever, and cast their crowns before the throne saying, Thou art worthy, O Lord, to receive glory and honor and power: for thou has created all things, and for thy pleasure they are and were created." Now that is worship!

In England they speak of the "worshipful" company of silversmiths or the "worshipful" guild of artists. They speak to a judge as "your worship." This common ordinary word is used in its old Anglo-Saxon sense to indicate the recognition of grandeur, nobility and character, or the acknowledgment of goodness, position and power. When we apply the word *worship* to God, of course, we're speaking in terms of an infinitely higher level. The words *worthy* and *worship* come from the same root word. The elders in Revelation said, "Thou art worthy, O Lord . . ." In worship of God, we are feasting upon who the Lord is. We are acknowledging Him in a sense of awe, wonder and glorification. This acknowledgment of the supreme wonder of the being of our God is a constant theme in the Book of Revelation.

William Lincoln, a famous figure in British religious life about three hundred years ago wrote, "To worship God we must be quite conscious of his love and grace. The more conscious we are of this, then the easier and better our worship." Worship is the overflowing of our hearts when we admire and adore Him. For as we read in Psalm 16:11, "In thy presence is fulness of joy." As we learn to worship we learn just to be occupied with the Lord. Then we can read the Bible, not merely to say, "I made it through another chapter," but to see in it something about the Lord; to lean back and let our minds go drifting up to heaven; to think, "Our God is on the throne. There is none like Him. He spoke and it was done. He commanded and it stands fast." When we go through life, and every once in a while see something beautiful, we might say, "Lord, you did that. Isn't it wonderful!" Well, that is worship.

We're all familiar with the pride of the small boy who says, "That's my pop!" The boy recognizes when his father is the champion of the block in something, or when his dad wins a golf game. He acknowledges and respects the words and accomplishments of his father. Since we are infinitely more closely related to our heavenly Father, we can, on a much greater level, acknowledge His wonder, His power and His might.

The full secret of worship lies in the guidance of the Holy Spirit. He is the one who brings before us the glories of the Father, the glories of Christ, and the glories of the Holy Spirit so that we just overflow with praise. Many of our hymns are hymns of worship. But how often do we really worship when we are singing? If our hearts can do more than say words, if we can lay hold of the words and translate them into thought that really grips our hearts so that we are thinking what we are saying, then we are participating in worship. Then we are honestly saying, "How wonderful is our God. How marvelous that He is what He is and that He has done what He has done. As we gave thanks for what He has done, we also adore Him for who He is. That is much more wonderful than what He has done. As we come to recognize who He is, then we can pour out our hearts in worship.

Psalm 27:4 says, "One thing have I desired of the Lord, that will I seek after; that I may dwell in the house of the Lord all the days of my life, to behold the beauty of the Lord, and to inquire in his temple." Now, with David, "dwelling in the house of the Lord" was a localized matter. At that time God, in a special sense, dwelt in a building. But we know that Jesus said to the Samaritan woman, "The hour is coming when neither on this mountain nor in Jerusalem will you worship the father. . . . God is spirit, and those who worship him must worship in spirit and in truth"[1] (John 4:21,24).

It is easy for us to worship God in natural surroundings, but nature is the mere display of His handiwork. When we see God through Jesus Christ, we see the visible expression of God Himself. Whether in nature, or in Jesus Christ, God delights to display Himself. He wants to spread before us the wonders of His being, so that we shall be drawn to acknowledge Him. In John 17:24, Jesus said this: "Father, I will that they also, whom thou hast given me, be with me where I am; that they may behold my glory."

Suppose someone acquired a beautiful estate through marriage to an heiress. If this person constantly said to people, "Oh, come out sometime and see *my* home," and took all the credit for himself, people would find him obnoxious and would eventually want nothing to do with him. But when the Lord Jesus Christ says, "I want to spread before you My holiness and My glory where you can see it," immediately it becomes the most wonderful thing in all the universe. Here is the exhibition of perfection and in perfection, there cannot be any pride.

A great singer is happy to sing in order that people may have pleasure from his voice. A great teacher in the university is delighted to answer the questions of his students that they may grow. But our great God delights in displaying all His glories and perfections because there is nothing better. His glory is the climax of everything there is in life and being.

If you visit a scenic spot, such as the Grand Canyon, and stay there for two or three days, you would hear the initial responses of people who came and saw that natural wonder for the first time. One after another, they would say, "Oh, how breathtaking!" "How wonderful!" "How beautiful!" Some would be just speechless. They would go aside to contemplate that awesome and wonderful beauty of nature. Here is something caused by destruction and erosion, and yet as we see it, we proclaim, "How wonderful!" How much more wonderful are the perfect glories of Christ as they are revealed to us by the Holy Spirit!

One day I was leaving England to fly home to America. The plane flew west in the direction of the setting sun, soaring high above the clouds. In that sunset, I saw the infinite billowing of the clouds, some of them rising up above us like mountains and some of them forming huge valleys below us. Occasionally, we would come right along beside a cloud and our wing would practically cut the edge of it. As we flew, I thought to myself, "Just think! For thousands of years before there were airplanes, all this beauty was up here and no one ever saw it, but God and His angels." God has never painted the same sunset twice. The shape of the clouds is always different. I thought of the fact that there were a million possible points on this earth where one could see a million different sunsets. Then I just sat there and said, "My what a wonderful God!"

Yes, it is possible to worship God in nature. For nature was created by the word of His power. But when we worship God in Christ, we are acknowledging the expression of His person. We are responding to His infinite love. The Holy Spirit reveals to our minds the glories of the Lord Jesus Christ and the beauty of the Lord as manifested in grace (love that stoops). We see Him leaving the throne of heaven saying, "I'll put myself in the hands of men and I'll let them nail me to the cross in order that I may satisfy God on the behalf of sinners." When we who are the sinners, realize what He did, we are overcome. Our hearts are lifted toward Him in praise for His greatness, His salvation, His holiness, His love—and we worship the Lord in the beauty of holiness.

True worship has certain characteristics. In Hebrews 10:22, it says, "Let us draw near." Worship is drawing near to God. There is nothing frightening about worship. In acknowledging the wonders of God in nature, people may be afraid of Him. They may tremble before the majesty of a storm, or the wonders of the great phenomena of nature. But in worship we are drawn to God. In fact, God has saved us in order that He might be closer to us. That is the nature of His love.

Worship needs no earthly house, no earthly form. I wonder sometimes if the very fact of the existence of churches doesn't block the spiritual reality of what the Bible teaches. Does a building with stained glass windows really induce worship? There's no doubt that natural man thinks so. He has built his cathedrals as symbols of greatness and beauty. I've been in buildings that all the artists say are the most beautiful cathedrals in the world. Yet I find that they do not draw my heart to God, and I don't think God wants them to. God doesn't need a fancy building or a picture of Christ in order to draw our hearts to Him. He doesn't need pews and pulpit and windows to draw our hearts to Him.

When Hebrews 10:22 says, "Let us draw near . . ." that "drawing" must be in our hearts. This involves the conscious exclusion of everything else in our surroundings. In worship, let your memory be active. Jesus said, in reference to the Lord's Supper, "Do this in memory of Me." The Lord wants you to be going over all the things that He's done for you. These things will tell you more about who He is. When your heart can think of who God is, it will be drawn to the last step of worship, which is hope.

In the Lord's Supper, Jesus links memory with hope—"You show the Lord's death till He comes." Our heart in worship turns to the hope of His coming to the day when we won't have to worship Him through the barrier of time or our senses, or the weakness of the flesh, fighting all the forces that would drive our attention away from Him. Then, we will really know what it is to worship Him in spirit and in truth.

Learning the lessons of true worship is the greatest factor in spiritual growth. You will grow faster by taking time out to think on things the Lord has done, and to think on the things He is, and to thank Him for these. Think of His condescension of leaving the throne of heaven to come and die for you. Think of His patience toward you. Think of His heart of love. Think of His holiness. Then think of whatever the Holy Spirit brings to your heart. In the fulness of the Holy Spirit, you will experience your greatest blessing—the true worship of God.

"Moses Wrote of Me"

"After these things there was a feast of the Jews; and Jesus went up to Jerusalem. Now there is in Jerusalem by the sheep gate a pool, which is called in Hebrew Bethesda, having five porticoes. In these lay a multitude of those who were sick, blind, lame, withered" John 5:1-3. Archeology has uncovered the ruins of a colonnade area that probably was the ancient pool. It was in the form of a *trapezium*—a four-sided area with no two sides exactly parallel.

In the shady section under the covered colonnade lay the town invalids. An ancient tradition held that, every so often, an angel came down from heaven to stir up the waters. The first person to enter the water after this agitation would supposedly be healed. For this moment of agitation, all the sick of the community waited.

In all probability, the waters *did* have some medicinal qualities, as do certain springs or baths the world over. However, the tradition about the angel (John 5:4) does not have too solid a foundation textually. Presumably it was a later addition to John's Gospel to explain certain healings that did take place at the pool. Most of the modern translations of the New Testament have deleted the verse on textual grounds.

Regardless of the existence or nonexistence of the angel who stirred the waters, the fact remains that sick folk lay in the sheltered portico waiting for the moment to step into the waters and find healing.

We have no idea how this is a picture of life today in many of the great cities of the underdeveloped world—the multitude of the impotent folk, the blind, the withered, waiting for something. Spiritually speaking, there is also a tremendous lesson here of the multitude of impotent folk who are waiting for God's moving of the water of life and bring healing to their souls.

One man at that pool had been ill for 38 years. And when Jesus came to that pool, He singled out that one man and asked him what appears to be a most ridiculous question, "Do you want to be healed?" (v. 6).

That's what the Lord Jesus Christ is waiting to say to men today. Oh, how many people are frustrated and have many longings which they know are not being satisfied in life. Many of them are not even being satisfied by formal Christianity. They recite creeds, they know all the orthodox answers, but they are impotent and they need to be healed by Christ.

The man replied with the same excuse that he had probably been relying on for a long while. (See v. 7.) He said he had no one to help him into the pool. Our Lord did not argue with him or waste any pity on him. He simply said, "Rise, take up thy bed, and walk." (See v. 8.) The man was healed and went on his way.

In a sense, this is a picture of the way God effects the miracle of the new birth. God chose us in Christ before the foundation of the world. (See Eph. 1:4.)

Then God arranges the factors through which we are confronted by the claims of Jesus Christ. He comes to each of His own in such saving grace— just as He came to the impotent man by the pool of Bethesda. We receive Him and become sons of God.

There was one difficulty in the healing of the invalid at Bethesda's pool: the work of mercy was performed on the Sabbath day! Jesus had purposely selected the Sabbath to heal the man, knowing full well the uproar it would cause.

We never need fear running counter to man's traditions and conventions. We have an excellent pattern for this in our Lord Jesus Christ. True, when He crossed the barriers and broke traditions, His contemporaries sought to kill Him (vv. 16,18). Yet, knowing their attitude, He deliberately invaded their hypocritical traditions and invited conflict.

This does not mean that we are expected to go about with a chip on our shoulders, as Christians. But, at the same time, it means that we are not to avoid controversy if it is inevitable.

Christ told the healed man to pick up his pallet,

or mat, and walk. In doing so, the man also broke the Sabbath. Whether he did not realize it was the Sabbath, or whether in his new joy of being able to walk, he did not particularly care, we cannot tell. The Lord of the Sabbath had issued the command; the man obeyed this order of his benefactor.

When he was challenged by the religious dignitaries for violating the Sabbath, the healed man did not even know his benefactor's name. Later, when he met Jesus in the Temple, and came to know who his Saviour was, he immediately returned to the religious leaders and told them.

This he did, not in any spirit of spite, but naively feeling that the religious leaders ought to know who this wonderful Man was. To the man newly made whole, this was his first witness to God's grace.

The Jews had contrived all sorts of rules and regulations for the Sabbath day that made it a nightmare instead of a blessing. The thousand and one restrictions were a constant thorn in the side of the people while their leaders delighted in catching the offenders. The law of man was replacing the law of God.

A man might spit on the ground on the Sabbath day, for example. However, if the spittle rolled in the dirt, it was considered "plowing a furrow." This was labor performed, and illegal on the Sabbath day. This sort of thing turned the Sabbath day, which had been "made for man," into a drudgery instead of a benefit. Consequently, our Lord Jesus Christ lashed out in unrestrained righteous indignation against the type of mentality that would devise these absurd restrictions.

This was why, on many occasions, He deliberately chose the Sabbath day to perform His works of mercy. And this was why the religious leaders hated Him and persecuted Him.

Then, when Jesus coupled with His violation of the man-made Sabbath rules, a declaration associating Himself with God (v. 17), this was the last straw. To the Jewish mind this claim was one of two things: it was either true—which was inconceivable to them, or it was rank blasphemy. They chose the second, and we read: "Therefore the Jews sought the more to kill him, because he not only had broken the sabbath, but said also that God was his Father, making himself equal with God" (v. 18).

In response to their angry charges, Jesus uttered this beautiful description of the harmony existent between God the Father and the Lord Jesus Christ.

At one of the turning points in our Lord's ministry, He said, "I do always those things that please him." (See John 8:29.) And again, as He approached the close of His earthly work, in the garden of Gethsemane, He said, "I have glorified thee on the earth: I have finished the work which thou gavest me to do" (John 17:4).

The idea of Jesus Christ as judge finds its way frequently into the pages of Scripture. (See Acts 10:42; 17:31; Rom. 2:16; 2 Cor. 5:10; 2 Tim. 4:1.) The Apostle's Creed states "From thence (heaven) He shall come to judge the quick and the dead . . ." Jesus reminded His listeners that God had seen fit to judge through the Person of His Son. (See v. 22.)

Verse 24 is a text of great assurance. Coupled with Romans 8:1, this verse guarantees, on the authority of our Lord's double "verily," that the fact of faith is the proof of life.

The judgment which has been committed by God to His Son, is escaped by the believer in Christ. (See Rom. 8:1.) Jesus Christ, by His death on the cross, bore our judgment in Himself, as our substitute. For this reason, we who have put our trust in Him are spared the necessity of facing the judgment for our sin.

When Jesus said, "He that heareth my word . . ." (v. 24) it was the equivalent of saying "he who hears My Father's word." And when He said, "And believeth on him that sent me" it was the same as if He said "he who believes in Me." Never forget that, because He was God the Son, He could say, "I and My Father are one." (See John 10:30.) So close is the relationship—so immediately identified are the divine Persons of deity—that what one says and does the other says and does also.

Jesus continued by hitting at the fake religiosity of the Pharisees. He said, "You have neither heard God's voice at any time, nor seen His shape. You do not have His word abiding in you, for you do not believe Him whom He has sent. (See vv. 37,38.) Now they knew all about the Old Testament. They had the whole thing learned *verbatim, liberatum, punctuatum*. They had studied every word, every letter, every jot and tittle. They had God's word, but they did not have it "abiding" in them. And the proof was that they did not commit themselves to Jesus Christ.

The phrase, "search the Scriptures," in the King James Version, is a wrong translation for verse 39. Very frequently you see it put up as a nice little motto over the fireplace or in the kitchen. Now, if you want a verse for Bible study, you can find many of them. But this verse is badly translated because the Greek verb is the same for both the indicative and the imperative. This is not a command, "Search the Scriptures," but a statement, "You search the Scriptures."

Now remember that Jesus is talking to the Pharisees—the graduates of the Jerusalem Theological Seminary, the Law of Moses Training School, and the Palestine Missionary Institute. They read the Bible just to establish their position, to build up their prestige, and to be able to look down their noses at the common populace who believed in Jesus, but knew little about the Law. These fellows always had their noses in the Bible, but they never got any further than the paper and ink.

Let me illustrate what happens when you look at the Bible this way. Suppose somebody were staying in an Atlantic City hotel and his room had a window overlooking a beautiful view of the Atlantic Ocean. Wouldn't you think something was wrong if they came to you and said, "Now I want to tell you all about the window in my room. This window has eight glass panes on one side and eight on the other side. It's a casement window which measures so many inches by so many inches. I want to take scratchings of the glass to give you a chemical analysis of my window." Someone who said that would be missing the whole point of having a window. The window is there so you can see the ocean; not so you can study the window.

Well, the Bible is a window. The purpose of the Bible is that you may look through it and see Jesus Christ. Some people stop with the Bible. I will yield to no man in my belief in the Bible, in its divine origin, in the fact that it is divine, verbally inspired revelation. But I say that the Bible is not a thing to be analyzed, criticized, outlined and examined, just for it's own sake. That would be just like sitting in a room and writing a book about a window, without seeing the ocean with its waves curling up the beach or the way the lights and clouds play upon the water. The Bible is not an end in itself any more than a window is an end in itself. The window allows us to see the beauty which lies beyond. The Bible is the way to life in Jesus Christ.

This chapter ends with one of the most astounding statements ever made about the Old Testament. In verses 45-47, Jesus Christ says to these theologians, "If you believe not Moses' writings—Genesis, Exodus, Leviticus, Numbers and Deuteronomy—how shall you believe my word—Matthew, Mark, Luke and John?" Here Jesus Himself is affirming that Moses was the author of the Pentateuch.

There was a time when people said, "Moses could not have written the Pentateuch because writing did not exist in his day." They claimed it hadn't been invented yet. Then, in the very place where Moses lived, in the Sinai peninsula, archeologists have discovered evidences of the existence of writing a thousand years before Moses' time. These discoveries merely confirmed Jesus' words. "Moses wrote of me." (See v. 46). Since He tied the whole Bible together, you take the whole Bible and the whole Christ, or no Bible and no Christ. You can't pick and choose. If you take a verbally inspired complete revelation of God's spoken word, you have the "words of eternal life." But if you try to have something less, you don't have anything at all.

"Something for Nothing"

It was springtime when Jesus lifted up His eyes and saw a great company coming to Him—five thousand it turns out. He said to Philip, "Whence shall we buy bread, that these men may eat?" (See John 6:5.) Now, of course, the Lord was on mission. It says in verse 6 that Jesus said this "to test him, for He Himself knew what He would do." The Lord had made the plan. He had ordered it as definitely as He orders the sunrise and the movements of the planets so that the eclipses come through at the appointed time. Jesus had worked all factors so that these thousands of men would come around the lake. He was there waiting to receive them because He had planned to do what He was going to do.

Philip answered Jesus, "Well, two hundred denarii worth of bread is not sufficient for them." Now a denarius was a day's wages. You remember in one of Jesus' parables, how the man went out on several occasions throughout the day and hired men to work for a denarius a day. Then there was the time Jesus paid His tax. He said to Peter, "Go fishing, and you will find a piece of money in the mouth of the fish. Use it to pay the poll tax for both of us." (See Matt. 17:27.) Half a denarius was the poll tax for everybody in the ancient Roman Empire. Two hundred denarii was two hundred days' wages.

I was talking once with a man who was getting $20 a day. Two hundred days' wages for him would have been $4,000. So, putting Philip's words in terms we can relate to, we can hear him say to Jesus, "What? Four thousand dollars' worth of bread (two hundred days' wages) would not be enough to begin to feed this crowd!"

Jesus was not disturbed by Philip's alarm. His purpose was to reveal to the disciples what they were in themselves, and what He was in Himself. You are never going to get any blessing from Him until you know what you are in yourself. And when you know you are nothing, when you really know you ought to go to hell, then you will be able to comprehend the way to heaven. But, as long as you think, "Oh, I'm not too bad," you are never going to know anything about Christianity—never—not a thing. And it is the same way in Christian work, for Christians. As long as you think you can do something by yourself, you will do absolutely nothing.

Darby made a brilliant statement when he said, "Any time a man gets out of his nothingness he gets into it." Now, at first, perhaps you don't understand what that means. If a person says, "I am absolutely nothing," then God says, "I can use you." But if a man steps out of his nothingness and says, "Well, I think I might be something," God says, "You are nothing." That person then moves from his own nothingness to the place of divine nothingness. Man trying is emptiness, but man trusting is fulness.

Then Andrew, Simon Peter's brother, said to Jesus, "There's a lad here who has five barley loaves, and two small fishes." Now, don't think of a barley loaf as a long loaf. Their barley loaves were about the size of our dinner rolls. Five barley loaves and two fishes—what is that among so many?

We can hear the boy's mother saying, as he set out for the day, "Well, Johnny, you must have some lunch. Here, take this with you." Then we see the boy going off for a rendezvous with the Lord Jesus Christ. Little did he know that what he had in his package was going to feed a multitude and furnish an illustration to demonstrate that Jesus Christ was none other than the Lord of Hosts, Jehovah the Creator Himself. I don't know how Andrew discovered that the boy had food. I don't know how he got the boy to be willing to give it up. But I do know that when a person has seen Jesus Christ, everything takes on a different value. Perhaps this was why the boy was willing to offer his lunch to Jesus.

Notice the faithlessness of the disciples. Oh, sure, Philip made a survey. That's the modern church's way of meeting a problem—make a survey, appoint a committee, investigate the problem. But that's not God's way. The boy only had a little, but a little surrendered to the Lord Jesus Christ is enough. As far as Jesus is concerned, the only way to get any place is to put whatever you have in His hands. Jesus keeps going around the world picking out people with a little nothing who are willing to give it to Him. Then He breathes on it and makes it something. When that happens, says Jesus, "My people get fed and they learn to know My power. That's the way I am doing it—and I'm doing it that way on purpose."

Jesus doesn't need your muscles, your loaves and two fishes, or any of the other resources you offer Him. He could have fed the crowd without the boy's bread. But He did it this way to show us He is never going to work apart from human instrumentality. God never saves a man directly from heaven. You and I are just little two-legged invertebrated metazoa—unfeathered and unfurred—who have to spend all our time merely trying to keep body and soul together.

When we go to Jesus and say, "Lord, all I have are five loaves and two fishes. What good will that do?" the Lord says, "Are you willing to give it to me?" The moment we say yes, people are fed! And then God says, "I took no cherub, no seraphim, no archangel, no angel. I didn't even take an unfallen Adam. I waited until man fell all the way. When I use him, it is obvious that I'm doing the work through him, and all the glory comes to Me. I am teaching man now that he who humbles himself shall be exalted, while he who exalts himself shall be abased. I am setting forth the proposition that little is much when God is in it. I am asking man to trust Me with his nothingness."

If you will say, "Lord God, here is my zero," God

will just come and stand in front of your zero and all of a sudden you will discover that your zero (0) is ten (10). If you can get an accurate enough picture of yourself to say, "Lord, I am two zeroes," He will come and stand in front of you, and all of a sudden your two zeroes (00) will equal one hundred (100). In rare instances in the history of the church, men and women have been able to say, "Lord God, here is my triple zero. (000)." That's how "one can chase a thousand and two put ten thousand to flight." (See Deut. 32:30.)

God is always willing to come and stand in front of your zeroes. But you know, if you put your zero on the other side of Christ, then immediately the decimal point is there and it's only a fraction and He won't do a thing. Come to the Lord and present your nothingness and He'll stand by you and will turn your cipher into power. When the disciples asked the question, "What are these loaves and fishes (my zeroes) among so many?" Jesus simply answered, "Let's get on with the job. Make the men sit down."

John's account says, "Now there was much grass in the place; so the men sat down, in number about five thousand. Jesus then took the loaves, and when he had given thanks, he distributed them to those who were seated; so also the fish, as much as they wanted" (John 6:10-11). In Mark's narrative of this same event, he wrote that Jesus "broke the loaves, and gave them to the disciples to set before the people" (Mark 6:41).

It is very interesting to know what happened at those moments when the food was being distributed. Jesus put some broken pieces of the loaves and the fish in each one of the twelve baskets. The creation took place in the basket—right in the hands of those who were working for Him. The disciples passed through the crowd and everybody began to take, and take, and take—the food was created as fast as anyone could take one handful. And if anybody had faith enough to come back and take three pieces off, why, it was filled right up again. When everyone had all he could eat, the Bible says, there were twelve baskets of fragments remaining.

When I was a small boy, I thought those twelve baskets were full of leftover scraps. As a child I was taught that I had to be very careful and eat everything on my plate because "the scraps were picked up after the five thousand were fed." However, I do not now believe that to be true. I wouldn't be at all surprised if there were quite a lot of scraps lying around on the grass and that the birds came and got them the next day.

The disciples' baskets were just as full when everybody was served as when they started. The Lord was saying to them, "I have put into your hands that which you can distribute. The more people take from your baskets, the more your baskets will remain full." The twelve baskets were not full of scraps, but of undistributed bread. What is Jesus teaching? He is teaching, "I am Jehovah God."

In my New York Bible class I was asked the question, "If God is all powerful, could He make a five-year-old tree grow old in ten minutes?" I said, "Why not?" Look at what He did in this case here.

In His fingers, the years and the seasons fell apart. He who was the God of eternity demonstrated that He was the Lord of the months and the growing seasons. The one who took the bread and put it in baskets was the one who had said, "While the earth remaineth, seedtime and harvest, and cold and heat, and summer and winter, and day and night shall not cease" (Gen. 8:22). While the seasons rolled on, the Lord of the harvest demonstrated that He was able to create, that He was the Creator. And He did the same with the fish. Creation happened in that moment, as His fingers broke the bread and the fish.

Jesus Christ is the Lord Jehovah of Hosts. He is the Creator. He can take not only bread and fish to feed your bodies, but He can also take you and break you and with you feed the world—if you're willing to be broken by Him, to be handed out day-by-day so that those around you may feed. And just as He said, "I am the light of the world" and "you are the light of the world," so He says, "I am the bread of life and so are you." When we are broken we can go out to feed others. The feeding, of course, will not be anything of our doing. It will be the work of the Lord Jesus Christ and Him alone.

Notice how Jesus elaborated on this in verses 48 and following. "Truly, truly, I say to you, he who believes has eternal life. I am the bread of life. Your fathers ate the manna in the wilderness and they died. This is the bread which comes down from heaven, that a man may eat of it and not die. I am the living bread which came down from heaven; if any man eats of this bread, he will live forever; and the bread which I will give for the life of the world is my flesh."

At this point, the Jews asked a very natural question. They said, "How can this man give us flesh to eat?" And we might ask the same question. But Jesus is not talking about cannibalism. When we say, "Feed on Christ," we mean that the life we receive from Him spiritually is that which makes us live spiritually. Jesus said it this way, "Truly, truly, I say to you, unless you eat the flesh of the Son of man and drink his blood, you have no life in you. He who eats my flesh and drinks my blood has eternal life, and I will raise him up at the last day." (See vv. 52-54.)

Let me give you an illustration about this. Suppose you are at a football game. You see a young fellow running out for a pass. All of a sudden he catches it and starts to run—broken field running—ninety yards down the field for a touchdown. What caused him to run like that? Well, that was the steak he ate two days ago. A little while later, he kicks a field goal. That was the mashed potatoes and milk he ate yesterday. The food that he ate yesterday, two days ago, last week, has been transferred into energy. Everything you do physically is done as a result of this chemical exchange—food being eaten and becoming energy. If a man knocks a home run, that's his steak transmuted into power.

Or maybe you see a young man who could make fifty thousand dollars a year as a surgeon. But he says, "I'm going out to the heart of Africa and I'm going to bury myself there for Christ." What makes him do that? Well, just as the beef steak makes the

football man run down the field, so feeding on
Christ transforms the life and sends that man to
Africa. And feeding on Christ, seven days a week,
makes a person live for Christ right in his own
hometown.

Those men, when they had seen the miracle that
Jesus did, said, "This is indeed the prophet who is
to come unto the world!" That shows you how blind
people can be. This was not a prophet. This was Jehovah God. Men look in the direction of Jesus, even
today, and call Him, "the Master," "the Nazarene,"
"the Galilean," "the Older Brother." How blind can
natural man be?

Oh, Christians, don't ever be guilty of calling the
Lord Jesus Christ "the Nazarene," and "the Galilean," and "the Master." Call Him, as the Scripture
through all of the epistles calls Him, "Lord Jesus
Christ," "Jehovah," "Saviour," "Messiah." He is our
Creator. He is our Saviour. He is our God. And
thus, it was demonstrated in that hour.

The lessons are there very easy to see. There is
the lesson of who He is. John said at the end of his
Gospel, "These are written, that ye might believe
that Jesus is the Christ, the Son of God; and that
believing ye might have life through his name"
(John 20:31). So I present it to you that you might
believe who Jesus is, and that believing, you might
have life. I am not talking only about eternal life. I
want you to have life for now, life that will enable
you to overcome sin, life that will enable you to say
no to the things you desire of yourself, life that will
enable you to be crucified with Jesus Christ, life
that will enable you to comprehend the nothingness

of yourself and your need for the creative touch. You need Christ to come and stand by the cipher of your being, the zero that can make you effective for Him. And when you comprehend this whole thing in relationship to this temporary, very temporary struggle between God and Satan, then you will know that you have been chosen to be on the side of eternity against time, on the side of God against Satan, on the side of supply over the demand of need. You and I have been called for His purpose.

John Bunyan's Text

Early in the seventeenth century, a hundred years after the time of Luther, the English Reformation launched the Church of England on its sweet and placid way. After it became quiet, calm, contented, and spiritually dead, there suddenly arose within the church a great movement for more strictness of life and for simplicity of worship. This religious Puritan movement paralleled the political movement which grew into the English Civil War and produced Oliver Cromwell.

Into this atmosphere, John Bunyan was born in November 1628. His father was Thomas Bunyan, a tinker of Elstow near Bedford. In those days, tinkers formed a hereditary caste, low on the social scale of England. John was educated in the village school, where he learned to read and write. He grew up in a strict atmosphere among people to whom religion consisted entirely of "Thou shalt not . . ."

When Bunyan was seventeen years old, he enlisted in the Parliamentary army and went through the military campaign of 1645, which defeated the forces of King Charles I. His officers were Puritans. Anyone in the army who swore was fined a shilling; if a man got drunk, he was deprived of two or three weeks' pay, and was put into the stocks where people could laugh at him. In 1646 Bunyan returned home from the war and about two years later married a poor girl who had, as her total possessions, the clothes that she wore and two books, *The Plain Man's Path to Heaven,* and *The Practice of Piety.* A year or two later Bunyan came into contact with someone who preached Christ to him. Bunyan said, "He did talk pleasantly of the Scripture; wherefore, falling into some love and liking to what he said, I betook me to my Bible and began to take great pleasure in reading, but especially in the historical part thereof. But as for Paul's epistles, and suchlike parts of Scriptures, I could not away with them." In other words, they were over his head!

There then followed a long period of tremendous conviction of sin. His head was full of Bible, and his heart was full of misery. The *Encyclopedia Britannica* article on Bunyan has a tremendous summary of the horror that filled this man's life during this period.

"In outward things he soon became a strict Pharisee. He was constant in attendance at prayers and sermons. His favorite amusements, were one after another, relinquished, though not without many painful struggles. . . . To give up dancing on the village green was most difficult, and some months elapsed before he had the fortitude to part with his darling sin. When this last sacrifice had been made, he was, even when tried by the maxims of that austere time, faultless. All Elstow talked of him as an eminently pious youth. But his own mind was more unquiet than ever. Having nothing more to do in the way of visible reformation, yet finding in religion no pleasures to supply the place of the juvenile amusements which he had relinquished, he began to apprehend that he lay under some special malediction; and he was tormented by a succession of fantasies which seemed likely to drive him to suicide or to bedlam."

Later he began to be plagued by an obsession with the unpardonable sin. He felt a strange haunting curiosity about it, and a strong compulsion to commit it. Day and night, whether at work, at meals, or in bed, he sensed strange demonic forms driving him to say the dreaded words which, he felt, would mean a renunciation of his faith. Finally, exhausted and defeated, he spoke the words, "Let him go if you will."

Bunyan grew more miserable than he'd been before. He thought he had done what could never be forgiven. Like Esau, he had sold his birth-right. Though strong in body, he trembled and shook for days, so captured was his mind by fear of death and judgment. He was so emotionally distraught that he was unable to digest his food, and he expected to "burst asunder" like Judas, with whom he grimly identified. In one of the most pathetic complaints ever written, Bunyan described his feelings. He felt like a blot upon the face of the universe; he had envied the toads, and the grass by the side of the road, and the crows that cawed in the ploughed land by which he passed. He thought they could never know such misery as that which bowed him down.

Thomas Macaulay, in his essay on Bunyan, refers to this paragraph by Bunyan as one of the greatest in English literature. "I walked to a neighboring town and sat on a settle in the street and fell into a very meek pause about the fearful state my sin had brought me to. And after long musing I lifted up my head, but methought I saw as though the sun shining in the heavens did grudge to give me light, and as if the very stones in the street and tiles upon the houses did band themselves against me. Methought that they were all banded together to banish me out of the world. I was abhorred of them, and unfit to dwell among them for I had sinned against the Saviour. Oh, how happy now was every creature over me, for they stood fast and kept their station, but I was gone and lost."

Finally, in desperation, he consulted an old Puritan and said to him, "I am afraid I have committed the sin against the Holy Ghost." And the old fanatic replied, "I am afraid that you have."

While he was thus lamenting his hopeless condition, the light broke. John Bunyan got his text! Oh, just one text out of the Word of God can explode in a person's life and make all things new. If you don't have a text, if you do not have something that you can turn to when you are sick, when you wake up in pain, when you get out on the wrong side of the bed—if you do not have something that you can turn to in your misery and say, "No matter how I feel, the promise of God is still true!" you had better go back to the Word of God and give diligence to make your calling and election sure.

F. W. Boreham, in telling the story of Bunyan's life, says that there is no doubt about what the text was. "For as a lover carves his lady's name on trees, signs it as his own, and mumbles it in his sleep, so Bunyan inscribes everywhere the text that wrought his memorable deliverance. It crops up again and again in all his writings. The characters in *Pilgrim's Progress*, in *Grace Abounding*, the dream children of his fertile imagination, repeat it to each other as though it were a password, a talisman, a charm; and Bunyan himself quotes it whenever there is the slightest opportunity for bringing it in. This text is the burden of everything he wrote and of every sermon that he preached. It sings through his autobiography like a chanting chorus, like an echoing refrain. . . . John Bunyan's text rushed to his memory as though an angel had brought it. This text sang its song of confidence and peace every morning; and its music scattered the gloom of every night. It was the friend of his fireside, the companion of his loneliness, the comrade of his travels, the light of his darkness. It illumined his path among the perplexities of life, it wiped away his tears in the day of sorrow, and it smoothed his pillow in the hour of death."

In 1649 King Charles I was executed, and Oliver Cromwell ruled England for eleven years. The Restoration came in 1660 when Charles II mounted the throne of England. The return of the monarchy signaled trouble for all Puritans, and in November, 1660, John Bunyan was put in jail. He was not a man to give up his stand for Christ just to avoid going to jail. Now there are times when the lines are so closely drawn that if we are going to stand for anything, it is going to cost us something. The great tragedy of our generation is that so few people have convictions: and even worse is the tragedy that those who have convictions will not stand for them. Jesus said, "Woe unto you when all men speak well of you."

In the first chapter of *Pilgrim's Progress*, we meet the principal character, Pilgrim, "clothed with rags, a book in his hand, and a great burden upon his back. . . . He was greatly distressed in his mind and burst out, 'What shall I do to be saved?' " When Pilgrim asks Evangelist the way of escape, Evangelist says, "Do you see yonder shining light?"

"I think I do," says wretched Pilgrim.

"Then keep that light in your eye, and go up directly thereto: so shalt thou see the gate; at which when thou knockest, it shall be told thee what thou shalt do."

And Pilgrim in due course did come to the gate and knock, saying: "May I now enter here? Will He within open to sorry me, though I have been an undeserving rebel? Then shall I not fail to sing His lasting praise on high."

Goodwill opens the gate, and says, "I am willing with all my heart. We make no objections against any notwithstanding all that they have done before

they come hither; *they are in no wise cast out.*"
Here at the very beginning of Christian's new life,
stands the first unmistakable mention of John Bunyan's text; "Him that cometh unto me I will in no
wise cast out."

In his autobiography, Bunyan said, " 'In no wise
cast out!' Oh, the comfort I found in that word! 'In
no wise cast out!' This Scripture did most sweetly
visit my soul." Did you ever have your soul visited?
Do you know what it is to have hope in place of despair? Do you ever feel, "Oh, I must go to a psychi-
atrist and find out what is wrong with me!" and
then learn that you can go to Christ and find out
what can be right with you? Have you ever given
up your burden in order to receive His joy? Do you
know what it is to have your life turned around because some word in the Bible did sweetly visit your
soul? And Bunyan now writes, "Oh, what did I then
see in this blessed sixth of John!"

What did he see in that sixth chapter? What comfort did he find so lavishly stored there? The matter
is worth investigating. Bunyan found three things
in John 6:37.

First, he found the approachability of Christ.
Now, if Jesus Christ came to Palestine today, you
could not get a booking for six months. The ocean
liners would be filled to capacity; every airplane
reservation would be taken. Everyone would want
to go to see Jesus Christ. But when Jesus went
away, He sent the Holy Spirit, who can bring Christ
right into your home. You don't have to phone a
travel agency or an airline and ask, "Can I get a
ticket to Palestine?" Jesus is nearer to you than

breathing, closer than hands or feet. "Him that cometh to me I will in no wise cast out." Even the most vile can easily go to the fountain of grace and find all that is needed, in the approachable Lord Jesus Christ.

Second, there is in this text the universality of Jesus. In his earlier life, Bunyan always thought that Christ would receive some more fortunate person than himself. There was a man whom people called "Holy Master Gifford." One day Bunyan heard Holy Master Gifford and some women discussing the things of the Kingdom of God, as they sat in front of their doors. Bunyan clearly believed in the salvation of these people, but he felt that he himself was forever excluded from the happiness and peace which they enjoyed.

"About this time," he says, "the happiness of these people at Bedford was a kind of vision to me. I saw on the sunny side of some mountains they were refreshing themselves in the pleasant beams of the sun while I was shivering and sinking in the cold, afflicted with frost and snow and dark clouds. Methought also, betwixt me and them I saw a wall that did compass about this mountain. Now through this wall my soul did so greatly desire to pass, concluding that if I could I would there also comfort myself with the heat of their sun, but I could find no way through or around or over the wall."

And then Bunyan discovered the text, "Him that cometh unto me I will in no wise cast out." "But Satan," he said, "would greatly labor to pull this promise from me, telling me that Christ did not love me, or such as me, but sinners of another rank that had not done as I had done. But I would answer him again, 'Him that cometh to me,' him, any him, with no exception, 'him that cometh unto me I will in no wise cast out.' " So the walls around Bunyan's mountains fell with a crash before that great and golden verse. The barriers were down, the way was open to anyone. This is the universality of Jesus. It doesn't make any difference what your past has been. Jesus says to you, "I will in no wise cast you out." Be not afraid to lift your eyes to Jesus Christ. He is approachable; He is universal; He is for *you*.

The final thing that Bunyan saw in this text was the reliability of Christ. How wonderful to know that you can deposit your money in a Bank that cannot fail, to know that you can invest in a Stock that cannot go down, to know that you can build upon a Rock that cannot be shaken! In Christ you have reliability.

Just by believing someone's word, you can experience complete relief of heart and mind. During the first week of World War II, in September, 1939, Hitler invaded Poland on a Friday and on the following Sunday morning at eleven Neville Chamberlain declared war. That same week I had left my family in France, to go to Belfast, Ireland, where I was to hold a series of meetings. Naturally, when the war broke out, I was concerned about my family. So the layman in charge of the meetings took me to see the postmaster general of Ulster where we asked about sending a telegram to my family.

He said, "We aren't sending any personal telegrams, but if you want to send a wire to the American consul, we will put that through."

I wired the consul, told him where my family was and asked him to get in touch with them. I assured him that I would guarantee their passage home.

After we had sent the telegram, my friend said to me, "What are you going to do for money?"

"Well," I said, "they have travelers' checks and they have their tickets for a ship which will sail a month from now, but they want to go home right away, as soon as possible."

My friend said to me, "You can count on me for anything you need, up to a thousand pounds." As soon as he said that, I didn't need to worry any more about the finances. If I needed extra money, it was there. I knew that person's character and I believed his promise.

In the same way, Jesus has given His word to us. "Him that cometh unto me I will in no wise cast out." We know what He did for us to guarantee that promise. He came and He died and He rose again to show us that we could rely on Him, that we could trust His word. Just as I felt relief and deep thanks to my friend in Ireland for his guarantee of funds, so you and I can say with great assurance, "Thank You, Lord Jesus for meeting all my needs." This is the reliability of Christ.

"Oh," said John Bunyan, "that word did sweetly visit my soul!" Do you have a word that sweetly visits your soul? Can you say, "My religion is not hope so, maybe, possibly, perhaps?" or do you say, "If I walk the straight and narrow way for twenty years, maybe I shall perhaps have eternal life?" None of that! Away with doubt! Away with basing anything on human experience! Jesus Christ is approachable. Jesus Christ is universal. Jesus Christ is reliable. On Him you can stake your soul! "Him that cometh unto me I will in no wise cast out."

This verse gave John Bunyan to the world. This verse can lift all weight from you. If you doubt, go back to the Word of God. Turn the pages and say, "O Lord, here is my need! Meet it. Here is my emptiness! Fill it! Speak some verse to *my* soul so that I can say, 'Here it is! this is for me!' " And when once you find the verse that speaks to your heart, you can base all of your life on God.

A "Reading" of John 7

PUBLISHER'S NOTE: Dr. Barnhouse's "readings" were extemporaneous commentaries delivered informally during the reading of the Scripture in the Sunday services at Tenth Presbyterian Church. The congregation grew to love and appreciate the practical, stimulating insights gained from his expressive interpretation throughout his ministry. Chapter 23 is also one of these Bible "readings."

Verse 1—"After this Jesus went about in Galilee; he would not go about in Judea because the Jews sought to kill him. Now the Jews' Feast of the Tabernacles was at hand." Oh, what a terrible sentence. In Leviticus 23 it says, "The appointed feasts of the Lord . . . are these"[1] (Lev. 23:2), but here one of the "feasts of the Lord" has disintegrated and degenerated until it is the "feast of the Jews." Today it is possible to have Easter instead of the Resurrection Day. And Easter is a cursed thing when compared with Resurrection Day. Too often we substitute "I could write a sonnet about your Easter bonnet" for "Christ the Lord is risen today, Hallelujah!" This is what had happened in Jesus' time. The Jews had made their own feast out of what was originally a feast of Jehovah.

Verse 3—"So his brothers said to him"—and this means the children of Mary by Joseph—"his brothers said to him, 'Leave here and go to Judea, that your disciples may see the works you are doing. For no man works in secret if he seeks to be known openly. If you do these things show yourself to the world.'" This is Madison Avenue and Hollywood, you see, the advertising agency. "Do things in man's way!" And you'll see in a moment the reason they thought that way.

Verse 4—"'For no man works in secret if he seeks to be known openly. If you do these things show yourself to the world.' For even his brothers did not believe in him." They hadn't understood Him, but they were interested in exploiting His power. Jesus had been the older brother in the family. They had heard Him call Joseph father, as any stepchild or adopted child would. He had performed miracles and they hadn't understood it. Undoubtedly they had lived close enough to Him to see that He was perfect, and certainly, that perfection had irritated them. Perfection always irritates the imperfect.

Verse 6—"Jesus said to them, 'My time has not yet come, but your time is always here. The world cannot hate you, but it hates me because I testify of it that its works are evil. Go to the feast yourselves; I am not going up to the feast, for my time has not yet fully come.' So saying he remained in Galilee.

"But after his brothers had gone up to the feast, then he also went up, not publicly but in private. The Jews were looking for him at the feast, and saying, 'Where is he?' And there was much muttering about him among the people. While some said, 'He is a good man,' others said, 'No, he is leading the people astray.' Yet for fear of the Jews no one spoke openly of him." When it says "for fear of the Jews" this means they feared the Jewish leaders.

"About the middle of the feast"—it was eight days long—"Jesus went up into the temple and taught. The Jews marveled at it, saying, 'How is it that this man has learning, when he has never studied?'" Now here is the answer to the modernist statement that Jesus had undoubtedly learned all the errors of His day and that's why He thought that Moses had written the Pentateuch and that the prophets were inspired. This is what modernists write about the New Testament and about Jesus. They say, "Well of course, He had the average education of a boy of His time and because He had learned the things of His time, beyond question. He believed that the earth was flat."

When this argument was brought to me in France several years ago, I said, "Isn't it strange that the man who created the heavens and the earth didn't know what shape it was?" The Lord Jesus Christ is Creator. "All things were made by Him and without Him was not anything made that was made." For a little two-by-four philosopher to say that Jesus thought the world was flat because the people of His day thought so, is simply to deny the

105

person of the Lord Jesus Christ. When you begin with Jesus Christ and believe that He is God, then you have no more difficulty in answering the question, "How is it that this man has learning when He has never studied?"

Verse 16—"So Jesus answered them, 'My teaching is not mine, but his who sent me; if any man's will is to do his will, he shall know whether the teaching is from God or whether I am speaking on my own authority."

It is a very unfortunate thing that in the ancient language the word *will* means a simple auxiliary verb of the future—I will go. If I say to you, "I will go," you don't know whether I am saying, "I intend to go," or "I am determined to go." You can say it both ways, "I will *go*" or "I *will* go." You see, the word *will* has many meanings. I would have translated this, "If any man *determines* to do His will, he shall know." God's will is the noun that He wants us to do. Now this is an extremely important verse and I suggest that each one of you learn this by heart, and always be able to say John 7:17, "If any man determines to do his will he will know of the teaching, whether it be of God, or whether I speak on my own authority."

This is the touchstone of men in dealing with their soul, especially with anyone who has been trained in any scientific research. For here Jesus Christ puts a simple qualifying statement on the knowledge of truth. He says, "If you determine to do God's will, you will have a supernatural miracle performed in you. God will show you whether or not the teaching is divine."

Now every science has its own instrument. In astronomy you have the telescope. In biology you have the microscope. In geology you have a hammer to knock off samples of rock. Now suppose an astronomer said, "I'm going to crank down the telescope and use it to look at some rocks." He wouldn't learn anything about them at all. Or suppose a geologist with his hammer said, "I'm tired of hitting rocks. I'm going to throw my hammer at the stars."

Well, that's silly. You cannot learn geology with a telescope, nor can you learn astronomy with a hammer. You won't find out anything about germs by beating them with a hammer, or looking at them with a telescope. The tool of the astronomer is the telescope. The tool of the biologist is a microscope. The tool of the geologist is the hammer. And the tool of the skeptic is determination to do the will of God.

"Well," you say, "I don't know whether all this about God is true or not." Then I suggest that you pray this prayer right in your heart, "O God Almighty, I'm going to do your will, no matter what it costs me." The minute you say that, He will show His will to you. You will know what He wants you to do. If you follow through and determine to do it, you won't have any more problems about believing Him. But if He shows you His will, and you decide not to do it, then you will become a skeptic again right away.

The only reason any man does not believe in Christ is because of sin. This verse, along with John 3:19, proves it: "Light has come into the world, and men love darkness rather than light, because their deeds are evil." If you put John 3:19 along with John 7:17, you've got any skeptic in the world backed into a corner—right in that minute. Don't let him get away from it.

God says your difficulty is sin. God says your deeds are evil. That doesn't mean you are robbing a bank; it may be that you've gone off in a corner of your mind and are full of pride. That's the way it is with the unsaved man. "But if any man determines to do his will, he shall know of the doctrine, whether it be of God or whether I speak of my own authority."

Verse 18—" 'He who speaks on his own authority seeks his own glory; but he who seeks the glory of him who sent him is true, and in him there is no falsehood. Did not Moses give you the law? Yet none of you keeps the law. Why do you seek to kill me?' The people answered, 'You have a demon! Who is seeking to kill you?' Jesus answered them 'I did one deed, and you all marvel at it. Moses gave you circumcision (not that it is from Moses, but from the fathers), and you circumcise a man upon the sabbath. If on the sabbath a man receives circumcision, so that the law of Moses may not be broken, are you angry with me because on the sabbath I made a man's whole body well? Do not judge by appearances, but judge with right judgment.' "

Verse 25—"Some of the people of Jerusalem therefore, said, 'Is not this the man whom they seek to kill? And here he is, speaking openly, and they say nothing to him! Can it be that the authorities really know that this is the Christ? Yet we know where this man comes from; and when the Christ appears, no one will know where he comes from.' So Jesus proclaimed, as he taught in the temple, 'You know me, and you know where I come from? But I have not come of my own accord; he who sent me is true, and him you do not know. I know him, for I come from him, and he sent me.' So they sought to arrest him; but no one laid hands on him, because his hour had not yet come. Yet many of the people believed in him; they said, 'when the Christ appears, will he do more signs than this man has done?' "

Verse 32—"The Pharisees heard the crowd thus muttering about him, and the chief priests and Pharisees sent officers to arrest him. Jesus then said, 'I shall be with you a little longer, and then I go to him who sent me; you will seek me and you will not find me; where I am you cannot come.'

"The Jews said to one another, 'Where does this man intend to go that we shall not find him? Does he intend to go to the Dispersion among the Greeks and teach the Greeks? What does he mean by saying, "You will seek me and you will not find me," and, "Where I am you cannot come"?'

"On the last day of the feast, the great day, Jesus stood up and proclaimed, 'If any one thirst, let him come to me and drink!' " Here is one of the great profound statements that shows what the Lord Jesus Christ thought of Himself. For this is the statement of an utter criminal megalomaniac—unless He is God. You cannot say that Jesus was a good man, and stop there. Here He is saying that He is the satisfier of all of the thirsts of humanity, "I am Jehovah God, the Eternal Spring. If any man

109

thirsts, let him come unto Me." None of us can say this. We all have to say, "If any man thirsts there's the fountain." But He said, "If any man thirsts, let him come unto me and drink. He who believes in Me, as the scripture has said, 'Out of his heart shall flow rivers of living water.'" (See vv. 37,38.)

One morning after church, while I was standing on the street, someone came up to me and said, "Dr. Barnhouse, I read an article in which the Bible teacher tried to say that this verse was talking about Jesus, and that if a person believes in Jesus, then out of Jesus shall flow rivers of living water." But to say that, is to lose the whole point of the story. Christ is saying that He is the main source, and that the water comes from Him to us through invisible pipes, and you and I are little faucets. Then, wherever we happen to be, rivers of living water flow out of us.

Are you a fountain? Is water flowing from you? Do people come to you in order to drink of Christ?

I believe that the Bible shows three kinds of faith. There is the faith of the unsaved man (the devil believes and trembles), a faith that only has to do with the mental recognition of facts. There is a second kind of faith, the saving faith, and in order to pass from the first to the second faith a man must be born again. That is justification. Yet there are multitudes of Christians who are born again but who are not springs for Christ. They haven't struck water in their lives. That comes with the third step from saving faith to flowing faith, arrived at by the process of sanctification.

When you are believing in this way, people will

110

instinctively come to you for help. In your school, in your office, in your hospital, you should so live Christ that others will approach you in their times of trouble; and then you can flow Christ to them. If people do not naturally turn to you for spiritual help, you may be sure that you are somewhere on the road to faith number two and that you have not yet arrived at faith number three. It doesn't say "Some that believe," but "he (anyone) that believes." This spiritual faith is so intense that out of the heart shall flow rivers of living water. "Now this he said about the Spirit, which those who believed in him were to receive; for as yet the Spirit had not been given, because Jesus was not yet glorified."

Verse 40—"When they heard these words, some of the people said, 'This is really the prophet.'" That is a reference to the book of Deuteronomy, where God said He would raise up another prophet like Moses. "Others said, 'This is the Christ.' But some said, 'Is the Christ to come from Galilee? Has not the scripture said that the Christ descended from David, and comes from Bethlehem, the village where David was?'" They didn't know that Jesus had been born in Bethlehem. "So there was a division among the people over him. Some of them wanted to arrest him but no one laid hands on him.

"The officers then went back to the chief priests and Pharisees, who said to them, 'Why did you not bring him?' The officers answered, 'No man ever spoke like this man!'"

Now if you translate that down into a police court in any city today, let's see what it would look like. Suppose the judge sent the sergeant of the po-

111

lice and a detail of men and said, "Go out and arrest so and so." And a few hours later, when they came back, the judge said, "Where is he?" And they answered, "Judge you've never heard anybody talk like that fellow. It's really wonderful how he talks." Well, you can readily understand the anger and amazement of the judge. How incongruous it would be! When the police are sent out to get a man, they bring in their man. What he says or does has nothing to do with it.

The reason they couldn't arrest Jesus was, of course, that He was in complete control of the judges and officers. No one could do anything until it was His moment.

"The Pharisees answered them, 'Are you led astray also? Have any of the authorities of the Pharisees believed in him?'" (vv. 46-48). This is the old argument from personal authority. Don't ever fall for this line. "Do the scientists believe?" "Do the Ph.D's believe?" "Do the professors believe?" If these people are ignorant, what can you expect from them? Remember that the Bible has met this argument in advance. In 1 Corinthians 1, Paul put it this way, "Where is the wise man? Where is the scribe? Where is the debater of this age? Has not God made foolish the wisdom of the world? For since, in the wisdom of God, the world did not know God through wisdom, it pleased God through the folly of what we preach to save those who believe'" (vv. 20,21).

Isn't it silly, this Christianity? Isn't it silly that any one could go to heaven because some Jew was put on a cross nineteen hundred years ago in Palestine? That's why Paul goes on to say, "Not many of you were wise according to worldly standards, not many were powerful, not many were of noble birth"[1] (1 Cor. 1:26). The world may think it is silly—until they discover that it works—and then they will believe.

The Pharisees went on to say "This crowd, who do not know the law, are accursed." Well as a matter of fact, it was the Pharisees who were accursed and the people (many of them) who were saved. Salvation is not by position or brains but by the grace of God in Christ.

Verse 50—"Nicodemus, who had gone to him before, and who was one of them, said to them, 'Does our law judge a man without first giving him a hearing and learning what he does?' " Poor Nicodemus! I wonder if he was saved. We find him three times in the Gospel of John. In John 3 he heard one of the greatest sermons that was ever preached. To him was made the revelation of the new birth, "Ye must be born again." He was the first one to hear John 3:16, but there is no record that Nicodemus believed. Many a man has heard good preaching and gone to hell. It isn't hearing good preaching that saves a man. It's laying hold of truth and letting truth lay hold of you.

At this second mention of Nicodemus, he shows himself to be a member of the Jerusalem Civil Liberties Union. "Does our law judge a man without first giving him a hearing?" Nicodemus was doing this very important liberal work defending liberties, and here was a man who was in danger of being crushed by force of these megalomaniacs who thought they had a patent and a copyright on God. Nicodemus spoke a kindly word (v. 52), but they replied, "Are you from Galilee too? Search and you will see that no prophet is to rise from Galilee." And Nicodemus didn't have courage enough to stand up and answer them.

Actually quite a few prophets came out of Galilee. These men told a lie to try and defend themselves.

Many a man in the heat of controversy gives forth an extravagant position and then seeks to maintain his extravagant position in spite of all objective truth to the contrary. That's what these men did at this point. Amos the herdsman was from Tekoa, which was in Galilee. Two other prominent Jewish prophets, Elijah and Jonah were also from Galilee.

The chapter concludes, "And every man went to his own house." May God bless to us this reading of His Word.

I Am the Light of the World

The first eleven verses in John 8 have been fought by many people. From the time of the Middle Ages people have tried to take them out of the Bible, because they're scared to death about the woman taken in adultery hearing Jesus say: "Neither do I condemn thee: go, and sin no more." People were afraid that this would teach people to treat sin lightly. However, when this is understood, we see it, not as a light treatment of sin, but as a tremendous illustration of salvation and righteousness, which is what the Lord intended it to be.

Now in order to understand the sequence of events, we have to look at what has taken place in the previous chapter. Never forget that the chapter divisions are not inspired. When you take together the last line of John 7 and the first line of John 8, it shows the obduracy of the men and it shows the wonder of the Lord Jesus Christ in His loneliness. "They each went to his own house, but Jesus went to the Mount of Olives"—where the "foxes have holes, and birds of the air have nests; but the Son of man has nowhere to lay His head" (Matt. 8:20).

I can understand why He went to the Mount of Olives. I think that sometimes He must have put his head down on a rock and said, "O Father, this is the place My feet are going to stand in these months ahead when Mine hour is come. Here is where I will ascend into heaven. I'll go back from this very spot." This evening He went out there and was alone all night with His mantle wrapped around Him, lying in the lee of some fallen tree or against a rock—alone with God.

Meanwhile those men went to their own houses. In the Gospel of Matthew, it says that they held a council against Him, how they might destroy Him. They all got together someplace for a committee meeting.

When I first began to realize that this council, this "get Jesus committee" was being formed among them, I began, as I read the Gospels, to see between the lines. I think it would almost be possible to write the minutes of their meetings. At the first meeting they got together and said, "We've got to get this fellow. How can we do it?" Someone said "I've got an idea. Let's go right out in public and ask Him if He pays taxes. If He says yes, we've got Him. We'll turn around and say to the Jews, 'Look, He says to support Caesar. What kind of a Messiah is this?' And if He says no, we've got Him. We'll go to Caesar's men and say, 'We're very sorry, but

Jesus is advocating that people shouldn't support the government, and we want to be loyal to the Romans. You'd better arrest Him and deal with Him.' "

So they went out the next day and said "Master, is it lawful to give tribute unto Caesar?" And He said, "Show Me the money for the tax." Then He asked them, "Whose image is on the coin?" They said, "Caesar's." "Well," said Jesus, "If you're going to accept the protection of the Roman government—their fire department, their police, their army—then you've got to pay the freight on it. Render unto Caesar the things that are Caesar's and render unto God the things that are God's." (See Matt. 15-22.)

At the next committee meeting they said, "Well, that one blew up in our faces. Now what can we do?" And they kept at it, time and time again, testing Him, to prove Him, to try Him, to catch Him. For they hated Him. And now they did one of the most despicable things human beings have ever done. One man said, "I've got an idea. You remember that old law from way back in the time of Moses that says anybody caught in the act of adultery should be stoned to death? Well, let's ask Him if He believes in it."

That law had not been put into practice for generations. Men are constantly passing laws that become obsolete after a few years, and then failing to take them out of their law books. For example, in the state of Delaware, there is a law that says anybody approaching an intersection in a horseless carriage must come to a full stop, get out, and go to the intersection, by day with a red flag and by night with a red lantern. You must be very careful not to scare the horses! They passed that law in 1902 and they never took it off the books. But no policeman will ever arrest you if you don't have a red flag and a red lantern in your automobile as you go through Wilmington!

There was a law back in the time of Moses that anyone taken in adultery be stoned to death. This was God's law, but little by little, because of the hardness of men's hearts, it had been allowed to go unnoticed. In fact, it probably had not been enforced for the last 1,000 years before the time of Christ. Even though the law was there, they just didn't practice it. But one of these men had studied law and knew about it.

So they said, "Suppose we get a woman in the act of adultery." I don't know which of them had a telephone number or knew where to go. Certainly at least one of them had the right information, because they were able, on a few hours' notice, to find just the kind of person they wanted.

And now the stage was set for this most dramatic and deeply significant confrontation. Early the next morning, Jesus came again into the Temple. All the people came to Him and He sat down to teach them. You can see such a picture today in the mosques of the Arab world, and in some of the synagogues of the Jews. In many places of the world, it's the religious custom for people to go for prayer as the sun rises. Since it was the custom among the Israelites, Jesus went there, and sat down and taught them. You see the eagerness of Jesus to teach the people, no matter where He was.

118

Now, get this scene. The sun is rising. It is just getting light outside. Jesus is seated, teaching a group of people squatted on the floor in front of Him, when all of a sudden, there is a commotion outside—the sound of rowdy men, shouting, pushing, forcing their way through the crowds. Jesus stops talking and everybody turns around to look at the door. Then come these Pharisees, dragging with them—a woman! Perhaps her veil has been allowed to fall down and everyone can tell what kind of woman she is—a woman taken in adultery! They have brought her, not because they hate adultery, not because they want to uphold Moses' law; not because they love righteousness, but because they hate Christ. They'll stoop so low that they are willing to take a poor woman and use her as a club to strike Christ with.

"And the scribes and Pharisees brought unto him a woman taken in adultery; and when they had set her in the midst, they say unto him, Master," (note the name they gave Him—not Lord, but Master) "this woman was taken in adultery, in the very act. Now Moses in the law commanded us that such should be stoned: but what sayest thou?" (John 8:3-5).

Well, what do you say? If He says, "Yes, stone her," they could turn around to the crowd and say, "Ha, ha, ha! This is your Messiah who says, 'Come unto Me all ye that labor, and are heavy laden and I will give you rest.' Come unto Him and He will really give you a stone and kill you! This man who talks about the meek and lowly says to stone a poor woman like this?" Had the crowd been given that

119

idea, they would have immediately become defenders of this woman.

But if He says, "No, don't stone her," well, they have their plan. They had said, "Here's what we'll do. We will have some of our servants there holding nice cobblestones behind their backs and the minute He says, 'No, don't stone her,' we'll yell, 'Oh, He's against the law of Moses. He ought to be killed!' Somebody will throw the first stone, and we'll be rid of Him. Then we'll say to everybody, 'Well, after all, He told us not to keep the law of Moses. What could we do? If a man right in the Temple of God tells us not to keep the law of Moses, we must be faithful to God and kill Him.' So we've got Him. Heads, I win, tails you lose. Let's go boys!" And that was their attitude.

"But Jesus stooped down, and with his finger wrote on the ground, as though he heard them not." Now, if you take a good concordance and look up the word *finger*, you will discover that three times the finger of God did some writing. The first time, the finger of God wrote the Ten Commandments on tablets of stone which were given to Moses. The second time, we read that in the feast of Belshazzar there came a finger of God in the form of a man's hand. It wrote on the wall, "Mene, Mene, Tekel, Parsin"—you have been weighed in the balances and found wanting. Judgment!

Now what does the finger of God write this day? In the first place, it's as though Jesus said, "Will you remind Me of the Law? I wrote the Law." Jesus is Jehovah. It was He who gave the Ten Commandments. I am convinced that when Jesus stooped over and wrote on the ground, He wrote "Thou shalt not commit adultery," or "The wages of sin is death." Or some other condemning words justifying God and pointing out the great fact that sin is sin and it must be dealt with.

They kept saying to Him, "Master, Master, what do you say? What do you say?" He simply looked at them and said, "Well, if you want to obey Moses' Law, go right ahead. Any of you who is without sin, cast the first stone." And all who heard it, being convicted by their own conscience, went out one by one beginning with the oldest, who had the most sins to remember, to the youngest, who "hadn't even lived yet."

Now, suppose Mr. Pharisee had come forth and said, "I am without sin." Everybody would have known better and just laughed at Him. Jesus is simply reminding us that they had all sinned and we have all sinned.

"And Jesus was left alone and the woman standing in the midst" of the congregation. Remember that this was an interruption in the middle of the sermon and those whom He had been teaching were watching all this. "And again, he stooped down, and wrote on the ground." What do you think He wrote the second time? I think He must have written something like, "The Lord has laid on Him the iniquities of us all," or "It pleased Jehovah to bruise Him; He hath put Him to grief," or "When thou shalt make His soul an offering for sin, He shall see the travail of His soul and shall be satisfied." (See Isa. 53:6,10,11.) "When Jesus had lifted up himself, and saw none but the woman, he said

121

unto her, Woman, where are those thine accusers? hath no man condemned thee? She said, No man, Lord" (John 8:10,11).

Notice that when the Pharisees came in they called Him "Master," but when she came in she called Him "Lord." And in 1 Corinthians 12:3, it says, "No man can say Jesus is Lord except by the Holy Spirit." This woman is going to be in heaven. The Pharisees are going to be in hell. They may have never committed adultery. She had.

"Oh," says someone, "what are you saying? Don't men go to hell because of their sin and don't they go to heaven if they don't sin?" No! They go to hell because they have inherited Adam's rotten nature. They go to heaven because they have been made partakers of the grace of God in Jesus Christ. "For by grace are ye saved through faith; and that not of yourselves: it is the gift of God: not of works, lest any man should boast" (Eph. 2:8,9).

Many people in the early centuries wanted to leave John 8:11 out of the biblical manuscript. They said, "Oh, no! Don't put that in. It is going to make it easy for people to sin." But when Jesus said, "Neither do I condemn thee: go, and sin no more." He was neither condoning adultery, nor was He making a detour around the Law. No one could ever be accused or condemned except by the mouth of two witnesses. Since there was no accuser, the Law could say nothing. If someone swore out a warrant for your arrest and then did not show up in court to accuse you, the judge would dismiss the case immediately. When Jesus stooped and wrote on the ground the first time, He was vindicating the righteousness of God. When He stooped again, He was vindicating great grace, the grace of Christ that can save the sinner.

So He says (and the order here is wonderful), "Neither do I condemn thee: go, and sin no more." "Neither do I condemn thee"—there is salvation; "Go, and sin no more"—there is sanctification. We would not have any gospel at all if He had reversed those two sentences. If Jesus had said first, "Go and sin no more," and second, "I won't condemn you," what gospel is that? You and I don't have the power to remain sinless on our own. Jesus was giving us an illustration of the gospel—the good news—of grace. There is nothing more calculated to keep us on the road to holiness than to know that "the love of Christ constraineth us; because we thus judge, that if one died for all, then were all dead. And . . . he died for all, that they which live should not henceforth live unto themselves, but unto him which died for them, and rose again" (2 Cor. 5:14,15).

Now, Jesus turns back to His audience again. The crowd of Pharisees and scribes had gone and the woman had left, but the original audience was still there. Remember back in verse 2, that the sun was just coming up. Now, time had gone by, and the sun had risen even higher, and it had come over the buildings around the Temple driving away the shadows, so that now they were all sitting in the bright golden glow of the morning sunlight. As this woman turns and goes out, Jesus turns back to His audience, after such an interruption, and says, "I am the light of the world! Light! Light! Just like the sunlight you are sitting in! I am the light of the world! Haven't you just seen the Light in action?"

We all know what light does. You turn a board over and all these squirmy things start slithering away to the darkness. Jesus had just turned a board over, and there went those Pharisees. When you put men with a heart of sin beside the Lord Jesus Christ, they cannot stand against the whiteness of the Lord of Glory! They scurry for cover. That's why men fundamentally hate Jesus Christ as God. If a man is not willing to bow before Christ, a man is condemned before Christ.

"I am the light of the world." That Light had just shown what these men were. "I am the light of the world." Like an X-ray, that Light had gone to the heart of this woman and had cleansed her of the cancer of sin. In one case, the Light exposed sin and brought condemnation to the accusers. In the other case, it exposed sin and brought grace to the sinner. Both times it was the same Light. The only difference was in their responses.

And then the same Light brought illumination to the audience. They saw before them this magnificent illustration that Jesus was the Light of the world. Jesus has all these functions. When He stands by men, He shows them they are sinners. When He comes to our hearts, He touches sin and deals with it lovingly. When we've been cleansed, He illuminates and instructs that we may bow before Him.

"I am the light of the world: he that followeth me shall not walk in darkness, but shall have the light of life" (v. 12). This is the heart of what John speaks of in 1 John 1:7. "If we walk in the light, as he is in the light, we have fellowship one with another, and the blood of Jesus Christ, his Son [keeps on cleansing] us from all sin." If you let that Light shine in your heart you will discover that it reveals everything you have hidden in the dark corners. When you open the closet doors, that Light will shine in, and cause you to go at the clean-up job. Do you have some tumor growing in your vitals? Let that Light come in and arrest its growth and bring death to those alien tissues. Then Light will come into your mind, Light will guide your feet, Light will illumine you. Jesus says, "I am the light of the world."

Restoring Sight to the Blind

Have you noticed that the Gospel of John emphasizes how the Lord Jesus dealt with the individual? Of course He taught groups, both large and small, from time to time, but He never was too busy to take time for the individual. The Gospel of John is full of individuals who became followers because they had private conversations with Jesus.

And whether the man was Nicodemus or a blind man, Jesus had time for him. In fact, He frequently was confronted by the blind, and it might be of interest to notice the various means He used to heal them. (See Matt. 20:30-34; Mark 8:22-25; Luke 7:21.) A part of our Lord's Messianic ministry required attention to the blind. (See Luke 4:18.)

This particular blind man set off a question with far-reaching implications. Quite casually, as Jesus and His disciples passed the blind man—apparently known to them—the disciples asked a philosophical question, *"Master, who did sin, this man, or his parents, that he was born blind?"* (John 9:2).

The question was based on the popular assumption that some sin, prior to birth, was responsible for congenital blindness. This idea came from pagan sources which held to reincarnation. If a person sinned in a previous existence, he might be reborn into a new life with some affliction or malady as a punishment.

Such a view was quite prevalent in the first century and, in its varied forms, is still held by cults of our own day. However, Scriptures lend no credence to the idea whatever, and positively teach that the issues of eternity are settled in his life for each individual.

The alternate idea the disciples suggested was that the man's parents had sinned and he, unfortunately, reaped the consequences for their sin in his blindness. This, of course, is a very real possibility. Many cases of congenital blindness have been caused by venereal disease, for example.

However, Jesus denied both possibilities. *"Neither hath this man sinned, nor his parents: but that the works of God should be made manifest in him"* (v. 3). Actually, what Jesus said was: "This man is blind because it was God's will for him to be blind at this specific moment, so that I might come and cure him and God might receive the glory."

We must ever realize that there are no "pat answers" for sickness and suffering in the world. There are those who try to tell us that it is God's will for everyone to be healthy, and the only reason a person is *not* healthy is his lack of faith. This is sheer nonsense! Here was a man—blind from birth —whom God had allowed to be born blind so that Christ could heal him and glory might go to God. It was God's will for him to be blind until that very moment.

Sometimes sin does have its repercussions. If a man gets drunk and falls down in the snow and isn't found until next morning, he may get his fingers frozen and have to have them amputated, or at least he will catch a severe cold. Other suffering is the lot of man because of the indirect results of Adam's sin which unleashed a whole wave of suffering on humanity in general. Still other suffering is punitive in nature or may be intended to teach us a lesson. Again, God may allow His people to suffer just to show the world how a Christian can "take it" by God's grace. In other cases, it is God's will to grant healing in answer to prayer.

Yet people have this horrible idea that if somebody has some natural catastrophe, God has been there sort of saying, "I am watching you. You did it! Bang for you!" Now this is not true. This is an absolute scandal on the name of God. God is not up in heaven trying to hit people. God is love. Anyone could testify to the fact that many times, he has sinned and has not reaped the fruits of that sin. God has been gracious in a wonderful way. How tender and patient He is with us!

My oldest son Donald was born with crossed eyes, which later were corrected by an operation. And, after we had had a baby sitter from a Bible institute, we learned that there was a lot of discussion among the students at the Bible school as to what sin we had committed that caused God to have our baby born with crossed eyes.

But, you see, this is not God's way. Don't ever think it is. The minute you do, you make yourself into a dirty little, nasty little judge, trying to say, "Well, what did they do," instead of saying, "In the providence of God all things come to God's people." The most holy and saintly woman that has ever lived for God may have cancer. Or one of the finest men of God may in his old age, have softening of the brain and lose his reason. A child of the most godly people may be born as a mongoloid. So don't ever fall into the great error that the disciples did.

Jesus continued, "We must work the works of him who sent me, while it is day; night comes when no man can work. As long as I am in the world, I am the light of the world" (vv. 4,5). Now get this fact. Because Jesus left the world, He is no longer the Light of the world. I know we have a hymn that says, "The whole world was lost in the darkness of sin; the Light of the world is Jesus." This is not true, Jesus Christ, while He was in the world, was the Light of the world. When He went back to heaven, He left us to be the mirrors to reflect Him. Jesus said to His disciples, "You are the light of the world!" The reason things are so bad today is because we do not reflect that Light of the world.

While Jesus was speaking these words, He spat on the ground and made clay of the spittle and anointed the man's eyes with the clay, saying to him "Go wash in the pool of Siloam." (See vv. 6,7.)

The Pool of Siloam is mentioned three times in

Scripture. (See Neh. 3:15; Isa. 8:6; John 9:7.) The present site of *Birket Silwan,* near the brook Kidron, is probably closest to the actual location of the Siloam of the past.

An oblong tank, partly hewn out of rock and partly built with masonry, the pool measured about 53 feet in length, 18 feet wide and 19 feet deep.

The adjacent Siloam tunnel was constructed in the eighth century B.C., by Hezekiah's engineers, who began at opposite ends and finally met a few feet apart in the center. The tunnel was to convey water, in the event of a siege, from Gihon to the Pool of Siloam.

Now Christ could have healed this man without this means. But He did it for a purpose. Perhaps He varied the manner of His miracles in order to show people that He was not bound to one way or another. When He made clay of His spittle and put it on the man's eyes there certainly was no healing power, no therapeutic value, in substance made out of spittle. No one else could have tried that. It had to be the spittle of Christ. It had to be the touch of Christ. It had to be the power of Christ that did this thing.

The Bible very simply tells what happened. "So he went and washed and came back seeing" (v. 7). People had become so accustomed to seeing him grope about in his blindness, they couldn't believe their eyes when he came along with sight.

Then, the Pharisees challenged him. Had Jesus merely spoken the word and healed him, there would have been no problem essentially. But *"Jesus made clay"* (v. 11) and this was work—on the Sabbath—and therefore, sin. These dirty, low down, religious leaders thought more of keeping the Sabbath than of healing a man who had been born blind.

You can stir up more hatred by going against men's little ideas than by doing almost anything else. Once I prepared a series of broadcast lectures on the Christian and the Sabbath. They were part of a study on Romans, and were broadcast nationally over the network stations of the Columbia Broadcasting System. During that series, we had more struggle with radio stations throughout the country attempting to censor my broadcasts about the Sabbath than we had had over issues discussed in any of the previous one hundred broadcasts.

Some people were furious! Why? Because those people hated the doctrine of grace. And by preaching the doctrine of grace in relation to the Sabbath, I was taking the ground out from anybody who thought he could do for himself what only God could do for him. Anything we do to earn our way to heaven amounts to nothing. God loves and Christ died and all we have is in Christ.

The man himself, and then his parents, were brought before the officials in an endeavor to evoke a testimony against Jesus. You see, the religionists needed a witness against the Lord in order to specifically charge Him.

The once-blind man did not know who Jesus was, He only knew that he had been given sight. Recall John 5:13 for another similar instance. When the man was asked his opinion of his benefactor, he ventured a guess, *"He is a prophet"* (v. 17). The man's parents, fearful of excommunication, wanted no part in the entire proceedings.

Oh, my, it's wonderful when you can get expelled from the synagogue! It would be an honor to be excommunicated from some churches. Wasn't it wonderful that Martin Luther was excommunicated? It's a great honor when a John Knox is crossed out. It's a great honor when a Hugh Latimer is burned at the stake by the bishops. To be accepted by some religious leaders is a kiss of eternal death. But this man's parents didn't feel that way, so they begged off with the excuse, "Our son is of age; let him speak for himself" (v. 21).

Failing to gain headway with the man's parents, the religious leaders recalled him for another session, attempting further to break down his resistance and get him to acknowledge that his benefactor was a sinner for having "worked" on the Sabbath.

"Give God the praise: we know that this man is a sinner" (v. 24), they said. However, the blind man was not interested in being drawn into arguments. He knew one thing for certain: he had been blind and was now able to see, and he stated this in no uncertain terms, "Whether Jesus is a sinner or not, I do not know. One thing I know, that though I was blind, now I see." (See v. 25.)

Brother, you may call yourself an atheist, a skeptic, an infidel, an agnostic or something else, but when you come face to face with a Christian—and I don't mean just a church member—when you come face to face with somebody who has been touched by Jesus Christ, who simply says, "Well, one thing I know, that whereas I was blind, now I see," you can't beat down that testimony!

In his zeal without a corresponding knowledge, the poor man was at a loss to understand the tactics of the religionists. He knew Jesus had worked a miracle and he loved Him for it. And, while he had respect for his religious elders, their continued haggling over what seemed to him to be a minor point was becoming extremely annoying to him.

He little understood the bitter hatred of the Pharisees for Jesus, or he might have been a little bit more judicious or tactful about his remarks. Instead, greatly irked at the insistence of the inquisitors, the man began to accuse them. "Why do you continue to ask for a repetition of the story? Do you want to join His movement also?"

Then, ultimately, his impudence turned to open arrogance and defiance as the man began to ridicule the elders of the Jews. (See v. 30.) The reaction was instantaneous! The man was excommunicated.

Unfortunately, the ex-blind man becomes a type of other believers who have zeal without knowledge. There are many young Christians, just fresh from a conversion experience, who go out to conquer the world for Christ.

In doing so, they frequently make the normal blunders which are easily overlooked and chalked up to naive enthusiasm. But, just as frequently, such new converts may antagonize and create hostility by their lack of discretion and, at times, even obnoxious mannerisms. The man in our story is an example. It is this sort of thing that Christians—

particularly those recently saved—must watch carefully. But, the man learned! In the Temple, he was again confronted by the Lord, who furthered his spiritual education.

The once-blind man had been excommunicated from the Temple—rejected by Judaism. He must have been a rather forlorn person when Jesus came upon him. But then, once he who had been rejected by Israel and He who was about to be rejected by His people, came into contact—a new convert was born, "*Lord, I believe. And he worshiped him*" (v. 38). Because the blind man had received and acted on what little truth he knew, God gave him more truth. Jesus met him again and revealed Himself as the Messiah.

This is an eternal principle that can be illustrated many times in the history of Christian missions. One such case occurred on the bloodstained island of Ono in the South Seas. One day the Ono chief learned from another chief that the only true God was Jehovah and that one day in seven should be kept in His honor. Every seventh day, as best he knew, he worshiped this unknown God.

Then his heart yearned to know more and he sent messengers to roam the seas to find teachers of Jehovah.

But while he was waiting to hear from his envoys, a storm drove a frail craft to shore. On this ship were Christians from the distant island of Tonga. God had sent them. And the islanders of Ono readily received the added truth regarding the great God Jehovah and His incarnate Son Jesus Christ.

135

The whole principle of Scripture indicates that God wants growth. All too many of the Lord's people are satisfied to remain on the first rung of the ladder, the ground floor of Christian experience. This is a sad commentary on our Christian living. Our Lord does not leave His own without additional knowledge and light. There can be no doubt that when any person lives up to such light as God has given him, God will see to it that he is given more.

Ripples on the Shores of Your Life

One Sunday morning, one of the elders in our service prayed, "Lord, we thank Thee that Thou art the God of the storm." That very weekend, a great thunderstorm had hit Philadelphia, and it had been followed by one of the most beautiful sunsets we had ever seen, with the lovely calm weather that often comes after a storm. So we understood what that elder meant when he said, "Lord, we thank Thee that Thou art the God of the storm in our lives, for it turns our thought to Thee."

This message has to do with how the storm affects our lives and the lives of those around us. In the eleventh chapter of John is the great story of Mary and Martha and the resurrection of Lazarus. I want you to note the effect of the death of Lazarus on different groups of people. Like a stone dropped in the water it began to ripple farther and farther and farther. Its effect went far beyond Lazarus, to his family, the household, and even into heaven itself.

First of all, let us remember the background. The sisters thought they had a right to expect help from the Lord. When Lazarus was sick, they sent a messenger who came to Jesus with the words, "Lord, he whom thou lovest is sick." They were claiming the help of Christ. A claim upon the power of Christ is the right of everyone of His children. Once we have been redeemed by Him, we belong to Him. An old man was once asked what he did when he was in trouble. He said, "I say, Lord, your property is in danger." It is a great thing to have just that simple faith: "Lord, your property is in danger." I belong to Him. I have been redeemed." "You are not your own, you are bought with a price," Paul said. Well then, do you think that the one who bought you does not have the responsibility for you? Of course, He has the responsibility. When the Lord Jesus died, He brought us out of the horrible pit. He set our feet upon the rock. He put a new song in our mouth. He established our goings. And if I may say it very reverently, it's up to Him to take us through. Certainly we cannot take ourselves through. I am as incapable of continuing my way to heaven as I was to start it in the first place. It is all of absolute sovereign grace.

When Lazarus was sick, there was first of all a tremendous effect upon himself. Naturally, when a man comes to the place where he is going to die, it has an effect on him. And afterwards, when he came out of the tomb, he was sitting at the dinner table, and though he didn't say a word, yet it says, "many people believed because of Lazarus." He just sat there and was the living witness to the power of God. And you may be absolutely sure that when you have passed through death and resurrection—I don't mean in the future, the death of the body and resurrection to heaven—when you have passed through the death that comes from the reality of, "I am crucified with Christ," and enter into the resurrection that is spoken of, "If ye then be risen with Christ, seek those things which are above," people will believe in Jesus because of you.

In a little wider circle, Lazarus' death affected his sisters. Before the time of Lazarus' death Martha had been preoccupied with much serving. She only had, so it would seem, one extra guest, but she was petulant because Mary was sitting at the Lord's feet. Martha was disappointed and said, "Lord, rebuke Mary. She is sitting here at thy feet instead of helping to serve." (See Luke 10:38-42.) But, a little later, in John 12:2, you see Martha again, and this time, she has at least thirteen extra guests at a big dinner. But the verse simply says, "Martha served." There's no reference whatsoever to any petulance. The death and the resurrection of her brother had taken her eyes away from the tasks she was doing and had put them on the Lord for whom she was doing them. And that's the difference between drudgery and devotion.

In the course of the years I have had to deal with families who come in and want me to help them patch up their home difficulties. Usually, when a couple is on the verge of separation, you can detect the killing of a special feeling that was there at the beginning of their marriage. In the mind of the wife, this would be the feeling that made her so delighted to bear her husband's child, to clean his house, to prepare his meals, to do anything that would please him. But one day, she started looking at dishes instead of at her husband. Then dishwashing became a task. The day she started looking at the tasks of the house and all the chores instead of remembering that she was a part of a great partnership in love, in that day her devotion turned into drudgery.

With Martha, it worked the other way. Her task of serving was drudgery until she saw Christ and then it became a way of showing her devotion. From then on, thirteen guests were easier to serve than one.

I want you to note, in a still larger circle, how the sickness and death of Lazarus affected the disciples. The great Physician, when He had heard that a patient was sick, waited two days in the place where He was. Now, that is not at all according to the oath of Hippocrates—that the doctors take—to do everything and to put themselves out for the patient, no matter what the hour. After two days, the Lord said, "Lazarus sleepeth." "Oh," said the disciples, "If he is sleeping, he's doing well." Then the Lord said, to make it plain, "Lazarus is dead—and I am glad." (See John 11:3-15.) Isn't that an amazing sentence? If you take out the punctuation and read the last part of verse 14 with the beginning of verse 15, you get, "Lazarus is dead and I am glad."

Why? why? why would You be glad of death? To that question, Jesus says, "Don't you think I know the end from the beginning? When something comes into your life, do you mean to think for a second that I haven't measured it down to the last detail?" The Lord knows what He is doing in your life. He knows when the investments that you'd made have stopped paying dividends. He knows when the boss says, "I think that in the next couple of months you'd better begin looking around for another place. Our business just can't stand your salary. I'll give you a couple of months, and if you want to take a lot of time and look around, go ahead." And you say, "At my age?" Do you think the Lord didn't know all about it? Do you think the Lord didn't know when He allowed death to come in your circle? Do you think the Lord did not know what He was doing?

Somebody came up to me once and said, "I've been looking everywhere for that verse in the Bible that says, 'He tempers the wind to the shorn lamb.'" I said, "Well, that was written by a poet in the seventeenth century, it's not from the Bible." But, believe me that is a good phrase because it's true. He does "temper the wind to the shorn lamb." And I can give that to you scripturally from 1 Corinthians 10:13. "God . . . will not suffer you to be tempted above that ye are able." He will never let a wind blow upon you that you cannot stand. He knew when you came to the end of your resources. Maybe He brought you there in order that you might depend on Him again. He knows all about the fever chart. He knows all about the doctor's diagnosis. He knows all about the bills that are coming. He knows how you stupidly got yourself

141

into the debts that you're trying to get out of now. And maybe He let you do it in order that He might begin to deal with you in the way that He wants to deal with you.

The disciples had to learn a very important lesson in the establishment of their faith. "I am glad for your sakes that I was not there so that you may believe." (See v. 15.) The death of Lazarus is going to affect their belief in Jesus. Romans 14:7 says, "No man liveth unto himself, and no man dieth unto himself." Certainly Lazarus didn't die unto himself. His death had an effect upon his sisters, it had an effect upon the disciples, and we're going to see the circle growing larger and larger.

At certain times when trouble comes to us, something that is just not the way we would have ordered it, we can say, "Perhaps this trouble is for some friend. I will trust in the Lord in this thing, because someone may be looking at me. And I pray that what is happening to me may not be light only for me but for someone else also."

Now, let's see how Lazarus' death affected the friends of the family. Since they were a large family, they had many friends. In John 11:19, it says, "Many of the Jews came to Martha and Mary, to comfort them concerning their brother." These were the family friends. We know that whenever there's a death, the friends gather around the family. As an act of courtesy, friends send flowers, they go to the viewing, they shake hands with the loved ones and express sympathy. This is a part of our lives and it was a part of their lives. And what happened? It says in verse 45, "Then many of the Jews which came to Mary, and had seen the things which Jesus did, believed on him." They came to sympathize and they remained to believe. So the effect of Lazarus' death now is seen in the family friends.

Now go a little farther still to the acquaintances when the Lord Jesus Christ reaches the tomb site of Lazarus. As He's praying He says, "Father, I thank thee that thou hast heard me. And I knew that thou hearest me always: but because of the people which stand by"—that would be the curiosity seekers—"I said it, that they may believe that thou hast sent me" (John 11:41,42). Here was a circle of people just standing by. They knew that Lazarus was dead. They knew that Jesus had come. Many of them were "the" important people of the community.

The name of Jesus Christ, of course, was widely known. He had spent time in Bethany. He had healed the sick of the town. He had touched the lepers. As soon as He came, there was a great crowd. There was such a great crowd when Jesus first came to the village. Martha, in verse 20, ran out so that she could meet Him, before He was surrounded by people. When she found Him, she said, "Lord, if thou hadst been here, my brother had not died." I think we can sense a tone of reproach in her voice. But, she continues, "I know, that even now, whatever you ask of God, God will give it to you." Jesus said, "Your brother shall rise again." And Martha replied, "Yes, I know he shall rise again—in two thousands years—but now he's been dead for four days and that's harder than two thousand years." Isn't it strange how people are? "I know he'll rise in the last day, but don't roll away the stone from

143

the door; by this time he stinketh." "I believe in the power of God to raise somebody from the dead in two thousand years, but not today."

That shows you, of course, the unbelief that had to be cleared away. Then Jesus announced, "I am the resurrection, and the life: he that believeth in me, though he were dead, yet shall he live: and whosoever liveth and believeth in me shall never die. Believest thou this? She saith unto him, Yea Lord: I believe that thou art the Christ, the Son of God, which should come into the world" (John 11:25-27). And at that point, Jesus said something to her which is not included in the text. But, I'll prove that He said it. He said to her, "Will you go call Mary?" Someone says, "How do you know that He said that?" In verse 28 it says that Martha "went her way, and called Mary her sister secretly, saying, The Master is come and calleth for thee." So then when Mary was called for, she rose quickly and came unto Him. And Jesus had not come into the town yet, but was in the place where Martha had met Him.

You see, the reason He had not reached the house yet was because—we see it all through the Gospels —the crowds had already sprung up around Him. You remember that Zacchaeus had to go and climb a tree because of the crowd. You remember the woman who wouldn't get near Him because of the press of the crowd, and she just reached through and touched the hem of His garment. You remember a time when He had to get in a boat and pull six feet off shore, and leave a natural moat between Him and the crowd. When He went on a

144

boat one way, five thousand of them went around the lake side to meet Him on the other shore. There was always this tremendous crowd—the hangers-on, the curiosity seekers, the ones who didn't come for spiritual reasons, but for bread.

These are the ones that are always ready to look out of a window when they hear the band and throw some ticker tape down on whoever is coming up Wall Street. They don't care whether it's a general or a golf player or an Olympic team or someone else. *Life* magazine one week had pictures of thousands of people who stood for hours and watched a bird, a hornbill, that came and sat on top of the Chase National Bank in New York City. The crowds just gazed and gazed for hours as a man from the Society for the Prevention of Cruelty to Animals tried to catch the bird in a net. Anything can attract a crowd. It doesn't make any difference what it is. The great contracting firms now build galleries for the sidewalk engineers who want to watch the excavations. People are built like that.

These were the kind of people affected by the death of Lazarus. When something happens to a Christian, it touches him, it touches his family, it touches his friends, it touches his acquaintances, it touches the casual observer. It is a phenomenon that must be explained. So Jesus, when He prayed at the tomb of Lazarus, said, for the sake of the crowd, "Father I thank thee that thou has heard me. And I knew that thou hearest me always: but because of the people which stand by I said it, that they may believe that thou hast sent me" (vv. 41,42).

145

I wouldn't be at all surprised that at the judgment bar of God, this dialogue will be heard, before certain men are sent to hell. Lazarus will be put in the witness box. "Did you die and were you raised from the dead?"

"Yes, I was. I did die and I was raised from the dead."

"And you, were you standing by, did you see this?"

"Yes, I saw."

"Did you believe in Christ?"

"Well, I was pretty busy. I had other things to do. My feet were pretty well in flypaper at that time. I was absorbed with the world, and I didn't make too much of an effort to get off. It would have interfered with my way of living. I didn't believe in Christ."

That's why Jesus could say, "The queen of the South will arise at the judgment with the men of this generation and condemn them"[1] (Luke 11:31). And so will Lazarus and so will we all. So the death of Lazarus had an effect upon the bystanders.

Then, most beautifully, this passage tells us that not only did this event affect Lazarus, his sisters, the disciples, the family friends, the acquaintances, and the bystanders, but it also had an effect on the Lord Jesus Christ Himself. Notice verse 4 in this chapter again. "When Jesus heard that, he said, This sickness is not unto death, but for the glory of God, that the Son of God might be glorified thereby." Jesus Christ Himself got a man into a predicament in order that He might get him out of it. I quite believe that God does that with everyone of us—all the time. That's the Lord's way. If God wants you to trust in Him, He puts you in a place of difficulty. If he wants you to trust Him greatly, He puts you in a place of impossibility. For when a thing is impossible, then we who are so prone to move things through by the force of our own being can say, "Lord, it has to be you. I am utterly, absolutely nothing."

Some of us are like the man who found a penny when he was ten and was hunchbacked by the time he was fifty looking for another one. In the course of that time he found two dimes, four pennies, three nickels, and an assortment of safety pins, bent nails and other things. But he never saw a sunset and never saw anything else, simply because of the fact that he had become stultified in all his life and living. Many people are so occupied with their noses to the grindstone that God sometimes has to put them on their backs to get them to look up. Therefore, you can thank God for the things that come into your life.

And the Lord says, "It is for you that this happened, for your disciples, for your family, for your friends, for your acquaintances and the bystanders, but it's also for Me; it's for Me." And God is saying, "I'm in the midst of an invisible war. The repercussions of what I'm doing will be known in eternity. 'What I do, thou knowest not now, but thou shalt know hereafter.'" Even the invisible world was watching this event. If He can say that there's more joy in heaven over one sinner who is converted than over ninety-nine just persons, do you think the angels weren't watching? Do you think the lord of death wasn't watching?

It says in the Bible that Satan used to have the keys of death. But suddenly, here in the midst of Satan's empire, the Lord Jesus Christ shouted, "Lazarus, come forth!" And all the forces of Satan shook, for they knew what was going to happen the next week. They began to realize that they were fighting the power of the resurrection. And they realized that before man, angels and demons, the whole universe was seeing Satan was just a "sawdust Caesar"—that he really didn't have any power except that which he graspingly took and boastingly vaunted. As Colossians 2 tells us, when Jesus died, He disarmed the principalities and powers, and triumphed over them, making a public example of them. (See Col. 2:15.) And thus, it was that Jesus Christ was glorified.

In the beginning Lucifer had said, "I will ascend into heaven, I will exalt my throne above the stars of God: . . . I will be like the Most High, I will be like the Most High." (See Isa. 14:13,14.) And God had said, "All right, here's your first problem. I'll make the earth without form and void and darkness shall cover the face of the deep. Take that darkness away and remove chaos from the globe." And Satan wasn't even able to do an engineering job on this the smallest of many little bits of dust that were on the universe. "I will be like the Most High"—but he was totally unable to solve problem one on page one. And thus was Satan's meat as it has been through the centuries and as it shall be.

Here once more it is proven that in the invisible realm he who had the keys of death was not able to withstand the Lord of life. "Lazarus come forth!" And Lazarus came forth bound. And as Jesus Himself said, in verse 4, "This sickness is not unto death, but for the glory of God, that the Son of God might be glorified thereby."

That's true of anything that ever came to you. I tell you it makes all the difference in the world, if you lose your job and say, "This catastrophe is not for my dishonor and my hurt, but it's for the glory of God that Christ may be magnified." The doctor comes and says to you, "I'm sorry to tell you that as far as I know, medical science can do absolutely nothing for you. Your case, from our point of view, with the present knowledge of medicine, is incurable." It's a wonderful thing to say, "My Father measured this. He it is that put the spoon to my lips. The medicine may be a little bitter, but He knows what He's doing. He's the Great Physician. And He's the Great Resurrector. He's the One who's constantly able to bring life out of death. And out of the death of my circumstances, He is able to bring the life of joy and victory and triumph."

And lastly, in verse 53 of this chapter, we see the divine purposes in all this. Having Lazarus be sick and die was the chain in the event that led to the cross of Christ and to the fulfillment of the eternal plan of Jehovah God. "From that day forth they took counsel together for to put him to death" (v. 53). It was this sickness and death of Lazarus that revealed the pretentions of the Pharisees and the Sadducees to be what they were. From that day forth, hatred mounted. From then on, they knew they could not have Him around. They had thought themselves white, until He came and stood beside them, and then the jaundice yellow of their position was immediately revealed by the contrast—and they hated Him. Everything they had ever pretended to be, was shown to be hollow. And now they said, "We will not have this man to reign over us. We'll kill Him." The sickness and death of Lazarus so revealed the glory of God, that they stirred the hatred of men.

The human logician may come along and say, "Well, if it hadn't been Lazarus, it would have been something else." But, that's not the way God does it. God used the sickness and death of Lazarus as the fuse that set off the cross of Jesus Christ. And it made all of the rest of these marvelous events of our redemption a fact.

Now then, here is the conclusion for you. The sickness and death of Lazarus, is still down through the centuries, like the expanding circle on the water when a stone has fallen into the pool. The fact that this man grew sick and died comes to you today to tell you that your sicknesses and your catastrophes are not too great; that you are in the hands of the Saviour; that nothing has ever touched you that has not passed through His will; that He wants you as you are for His honor and His glory; that He is able to take care of that situation in your home; that He is able to give you triumph in a body that is crippled or that is diseased or that is losing some of its faculties; that He knows what He's doing. He's with you in your loneliness. He knows all about it. Let the ripples of Lazarus' experience wash the shores of your life today.

And as you go on in life, you can go with a renewed certainty in the sovereignty of God that He doeth all things well, that nothing has ever come to you that wasn't tailor-made and measured to fit your exact circumstances and your exact need. Our Lord is on the throne!

Let us bow in prayer. Our God and Father, we do thank Thee for the greatness of our Saviour and for the wonder that all that we have comes from Thee. And whether it be good or ill, Thou knowest and has prepared it for us because Thou seest our true needs. How we thank Thee, our God, that we come to this fountain, this deep sweet well of love, and that all Thy glory awaits us when we're through this little day of trial. In Jesus' name we pray, Amen.

The Challenge of the Cross

"Six days before the passover" (John 12:1)—the Passover which was to claim the Lamb of God as the sacrifice for sinners—Jesus paid a visit to Bethany once again. There He enjoyed supper with His close friends—the last really enjoyable meal He was to have.

Mary of Bethany anointed Jesus' feet, much to the disgust of Judas who saw not ointment but shekels flowing out of the container over Jesus' feet (12:4-6). (Notice that Mary is at the feet of Jesus again, just as she always is when we see her in the New Testament.) The rebuke of our Lord (v. 7) silenced Judas, but the greedy thoughts of an unregenerate heart were still there.

The next day (five days before the Passover) the triumphal entry into Jerusalem took place on what is traditionally called "Palm Sunday."

Everyone was in a state of excitement or agitation. The disciples—delirious for joy; the religious leaders—furious to the point of murder; the general

153

population—thrilled with anticipation. At such a moment, a day or two after the triumphal entry certain Greeks came, requesting an interview with Jesus.

When Jesus first sent out His disciples, He had specifically instructed them, "Go not into the way of the Gentiles, and into any city of the Samaritans enter ye not: but go rather to the lost sheep of the house of Israel" (Matt. 10:5,6).

This was not because of any racial bigotry on our Saviour's part. It was simply that He had come to offer Himself to His people Israel as a King, in accordance with Old Testament prophecies. He knew they would reject Him on the terms He offered, but legally, this offer had to be made to Israel.

It is true that periodically Jesus ministered to non-Jews. The Syrophoenician woman was a case in point (see Mark 7:26) but only after she stopped calling Him "Son of David" and addressed Him as "Lord." His conversation with the Samaritan woman at Jacob's well was another. But He was careful to say to her, "Salvation is of the Jews" (John 4:22). These incidents had been few, and were merely prophetic examples of universal grace.

But now, a new factor appeared on the horizon. Some Greeks came to Jerusalem to observe the Passover ceremonies. They were Gentiles, but perhaps Gentiles who had become dissatisfied with the paganism of their own idolatrous religion and were seeking solace in Judaism.

They came to Philip, possibly because he had a Greek name (*Philhippos,* "lover of horses"), and they may have felt he might be more sympathetic to their request. Understand, most Jews would look with disdain upon a Gentile and call him a *goy,* the lowest form of contempt. These men probably realized this and felt that if anyone would listen to them, Philip might. Then, too, it is possible that they may have known Philip from his home in Bethsaida.

Observing that they were Greeks, Philip was not sure just how Jesus would receive this request for an interview (see v. 21). So he asked Andrew (also a native of Bethsaida). He didn't know what to do either, so both of them approached Jesus with the news that some Gentiles were requesting an opportunity to talk to Him.

Our Lord recognized in the coming of these Greeks a certain divine sign. Up to that moment He had been insisting that His "hour had not yet come" (John 2:4; 7:30; 8:20). But now, the picture changed. The sudden, unexpected appearance of these inquirers was received as from the Father. His hour had now arrived!

Verse 24 suggests, in metaphorical language, the Lord's own death and its effectiveness. *He* was the grain of wheat, about to fall to the ground in death and burial. But because of His death, multitudes of every tongue and nation would come forth to eternal life in Him, as fruit. How true this has been as we survey the pages of church history. Wherever the message of Christ's atoning death has gone, it has borne fruit in abundance. This is the very heart of the Christian gospel.

George Muller, that remarkable man of prayer, who established orphanages and maintained them on faith, experienced wonders through prayer over and over again.

But when Muller was asked the secret of his service, he replied, "There was a day when I died." And as he spoke, he bent lower and added, "Died to George Muller, his opinions, preferences, tastes, and will; died to the world, its approval or censure; died to the approval or blame even of my brethren or friends; and since then I have studied only to show myself approved unto God."

This is what the Lord Jesus meant when He said, "But if it die, it bringeth forth much fruit" (John 12:24).

Verses 27-30: Then suddenly, the mood changed. A moment before our Lord had been elated: "The hour is come, that the Son of man should be glorified" (v. 23). But, in verse 27, we can almost see the clouds of darkness hovering over Him.

Perhaps He began to consider afresh, because of its increasing proximity, the horror of the cross. Certainly our Lord's death never came as a surprise to Him, as some have suggested. The cross had been planned in the mind of God from all eternity. It was designed that God the Son would adopt the form of humanity and die on a cross for sinners.

When Jesus came to earth, therefore, His whole ministry was focused upon the cross. He set His face like a flint to go to Jerusalem, where He knew the cross was awaiting Him. Yet, it must not be overlooked that He was human. Perfect humanity, it is true! But human, nevertheless. Our Lord was no automaton who could endure pain and suffering without any feelings.

Thus, even the thought of the cross must have filled His holy soul with revulsion. The physical agony would be horrible enough, true! But the agony of soul which would be His probably seemed unbearable in prospect. For the Father would abandon His Son as He bore our sins on the cross. The vision of *this* suffering was enough to make the Saviour troubled. Is it any wonder that He said: "Now is my soul troubled"?

Yet, not for a single instant did His determination waver. In eternity, before time commenced, when the plan of redemption was charted, He was the same as He is today. (See Hebrews 13:8.)

This was the eternal plan and there can be no thought of change, no turning back. Jesus could not have turned back because He would not turn back. His heart of love ever urged Him forward. So, He said, "Shall I ask to be spared from this hour? Never! It was for this purpose that I came to this hour. Therefore, Father, My request is, Glorify Thy name!" (See vv. 27,28.)

The response which came upon Jesus' restatement of His purpose—the answer to His petition for the glorification of the Father's name—was variously interpreted (v. 29). Some said a storm was brewing and it had thundered. Others felt it was the voice of an angel.

So do the unregenerate hearts of men always misinterpret the voice of God. When God speaks, man gropes about for some natural, scientific or pseudo-spiritual explanation which will nullify the effectiveness of the divine message. Jesus said, "This voice came not because of me, but for your sakes" (v. 30).

Verse 31 contains two very bold statements: (1) The world is judged; and (2) The ruler of the world shall be cast out. Taken at face value, these are two very difficult statements to understand. For, after Christ spoke these words, there was no thunderous explosion or clap of doom that might indicate the Judgment Day had arrived.

Through the years since, there does not seem to have been any lessening of evil in the world which might indicate that Satan has been dethroned. Furthermore, our Lord said that in His being "lifted up" He would draw all men to Him (v. 32). Over 1,900 years have passed, and the world still seems a long way from having been "drawn to Christ."

Paul's testimony was (Gal. 6:14) that he had no glory except in the cross. As he preached to the Corinthians, he determined not to know anything but the Lord Jesus and Him crucified. (See 1 Cor. 2:2.)

There is a strange power in the cross of Jesus Christ. Bloody, indelicate, crude and nauseating though it was, the crucifixion of Jesus Christ has power even today. As Christian witnesses, our responsibility is not to promote "easy living" throughout the world, nor to bring a certain psychological release for mankind's guilt feelings; rather it is to uplift the cross of Christ.

Too many Christians today who are steeped in the Word and are concerned about spiritual things might just as well be atop a 60-foot pillar for thirty-seven years as was Simeon Stylites of the fifth century. We too are virtual hermits. We must keep our lines open to the unsaved. The first rule of winning souls for Christ is to be a sincere friend.

The cross speaks of judgment as well as salvation. Throughout John's Gospel judgment is juxtaposed with salvation. (See John 3:18; 3:36; 5:22-24; 9:39; 12:48.) How do we explain these apparent contradictions? What, exactly, did our Lord mean?

In a sense, the world has been under the curse of God's condemnation ever since Adam first sinned. Yet, in His grace God had withheld His judgment in view of the fact that the Saviour had not been provided in the Person of Jesus Christ. In fact, the Old Testament Hebrew word for "atonement," *kaphar*, suggests a covering of man's sins by the blood of the slain animals till such time as Christ would come to put away sin by His own sacrifice.

However, once Christ had come, once His offering of Himself on the cross became a reality—the former method of putting sin away by animal sacrifices was ended. Since Christ's sacrifice there is only one way of forgiveness and cleansing from sin—through Jesus Christ. Anyone who refuses to come to God by the way of the cross rightly stands under the just judgment of God for sin. (See John 3:18.) Thus, Jesus could cry out: "Now—because of My imminent death on the cross—*now*, the world stands judged as never before."

And the devil? He was to be dispossessed. Originally, Satan was Lucifer, highest of the angelic beings. (See Isa. 14:12-15.) But he allowed pride to enter his heart and determined to usurp the place of God, "I will be like God!" he said.

Lucifer became Satan by attempting to ascend into heaven. (See Isa. 14:13.) Satan is still in the lower heavens (Eph. 1:21; 3:10; 6:12), an invisible spirit with numerous demons at his beck and call. These demonic forces surround us today and the devil is the "prince of the power of the air" (Eph. 2:2). The Bible teaches us that he will, in the future, be cast from heaven to earth. (See Rev. 12:7-12.) This will take place during the great tribulation period. Our Lord Jesus Christ once prophetically described this phase of Lucifer's fall. (See Luke 10:18.) And finally, Satan's ultimate destiny and doom will be the lake of fire (see Rev. 20:10) which Jesus said had been prepared for the devil and his associates. (See Matt. 25:41.)

However, Christ signed Satan's death warrant and broke his power over the redeemed when He declared, "Now, because of my imminent victory over the forces of evil, the prince of the world shall be cast out." (See Col. 2:15.) When a person becomes a Christian, he is delivered from Satan's grasp, and the chains of sin which had shackled him are instantly broken.

Finally, Jesus said: "And I, if I be lifted up from the earth, will draw all men unto me" (John 12:32). The Greek text does not have the word *men* in it, so that actually the text says: "I will draw all to myself." Christ did not promise to draw every person to Himself; there is no universal salvation involved at this point.

Christ was lifted up on the cross, lifted up from the grave, lifted up at the Ascension. In our lives and preaching today, He is again lifted up and exalted by us. In every instance, He draws to Himself those who truly repent and receive Him as Saviour.

Art Not Thou Also One of His Disciples?

I want to take you to the Word of God and study with you for a few moments something in the New Testament of what it means to be a disciple of our Lord Jesus Christ. In preparation for this sermon, I just took the concordance and looked at every verse in the Bible where the word *disciple* is found. And after I had them all together, I saw that the word *disciple* is used in two ways, the loose way and the tight way. The loose way is a wide sense—it refers to those who favor a teacher, who join his party and become his adherents, in a general sense. Then in the smaller, tighter sense, the word *disciple* is used of those who seek to learn the mind of the one they follow so that they can know their leader and conform their lives and actions to his. The word *disciple* means follower or learner. It is frequently used in conjunction with the word *teacher*.

Now it is in the second sense, the tight sense, that I wish to put before you your relationship to the

161

Lord Jesus Christ and show you what the New Testament has to teach to those who are the followers of the Lord Jesus Christ. Perhaps, we can see it by looking in John 9 at the ironic use of the word *disciple* by the man who had been born blind. You remember that when Jesus healed him, the miracle was so startling that the Pharisees came and tried to dissuade the man from his testimony by making him admit that he had been healed in some other way. And they questioned him, and questioned him about Jesus. In John 9:27, with some degree of sarcasm and irony, the man who had been born blind challenged the Pharisees with, "Will ye also be His disciples?" Of course, this made them furious. For the last thing in the world they wanted was to follow the Lord Jesus Christ. So they reviled the man and claimed, "We are the disciples of Moses." In that ironic utterance you can see that the disciple is the one who follows, who believes the doctrine of an individual, and conforms himself to his teacher.

Now the question I put to you, without irony, is that question, "Will you be a disciple of the Lord Jesus Christ?" The man had said to the Pharisees, "Will *ye also* be His disciples? but I stress it: will you *also*—in addition to your belief in Christ—be His disciples?" For I suppose that if I talked individually to many Christians, each man, woman and child, and asked, "Do you believe in Christ?" they would all say, "Yes, I do." Then I would ask another question, "In addition to your belief, will you also be His disciples?" You say, "Is there a separation between believing and being His disciple?" Yes, there is. In the Book of Acts, a verse says, "The dis-

162

ciples were called Christians first in Antioch" (Acts 11:26). But today the question must be asked, "Can the Christians be called disciples?"

Originally the people followed Jesus so closely that when the name "Christian" was invented, it was put upon those who were following Him. People said, "These are Christ-ians. They follow Him. They're His!" But today, everybody calls himself a Christian. America is even called a Christian nation by some people. Anything that has a vague flavor of Christiandom gets the name. But how few people who call themselves Christians are indeed His disciples. So will you also be His disciple?

The minute you speak of being His disciple, this implies ownership. We belong to Him. To be His disciple recognizes His claim on us. We are to follow Him. Everything a disciple has belongs to his owner. He is always in readiness to do whatever the owner wants him to do. *slave*

Many people do not consider it that way. I was once talking with someone concerning the attitude of a group of people who were in a phase of Christian work. I mentioned the fact that they did not seem to be on their toes and active in what they were doing. The person said to me, with an air almost, of wonder, "Well, I don't think the thing was ever put up to them in that way. I think they looked upon what they were doing as more or less a job."

When one is a disciple of Jesus Christ, one does not look upon his work for God as just a job. If you're a disciple of Jesus Christ, you're just as much interested in a hole in the carpet in your church as you are in a hole in the carpet in your home. You're just as much interested in the plumbing and the heating of the church as you are in your own home. Of course, in most cases, you can only be interested vicariously, but I'm using this as an illustration to show that a disciple is interested in everything that concerns the life and the work of the Lord, and not merely in giving the Lord the shag end of what is left over.

Years ago I heard a story that shows what so many people do in relationship with their surrender of Christ. There was a girl who lived in a rich sub-urb of one of our great cities. She went to a certain church and belonged to a certain Sunday School class. One day a big car with a chauffeur came up to her house. The chauffeur came in and handed her a box from her Sunday School teacher, who was a very wealthy woman. The box contained roses, but instead of being fresh and dewy, they were just beginning to fall. The petals were discolored, the leaves were withered and one could see that the roses had been picked for several days. Well, the girl thought to herself, maybe Mrs. So-and-So gave the chauffeur that box several days ago and he just forgot to deliver it. So when she met her Sunday School teacher on the street, she emphasized the word *today* and said, "Oh, I want to thank you for the roses you sent to me today."

The woman said, "Yes, several days ago I was out in our greenhouse and I saw these roses. They were so beautiful, they made me think of you, so I cut them, and I've had them in our room and we've been enjoying them tremendously the last two or three days. When I saw that the petals were beginning to fall, I put them in a box and sent them over to you today."

The girl looked at her and said, "But, but, I don't understand."

And then the woman explained. "Listen dear," she said, "the other night my husband and I were driving down in the village, and he went into the store to get something. While I sat in the car waiting for him, half a dozen high school girls came along, talking about the special meetings over at the church. I heard one of the girls say, 'Well, of course, I expect to be a surrendered Christian some day, but while I'm young I want to have a good time.'"

Then the stunned girl said, "Why, why, I said that! But I didn't know that you were in the car and heard it."

And her teacher said, "Yes, I heard it and I thought to myself: There is Mary, just like a bouquet of beautiful roses. And she says, 'Lord, here is the blossom of my life; it is so fragrant and so beautiful, I wish to enjoy it. In a little while, when the beauty of it has worn off and when it is beginning to droop, then I will hand over to Thee that which is remaining. But in the strength and vigor of my life I wish to live it for myself.'" That incident was the means of turning the girl to see exactly the way she was treating the Lord Jesus Christ.

There are too many people who are like this with the Lord. We give Him a wilted flower, but we do not give Him ourselves. Now, Christ gave Himself for you—and there was no holding back. It meant the cross. It meant the tearing of nails in the flesh. It meant the hanging of the weight of a body on those torn places in the hands and the feet. The Bible says, "Christ gave Himself for *you*." Yet it is a fact that most Christians would have to say, "I believe that Jesus Christ gave Himself for little bits of me, and I give Him little bits of myself from time to time when I have something left over. I give Him a tip Sunday morning from 11:00 to 12:00. And I give Him some more once in a while here and there." But, true discipleship is something far different. True discipleship is expressed in 2 Corinthians 8:5 where it says they "first gave their own selves to the Lord, and unto us by the will of God." They first gave their own selves unto the Lord.

When Christ was on trial before Caiaphas, the high priest, He was questioned. We read in John 18:19 that the high priest asked Jesus "of his disciples, and of his doctrine." Interesting, isn't it? The high priest didn't ask Him of His doctrine and His disciples, he asked Him of His disciples and His doctrine. That's the thing that challenges the world —what they see in the disciples. The doctrines they will look at later. There's no doubt of the fact that men look at you before they look at your creed. They look at the disciple before they look at the doctrine. They see us, they see our lives, they see our habits, they see our bearings, our attitudes. They know us by what they see us doing day by day. And they will form their conclusions about our beliefs when they see in us what we do and what we don't do. If they like what they see, then they may look past us to Jesus Christ. But believe me, if

166

they do not like what they see, they will never look past us to see Jesus Christ.

Too often we alienate men by our inconsistency. Instead of adorning the doctrine, as we read in Titus 2:10, we detract from it. The gospel goes out into the world with two strikes against it. God Himself speaks of the offense of the cross, and it is bad enough to have the offense of the cross without having the offense of the disciple. Be sure when someone is offended by Christianity, they are offended, not by you, but by your doctrine. I can take it, I can stand it, if someone hates Christianity because of what Jesus Christ did and because of what we preach. That we're to expect. What makes me tremble is that anyone should dislike Christianity because of me. Everyone of us must keep this in mind as we remember that the world looks at the disciples before it looks at the doctrines.

Now, there are three texts in the Scriptures that show the marks of the disciple. First, in John 8:31, Jesus said, "If ye continue in my word, then are ye my disciples indeed." So, the first mark of a true disciple is continuation in the Word. Jesus had been teaching some very startling things, and the people were in a riot of questions. "How can a man be born when he is old?" "How can this man give us His flesh to eat?" "What manner of saying is this, 'Ye shall seek me and not find me and whither I go ye cannot come'?" These were the questions raised by His teachings. And in John 10:19 we read that there was a sharp division among the Jews. Now note this: it was not the disciples who asked these questions. The disciples followed Him. They did not know all the answers. They certainly did not understand all that He said. On one occasion, it's almost a laughing matter, but, in the thirteenth chapter of Matthew, after Jesus had given seven parables, He said, "Have you understood all these things?" They said, "Yea, Lord." (See Matt. 13:51.)

That's like the story of an eight-year-old girl who was joining a church. One of the elders asked her, "Have you read the Bible?"

"Yes, I have."

"Do you understand it?"

"Yes," she said, "all of it!"

Well, that's nice. For her eight-year-old age and mentality, she understood what she had read: it had spoken to her heart, and she had followed it. There is no doubt of the fact that if you can understand and follow what you know when you're eight, then certainly you can understand and follow what you know when you're eighteen or thirty-eight or seventy-eight.

Obviously the disciples did not understand everything, but they believed what they knew and they continued in His doctrine. As soon as they learned more, they believed that also; for that's the method in Christian life. We are not born again with the full content of doctrine neatly stored in categories in our brain cells, but we go on as babes. We walk as children, desiring the sincere milk of the Word that we may grow thereby, entering into the doctrine. (See 1 Peter 2:2.) Unquestioning faith was the mark of the disciple.

"Is it something Jesus said?" "All right," says the disciple, "I may not know all about it now, but I shall know hereafter." As disciples, we take Him at His word. Whatever He says, we will obey Him. Even when we cannot comprehend, we say, "Lord, I'll follow Thee." "Continue in My Word, then are ye My disciples indeed." He was not teaching them legalism but grace. They were not to be disciples of Moses, but disciples of Christ. They were not to follow the tradition of the elders, but the Word of the eternal Son. This is what they received and this is that in which they continued. So the first mark of a disciple is summed up in Christ's statement, "If ye continue in my word, then are ye my disciples indeed."

Secondly, the mark of the disciple was that they loved one another. In John chapter 13:35, we read this (it's a wonderful verse, especially since selfishness so frequently marks the Christian): "By this shall all men know that ye are my disciples, if ye have love one to another." "By this shall men know that ye are my disciples" the fact that we're willing to sacrifice for other Christians will tell the world whose disciples we are.

In my Monday night Bible class in New York, we had a question box period. One night this question came in, written in a rather scrawly hand as though submitted by someone who had come in from a nearby street and was not too interested in Christianity. "You announce that you're taking an offering for Korea. What about giving it to some of us who are in need right here? Why doesn't the church do something like that?"

I spoke immediately of the fact that the church had done just that. The church has built hospitals, and places where people can go in time of need. No member of our church has ever had to go on relief. No member has ever become sick without having a bed, free if necessary, in the Presbyterian Hospital. There's no person in our church who could die and be left without friends. The church has taken care of, I suppose, everything from a newborn babe, in fact, from an expectant mother, all the way through to burying people, in the course of the years. And this is a mark of the disciples of Christ. The world has learned it somewhat from us. But when the world gives care, it is never given in the same way that it is given by Christians.

Once when I was in Nigeria, in Africa, I saw a man in a leper colony. One of his legs was eaten off at the knee, the other leg at the ankle, because of leprosy. He had no feet. And yet with pads under his knees and with some sticks to push himself along the ground, he had escaped from a leper hospital run by the government and staffed by unsaved men as the wardens and keepers. This leper had crawled on the ground for thirty miles to get into a leper colony that was run by Christians, because he knew that when a government employee put his hand on you in a hospital, it wasn't the same thing as when a Christian puts his hand upon you. There is a softness and love in the hand of a believer towards the ills of the world.

As I was driving in India, a few years ago, I came to a village where I knew there were missionaries, and a hospital. As I came in to the hospital I happened to see an American woman, a doctor, with her arm over the shoulder of a girl, a victim of leprosy who had no nose. The doctor had her hand on her and they were laughing together. I never forgot that—the love of Christ in the hands of a doctor touching a leper. "By this shall men know that ye are my disciples, if ye have love one to another."

You see, the Holy Spirit that lives in one disciple lives in another disciple and the Holy Spirit must get together with Himself. And if there is not that drawing of love on the part of the believer, do we have a right to call ourselves the followers of Jesus Christ?

Paul said, "I have you in my heart." (See Phil. 1:7.) I've seen missionaries who told me that, when the time came for them to leave their mission stations to come home, it broke their hearts. They had arrived in the midst of one of the spiritually dark and sordid places of the earth. The missionaries had preached and people had been saved. People had come from paganism, through baptism, through growth, through the Communion service and into the first steps of the Christian life. Then suddenly, furlough time came, and sometimes there were no replacements. The missionaries knew they would have to go, or their health would suffer. But to leave the flock was a terribly wrenching thing. A bond of love had been built between them. And so it should be with everyone of us.

This should help us to understand the Lord Jesus a little better. He was going to leave His disciples, and He knew that the prince of this world was on the move. In fact, the Lord said that Satan would seek to scatter the sheep. And so, in the face of this kind of opposition, Jesus said the mark of true loyalty, of true discipleship after He had gone and the Holy Spirit had come, would be that His followers love one another.

In John 15:8, we read this: "Herein is my Father glorified, that ye bear much fruit; so shall ye be my disciples." Fruit bearing is the third mark of being a disciple. Now, the context gives you a series of steps for fruit bearing. "Without me ye can not do very much." No, no, that's not it, "without me ye can do nothing" (John 15:5). We must first recognize our own nothingness. There are those who talk and who preach and who have multitudes of meetings but there's no fruit. Activity is no substitute for fruit bearing!

A man said to me once, after he had given a certain portion of his life to Christian work, "It's all been fruitless."

I said, "How did it begin?"

He said, "I remember so well. I was in my room studying, and as I was looking at the Bible, the Holy Spirit started to speak to me. He was putting His finger on things in my life that shouldn't have been there. It made me restless and I closed the Bible, got up, and went out in to the other room and picked up the telephone. I called another Christian and said, 'You know, I am greatly moved at the need for such and such a thing; couldn't we start a Christian work for them?' Well, we got together and we started a Christian work and we gave ourselves to that great activity—work, work, work—and nothing ever came of it."

The reason there was no fruit bearing is because there was no true discipleship.

There in the heart of the room when the Holy Spirit speaks, then is the moment to have the roots in, then is the moment to recognize that we are joined to Him, that the "sap should run," that we are His disciples indeed. And the key to fruit bearing is in the context—if you abide, abide, abide—"If ye abide in me . . . so shall ye be my disciples." (See John 15:7,8.)

Now, let us face each other with the words that were spoken at Christ's trial. Peter had followed afar off. The troops had marched in the big opened door into the courtyard and they had shut the door behind them. In the architecture of the building, there was a little protruding door of a gate house. Peter wandered up to this door, since the main door was closed, and intended to walk through this kitchen-like place and go out another door into the courtyard. As he walked in, a girl who was the gatekeeper looked at him and said, "Art not thou also one of this man's disciples?" (John 18:17). And that's the question I leave with you, "Art not thou also one of His disciples?" Peter said, "No, I'm not, and he went inside to warm himself at the fire with the soldiers and to deny Christ two more times. It shows that one may belong to the inner band of the twelve, yet he may deny Christ, and not act as a true disciple.

"Art not thou also one of His disciples?" Now, you will not deny it like Peter. Right out you gladly say, "Yes, I am a disciple of Jesus Christ." Well then, can you show your faith by your works? As James said, "Faith without works is dead." (See James 2:26.) What works am I to show? These

173

three things: continuing in His Word; loving one another; and bearing fruit. There is the Word of God.

In John 19:38 we read that Joseph of Arimathea was "a disciple of Jesus, but secretly." Interestingly enough, this is the only time in the New Testament where the word *disciple* is mentioned without calling it *His* disciple or *My* disciple. Every other time you find the word *disciple,* it is "His disciple" or Jesus says, "My disciple." Only once does it say, "A disciple." In other words, he was a coward. Joseph fits the words of John 12:42,43, "Nevertheless among the chief rulers also many believed on Him; but because of the Pharisees they did not confess him lest they should be put out of the synagogue: For they loved the praise of men more than the praise of God." Such disciples are not happy ones.

I wonder if some of you work in surroundings where you do not let the boss know you are a believer. "Oh," you say, "but he is a member of the Knights of Columbus—a faithful knight—and if I let him know that I was a strong Protestant I might lose my job." So what? Do you think God is not able to keep you in employment for Himself? He calls you to witness for Him. You don't have to flaunt it. You don't have to come in and call him names, but you can point out the fact that you're a follower of the Lord Jesus Christ, that you believe in Him.

In John 6:66 it says, "Many of his disciples went back, and walked no more with him." That's one of the saddest verses in the Scripture. "Many of his disciples went back and walked no more with him."

174

All the joyful times were passed. Why? Simply because He taught them some new doctrines and they were afraid. Things weren't done exactly the way they were accustomed to have them. I wonder sometimes that these people would destroy fellowship.

I once published in a magazine an article entitled, "I Have Read the RSV." Because I pointed out that there were people who were ignorant, who were damning the *Revised Standard Version* without having read it, and therefore, didn't know how good a tool it could be, we had three people write in and cancel their subscriptions. "Oh no, if you don't cross the *t's* the way we cross them, we will no longer fellowship with you!" (Fortunately, we had, from several parts of the country, people who sent in ten dollars and said, "Here are three subscriptions for the three that were cancelled." So we came out better in the end, perhaps, than we were before.)

I thought of the timidity of people who won't talk with anybody that doesn't walk exactly the way they walk; that do not understand the love of a disciple; that perhaps do not understand how people can be very good Christians, and not belong to what they belong to. They may not believe in the second coming of Christ as you believe it. They may not believe in baptism as you believe it or in church policy as you believe it. So what?

As long as we believe that Jesus Christ is God and that salvation is by the blood, we can be Presbyterians when we come to 18th and Spruce in Philadelphia, but when we go outside we can be Christians—disciples. Everywhere we go, let men and women understand that we are continuing in His Word; that we would be His disciples indeed; that we will be marked by our love for one another; and marked by the fact that we bear much fruit. These are the phrases that Jesus Himself has added to the word *disciple*. "If ye continue in my word, then are ye my disciples indeed." "By this shall all men know that ye are my disciples, if ye have love one to another." "If ye abide in me . . . that ye bear much fruit; so shall ye be my disciples."

May God search our hearts that we may walk very close to Him.

Another "Strengthener-Wither"

I want to give an exposition from John 14 beginning with verse 15, "If ye love me, keep my commandments. And I will pray the Father, and he shall give you another Comforter, that he may abide with you forever; even the spirit of truth; whom the world cannot receive, because it seeth him not, neither knoweth him: but you know him; for he dwelleth with you, and shall be in you."

Now in order to understand the fourteenth chapter of John, you need to look at something in the thirteenth chapter. The Lord had come with His disciples to the upper room. Remember that the disciples were rather ignorant fishermen, quite capable of great mistakes and failure to understand.

177

They had come to know the wonder that was in Christ, yet they did not understand much spiritual truth yet. Suddenly, as they were sitting up there in the upper room, Jesus dropped this fantastic bombshell. He said, "Little children, yet a little while I am with you. You will seek me; and as I said to the Jews, so now I say to you, 'Where I am going, you cannot come'" (John 13:33).

Well, this caused utter consternation! "Why, what do you mean He's going away?" Now He went on talking but I'm going to prove to you that they didn't hear what He said to them.

"A new commandment I give to you, that you love one another"—they didn't hear any of this—"as I have loved you, that you also love one another. By this shall all men know that you are my disciples, if you love one another." If the Holy Spirit hadn't brought these words later to John's mind and had him write them down, we would not have this.

If you look at the next verse, you see that Peter came back into the room. His mind had been down the street with the idea: "He's going to leave us. Where's He going to go? What's He going to do?" As Jesus' voice went on, Peter jumped in and said, "Lord, where are you going?" See where his mind has been?

Jesus said, "Where I am going you cannot follow me now, but you shall follow afterwards."

Peter said, "Lord, why can't I follow you? I'd lay down my life for your sake."

Jesus said to him, "Would you lay down your life for My sake? I tell you before the rooster crows tomorrow morning at break of day, you will have denied Me three times." (See John 13:36-38.) Oh, consternation! And Jesus said, "Let not your hearts be troubled; you believe in God, believe also in me." "Don't worry, now, don't worry," Jesus is saying.

"Yes," reply the disciples, "but what is this fantastic thing?"

I want to first establish the principle that when a speaker speaks, you don't hear all he says. That's why it's worthwhile to preach the same sermon over in a different way. A preacher's job is somewhat like that of a writer of a musical comedy or a popular song. He has to say the same thing over in fifty thousand ways. Many of the popular songs follow this pattern: boy meets girl—I love you—there's trouble—now the trouble's over—you're back—we love each other. Just as they have to say this over in fifty thousand different popular songs, so we have to say the divine truths over and over again always showing with a different facet of the same diamond. But we have it a little easier than they do because divine love has so much more than human love.

You see when people are talking, it's so easy to leave the room with your mind and not hear a part of what is being said. One Sunday morning after I had preached a sermon one of our members, a very thoughtful man, came to me and said, "I don't think you were logical. You said this and then you said this—and these two things just don't follow."

I said to him, "But in between I said this and this."

"No you didn't."

"I pulled out my notes and said, "Remember when I said that?"

"Yes."

"What about that?"

He said, "I didn't hear that."

I said, "And this?"

He said, "I didn't hear that either."

I looked back up above to ask him what was the last thing he had heard. Then he interrupted me—"Oh, yes, I remember! When you said so and so, I began to think about it because it was a new thought to me."

I said, "While you were thinking about that— point 2—I was going through points 3 and 4, and you shook your head and came back into the sermon at point 5."

Now this is possible and it is exactly what happened here in John 13:33. Jesus said, "I'm going to leave you," and the disciples' first reaction was terrified amazement! Then as Jesus talks and talks and talks, Peter comes back into the room and asks, "Lord, why can't we go where you are going? What are you going to do? What do you mean?"

I could give you an analogy. Some of you have little children. You all know what happens on those nights when you've got the babysitter coming and you are getting ready to go out for an evening. Mother puts eighteen-month-old Junior to bed quickly tonight. "Now, Junior," she says, "Be good . . . stop crying . . . eat your dinner . . . get going . . ." Then when mother suddenly comes around and warns, "Don't touch me—I'm all made up!" Junior begins to recognize that something is happening!

He sees Mother putting on her gloves and hat and hears her wishing out loud for that baby-sitter to arrive so they won't be late.

All of a sudden the doorbell rings and in comes Miss Baby Sitter. "Now, Junior," says Mother, "she's a lovely lady and—"

"Waa! Waa!" Junior interrupts.

"But Junior," says Mom, "she's nice. You should have as much confidence in her in ten seconds as you've learned to have in me for eighteen months!" It doesn't work that way, does it?

Now this is exactly what the Lord Jesus Christ was saying. "I am going to leave you and the Holy Spirit is coming as the divine baby-sitter.

"Waa! Waa!" cried the disciples. "We don't know anything about that!"

"Let not your heart be troubled," replied Jesus, "ye believe in God, believe also in me. . . ."

With this in mind, we can go back to our text in John 14:15, "If you love me, you will keep my commandments. And I will pray the Father, and he shall give you another Comforter." The Lord has just announced that He is going to leave. And He says, "While I am gone the love that I bring into your heart is to direct you." What is to be the fuel on which our Christian life travels? What is to be the oil which keeps the motor lubricated? What is the source of everything that we have and do? It is the love of Christ constraining us.

Jesus said, "You're not to live in inconsolable regret after I leave." Some of you may have learned this hymn when you were children—what a terrible hymn!

"I think when I read that sweet story of old,
How when Jesus was here among men
And they brought little children and lambs
    to His fold,
I would have liked to have been with Him
    then.
I wish that His hands had been placed on my
    head,
And that His arms had been thrown about me,
And that I might have seen His kind look
    when He said,
'Let the little ones come unto me.' "

Well, to me dear friends, that hymn is false! I don't want anything to do with the life of Christ as He lived before He died and rose again. Paul says in 2 Corinthians 5, "Yea, though we have known Christ after the flesh, yet now henceforth, know we him no more" (v. 16). Jesus said in another passage, "It is expedient for you that I go away" (John 16:7). The *Revised Standard Version* translates this verse: "It is to your advantage that I go away." You and I are ten thousand times better off than was John the Baptist or Peter, James and John before Pentecost. For we have Him living in our hearts.

Now, just before He goes to die and rise from the dead, He's announcing the motive and the goals and the course of our lives. We are not to live in regret, but in complete compliance with His commandments, "If you love me, you will keep my commandments" (John 14:15). This love is the source of true faith. If you look back you will see that this love is the goal of our prayers. Verse 14 says, "If you ask anything in my name, I will do it."[1] Now what does this mean, "If you ask anything in my name"? Well, what are you going to ask— "Lord, give me this, give me that, give me this, give me that, give me this, give me that"? No! You're not going to say that. You are going to say, "Lord, what do you want me to have?"

You wouldn't ask someone you love to do something absurd, something completely selfish for yourself. But someone says, "Doesn't the Bible say, 'Delight thyself in the Lord and He'll give thee the desires of thy heart'?" What heart? Your foul heart? Your lustful heart? What if your desire is that your aunt will die and leave you that oil well? You've got to understand that love "worketh no ill to his neighbor"; that the fulfillment of the law is love; that His love is to dominate our praying; and that in all things love is the aim of prayer.

In 1 John 3:22 it says, "And whatsoever we ask, we receive of him, because"—because—because— because—because—"we keep His commandments, and do those things that are pleasing in his sight." In other words we are surrendered to His will. We are yielded to Him, and if we are yielded to Him, our attitude in prayer should be, "Lord, I don't want anything that's not for my own good. Lord, I'd like to have this; humanly speaking, I'd like to have this, but I don't know whether this is best for me."

You might see a glass of liquid and you might say, "Oh, that makes me thirsty. Please may I have it." Well it happens to be a solution to kill leaves, plants, crabgrass and dandelions in the lawn. "Yes, but it looks nice. It looks somewhat like limeade." But it isn't limeade. If someone gives that to you, just because you ask him to, and you take it, that nice-looking liquid may do more than kill dandelions in the garden.

Many times we pray in just such silliness. Therefore, we must always say "Lord, keep me from even asking for something that is to my detriment."

Now I want you to note that this text, "If you love me, you will keep my commandments," is a great rebuke to the antinomianism of our day. That is a theological term which means one is against the *nomas,* the law. In some fundamental circles, there are people who say, "Well, the law is not for us. The law is gone now. We don't need to have anything to do with the law. We live under grace and therefore we can do as we please."

I once was talking to the dean at a big Bible institute, where there were several hundred students. Thinking in terms of a sermon I was preparing, I said to him, "Do you have moral problems with your Bible institute students?" And he said, "Oh, yes, all the time, and increasingly so." The number of cases of fornication among Bible institute students is very great. And every Bible institute in the country knows it. It's possible for Christian young people to come to church saying, "I love him," "I love her," and then go out—and commit sin. This antinomianism is a cursed thing.

We must understand that if we love Christ, we've got to keep His commandments. The Lord that gave the Law to Moses is the same Lord who died for us on the cross. Mt. Sinai and Mt. Calvary are in the same range of mountains, spiritually speaking. You cannot divorce Mt. Sinai from Mt. Calvary. In the Old Testament, in Exodus 20:6, after saying that God visits the iniquities of the fathers upon children of the third and fourth generations of those who hate Him, it says that He shows mercy "unto thousands of them that love [Him] and that keep [His] commandments." So in the Ten Commandments, He says, "Love Me and keep My commandments," and in the upper room He says, "Love Me and keep My commandments."

Now what are the commandments? "The commandments" is the whole of the divine revelation—the Old Testament and the New Testament. Now this doesn't mean that you are to kill a lamb for the remission of sin, or that you must observe Saturday, or that you are to go around observing the legal prescription of the Old Testament that says you can't make a suit of clothes out of two different kinds of cloth. If you can't mix linen and wool—why, who knows what you're wearing these days? Dacron, nylon, orlon, pine tree root, cold tar products, sour milk—today chemistry has given us so much that nobody in the world knows what we have on our backs. If you were a good Jew living in an orthodox manner, you couldn't wear most of the clothes you wear, because it would be a violation of the kosher elements concerning dressing. You couldn't have bacon with your breakfast or ham with your lunch if you were keeping the Old Testament commandments.

When it says, "If you love Me, keep My commandments," this is referring to the whole of the divine revelation. We must understand that the Lord Jesus Christ is living in our lives and leading us on

185

moment by moment into a life of holiness according to the principles set forth in the whole of His Word. Who was it that was with the children of Israel for forty years in the wilderness? It was Jesus Christ.

"Oh," someone says, "is that in the Old Testament? Christ?" In 1 Corinthians 10:9 it says, "Neither let us tempt Christ, as some of them also tempted, [in the wilderness] and were destroyed of serpents." Back in verse 4 of that same chapter, it says, "And they did all drink the same spiritual drink; for they drank of that spiritual Rock that followed them: and that Rock was Christ!" So we see very definitely then, that the Lord God Almighty has given us the expression of His will, which He calls "His commandments," and that we are not to take them in the servile sense of slaves, but in the joyful sense of sons who find out the will of the Father and seek to put into practice that which would be pleasing to Him. "If you love me, keep my commandments."

Now notice verse 16, "If you love me, keep my commandments. And I will pray the Father, and he shall give you another Comforter." Back in verse 15, He asks love and obedience from us. In verse 16, you see that His love "through the Comforter," gives us the power to obey. How are you going to obey Him? You can't obey Him by yourself. "The carnal mind is enmity against God: for it is not subject to the law of God, neither indeed can be" (Rom. 8:7). But in Romans 5:5 it says, "Hope maketh not ashamed; because the love of God is shed abroad in our hearts by the Holy Spirit which is given unto us."

So you can see just the logic of this thing. First, the Holy Spirit comes—Romans 5:5. He brings the love of God. This love is shed abroad in our hearts. And if we have this love of God, we keep His commandments. It's all interrelated in an interlocking direction—the Holy Spirit brings love, love enables us to keep the commandment, and following the Lord Jesus Christ takes us on to daily power and life. "I will send you another Comforter."

In order to understand this word *comforter*, we've got to get away from the false, American idea of what a comforter is. I was walking in downtown Philadelphia one noon, and as I came back from lunch, I crossed on the west side of 17th Street and looked in a window where they were having a sale of Irish linen and other things. In the window was a sign which said: All Comforts on Special Low Price! That use of the word *comfort*, refers to a comforter, a soft, downy quilt.

But that's not a comforter, in the Bible sense of the term. The first syllable *com* is the English application of *cum*, the Latin word for "with." And then the Latin word *fortis* is the word we have in fortification, flying fortress, fortify. It means to strengthen. The Comforter is a "strengthener-wither." A Comforter is not a downy quilt that you pull up on a cold night. A Comforter is a ramrod down your backbone to make you stand for the truth; to make you take the right side, even though it's the minority side. The Comforter gives you strength to stand up in face of something that is vile and evil.

I once went to a lunch counter in Pennsylvania Railroad Station in New York, and there was evidently a new employee on the job. It was the middle of the night. I had come in while waiting for a late train. The top man-for-the-moment was giving orders to this new person and said, "Now look. Just don't work too hard. If you do, there aren't going to be enough jobs. Take it easy. If there are a lot of customers around, just serve them slowly enough, so that the boss will have to put on another person. We've got to get one more job and one more set of wages." In other words he was saying ,"We have to steal."

Well this is the kind of thing you must stand against if you are an employee and the rest of the people say, "Oh, come on. Don't come in before 9:00; you make the rest of us look cheezy. We get in at 9:00 and hang up our coat on company time. Now we take fifteen minutes off for morning coffee break, and brother, we stop working at ten minutes to twelve, to get ready to go out for lunch."

"Well," you say, "I'm a Christian. I'll be here at 9:00 with my coat off. And if I'm paid for so many hours' work, I'll work so many hours."

"Oh," someone says, "you're not going to be popular."

Well, I don't find any verse in the Bible that says: In this world you shall be popular. I find that in this world you shall have tribulations. Do your work quietly, in Jesus' name. And if someone says, "Why do you do this?" you can say, "I'm a Christian and the Lord tells me that I am to live for Him, and my way of living for Him is to be honest with the boss. I'm paid for forty hours' work a week and I'm going to work for forty hours." If you steal 5 minutes each morning, that is 25 minutes in 5 days, and 5 minutes each noon, makes 50 minutes; and if you are 5 minutes late getting back to work, that totals 75 minutes, and you leave 5 minutes early in the evening, that makes it 100 minutes; then if you waste 20 minutes throughout the rest of the day it means you are stealing 3 hours and 20 minutes a week! The Comforter enables you to stand firm in that kind of situation.

Now in the Scripture Jesus says, "He shall send you *another* Comforter," and He will strengthen you in the midst of any problem you have. This means He has personality. He shall send you another personality—another Comforter. In Greek there are two words for another. There is another which is exactly alike, and there is another which is completely different.

I go into a store and I buy a fountain pen. It's the best fountain pen I ever had. Oh, this is a wonderful fountain pen. I'm walking down Chestnut Street one morning, and a man says to me, "Dr. Barnhouse, it's been a long time since I've seen you. I've been meaning to write to you because I get so much joy out of your radio hour and I want to give you a check for your work. I've got a check here and—" he looks in his coat pocket "—oh, I forgot my pen."

I say, "Here, use mine."

So he writes out a check and I sort of look to see and—oh, goodness, he put an extra zero! He's giving me a hundred dollars for the Bible Study Hour. "Well," I say, "I certainly appreciate it."

Then he says, "My, that's a nice pen. I have such

trouble getting a good pen. That's the best pen I ever 'writ' with."

I say, "Look, let me give it to you as a present. You've been a long friend of our work."

"Oh, no, no," he says.

"Look, if you don't take it now, I'll merely take it over, have the secretary wrap it up, mail it to you. That may cost us fifteen cents more, but you're going to have that pen!"

"Well," he says, "that'll remind me to pray for you and write more checks."

Well, I go back into Pomerants, where I bought the pen, and I say, "Joe, remember that pen you sold me the other day? I want another." What does that mean? It means I want another exactly like that good one he sold me the first time. But then the second pen turns out to be a fountain pen—it "founts" all over me—ink everywhere—leaky, nasty thing.

So I go back and say, "Joe, remember that pen I bought from you the other day? I want another!" Now what does that mean? I want another—absolutely different.

In the Greek, since there are two words, you could never be confused about this. In John 5, Jesus Christ said, "I am come in my Father's name, and ye receive me not: if *another* [the antichrist] shall come in his own name, him ye will receive" (v. 43). Which word do you think He used there? "Another will come"—*another*—absolutely different. Now, says the Lord in John 14:16, "I am sending you *another* Comforter—"like Me."

The Greek word for Comforter is *paraclete. Para,*

190

in Greek, means "along side." You see it in *parallel* and *paradox*. The second half of *paraclete* is from the Greek *kaleo,* to call. The same word is in *ecclesia,* the "called out ones" of the church. And what He's saying is, "I'm going to give you another personality who is called alongside of you." In Latin the word for "alongside" is *ad.* And the word for "call" is *vocare,* so you get *advocate. Advocate* is pure Latin for "call alongside." And *paraclete* is pure Greek for "call alongside."

Let's say you get into legal trouble. You go down the street and you see a sign that says: "Smith, Jones, Brown & Smith—Lawyers." You go in and you say, "Help! S.O.S." You've just called the lawyer alongside because you are in trouble. The lawyer is your paraclete. "Now," says the Lord, "I will send you another Advocate, another 'Strengthener-wither,' who comes alongside of you." Now we have two of these. The remarkable thing is that this word *paraclete* or *comforter* appears twice in the Bible. You only see it once in English though, because in 1 John 2:1 the same Greek word is translated by another phrase. "My little children, these things write I unto you, that ye sin not." And if any man sin, we have an advocate"—a paraclete, a comforter—"with the Father, Jesus Christ the righteous." So the Scripture tells us that we have this advocate, this firm of lawyers, this partnership of magnificent attorneys, Christ and the Holy Spirit. And Christ is in charge of the branch in heaven and the Holy Spirit is in charge of the branch on earth.

These two are working for us. In fact, right this minute, both of them are praying for us. In Hebrews 7:25 it says, "Wherefore he [Christ] is able also to save them to the uttermost that come unto God by him, seeing he ever liveth to make intercession for them." So who is praying for us in heaven? Jesus Christ is right this minute praying for us in heaven. Now over in Romans 8:26 it says, "Likewise the Spirit also helpeth our infirmities: for we know not what we should pray for as we ought: but the Spirit himself maketh intercession for us with groanings which cannot be uttered." So we have in Hebrews 7:25 that Jesus Christ is praying for us in heaven and we find in Romans 8:26 that the Holy Spirit is praying for us here on earth. So we have "another Comforter."

Now let's go back to John 14. "I will pray the Father, and he shall give you another Comforter, that he may abide with you forever; even the Spirit of truth; whom the world cannot receive, because it seeth him not" (vv. 16, 17). That means He is not a physical person. This is very important because the whole heart of the Roman Catholic error is that they say God replaced Christ on earth with the Pope. Well, what this text is teaching us is that God replaced Christ on earth with the Holy Spirit. This is why the whole Roman Catholic system is a vast blasphemy, in spite of the fact that they believe in the virgin birth, and that Jesus Christ is God, and that He died on the cross and that He rose again from the dead.

It's possible to believe all that and yet have a system that is based on error because they say Jesus went to heaven and Peter came to be the vicar of Christ. The word *vicar* means "instead of." It's from

192

the Latin word *vicarious*. You have it in the phrase "vice-president." When a president dies, the vice-president becomes president "instead of" the man who died. But when the Roman church says that the Pope is the vicar of Christ, this is the most fantastic blasphemy that the world has ever seen, because it gives you a man who says, "I am God Almighty and when I speak, God speaks." But Jesus says, "My vicar is not a visible person. The Holy Spirit is My Vicar, whom the world cannot see."

Now notice that He is called "the Spirit of truth"; in fact, in Greek it's "Spirit of *the* truth." What is the truth? In John 14:6, Jesus said, "I am the way, the truth and the life: no man cometh unto the Father, but by me." So the truth is Jesus Christ. But in John 17:17 it says, "Sanctify them through thy truth: thy word is truth." So "the truth" is Jesus Christ and "the truth" is the Bible. And the Holy Spirit will always work in connection with these two.

Then in John 16:7 we read, "Nevertheless I tell you the truth; it is expedient [it is advantageous] for you that I go away: for if I go not away, the Comforter will not come unto you; but if I depart, I will send him unto you." The Holy Spirit is sent to us by Christ, the Truth. And the Holy Spirit therefore becomes the agent of the Truth. Jesus said in John 16:14, "He [the Holy Spirit] shall glorify me: for he shall receive of mine, and shall show it unto you." So you see, the Holy Spirit is the Spirit of Christ, the Spirit of "Christ, the truth."

He is also the Spirit of the "Bible the truth." It says in 2 Peter 1:21, "For the prophecy came not in old time by the will of man: but holy men of God spake as they were moved by the Holy Spirit." So the Bible comes from the Holy Spirit, the Holy Spirit comes from Christ and "when he, the Spirit of truth [Christ and the Bible], is come, he will guide you into all truth [Christ and the Bible]: for he shall not speak of himself; but whatsoever he shall hear, that shall he speak: and he will show you things to come" (John 16:13). In John 14:26 the function of the Holy Spirit is clearly defined: "But the Comforter, which is the Holy [Spirit], whom the Father will send in my name, he shall teach you all things." So you see, the Holy Spirit replaces Christ as the teacher of truth.

Now, for the last point, let's go back to John 14:17: "Even the Spirit of truth; whom the world cannot receive, because it seeth him not, neither knoweth him: but ye know him; for he dwelleth with you, and shall be in you." Now why can't the world receive Jesus Christ? The reason is that the world and Jesus Christ are diametrically opposed to each other. If you take a good concordance you can discover the following facts: That the word *world* is found in Matthew four times; in Mark three times; in Luke four times; and in John seventy-nine times! The word *world* is the key to the Gospel of John— you and the world, the believer and the unbeliever, the church and the world, the true Christian and the world. God alternates and puts them against each other and says, "If you were of the world, the world would love its own. But because you are not of the world, because I have elected you out of the world, therefore the world will hate you." And if the world hates God, if the world hates Christ, if the world cannot receive the Holy Spirit, then the world cannot receive us.

In 1 John 2:16 we read, "For all that is in the world, the lust of the flesh, the lust of the eyes, and the pride of life, is not of the Father, but is of the world." Now what does this mean? This means that "Hollywood is not of the Father." This means that Madison Avenue with its advertising techniques and its hidden persuaders "is not of the Father." This means that high society "is not of the Father." This means that business which exploits and will seek anything to get a profit "is not of the Father." This means that the television industry "is not of the Father." This is the world that crucified Christ.

But if you look over in 1 John 5:19 we read this: "We know that we are of God, and that the whole world lieth in wickedness." A literal translation of this would read, "the whole world lieth in the wicked one." And the Greek word for *lieth* is the same word that is used by the Greek poet to describe a man lolling in the arms of a prostitute. So here it says, "We know that we are of God, and the whole world lolls in the embrace of the devil." Now this is the reason why the world cannot receive Christ.

We must understand that the world cannot see Him—"it seeth him not" (John 14:17). Seeing doesn't mean seeing merely with a visible eye. It means, of course, seeing spiritually. In 1 Corinthians 2:14, it says, "The natural man [the unregenerate man] receiveth not the things of the Spirit of God: for they are foolishness unto him: neither can he know them, because they are spiritually discerned." The seeing is a spiritual discernment. This is what Jesus meant in John 3:3 when He said to Nicodemus, "Except a man be born again, he cannot see the kingdom of God."

Now why is this verse (John 14:17) put at this spot in the Gospel of John? The Lord has said, "I am going to heaven, and I'm going to send you another Comforter, whom the world cannot see." Why is this put here? It's put here in order to point out to us that the Church is not to expect fantastic triumphs. We are to be a despised and a persecuted people. You may be sure of the fact that anything that calls itself "church" and wants to wear fine robes and say, "Kiss my ring," or "You are Mr. Pope," or Mr. Bishop or Mr. Dignitary, is not of the Holy Spirit. The Lord Jesus Christ was meek and lowly, and He said, "If the world hate you, ye know that it hated me before it hated you." (See John 15:18.)

This fact destroys any false hopes that the Church might have about bringing in the millennium. Someone says, "Isn't the Church to convert the world?" Of course not! Brother, we have certainly made a botch of converting the world, because we're not even up to 50 percent of the population growth. Fifty years ago we might have said that there were a billion people who had not heard of Jesus Christ. Today, there are close to two billion people who have not heard of Jesus Christ. The missionary task is fantastically greater now than it was then. And always the number of births and the increase of population is greater than the increase of the Church.

This trend will continue, for Jesus Christ said, "When the Son of man cometh, shall he find faith on earth?" (Luke 18:8). But as it was in the days of Noah, Sodom and Gomorrah, so shall it be!

Now for a closing thought from John 14:17, where Jesus says, "for he [the Holy Spirit] dwelleth with you, and shall be in you." Oh, how wonderful this is! He dwelleth with you and shall be in you. This does away with those branches of Protestantism, that say the Holy Spirit can't dwell with us if we are sinners. They say, "Well, the Lord has got to come and dwell in us, but since we are sinners, we have to have a second blessing, an experience that makes us sinless." But this is not true. While we are on this earth, we are sinful. The Lord dwells in a body that is decaying and disintegrating. He dwells alongside my carnal nature, which is enmity against God.

Let me show you how this was in the Old Testament. The Lord was to come and live with His people, but here's what He says in Leviticus 16:16: "He shall make an atonement for the holy place, because of the uncleanness of the children of Israel, and because of their transgressions in all their sins: and so shall he do for the tabernacle of the congregation, that remaineth among them in the midst of their uncleanness." In other words God says, "Before I can come and live in the Tabernacle, I want Aaron to kill a lamb, take the blood, and put one drop of blood on the veil, one drop of blood on each stave, one drop of blood on the altar, one drop of blood on the laver, and one drop of blood on every stick and piece that is in the Tabernacle, because," God says, "I'm coming to live there." Well how can You come and live with these stiff-necked, stubborn, rebellious, fornicating, idolatrous Israelites? "Oh," says God, "look at the drop of blood down at the corner of the tent. I'm looking at this dwelling place through Jesus Christ."

How can God come and live in Donald Barnhouse? Look at what he is in himself. "Oh," says God, "the blood of Christ is between Me and what Donald Barnhouse is in himself." The Holy Spirit comes to dwell in these human "tabernacles" in order to manifest Christ. And in spite of the fact that when you look into the mirror and see yourself you say, "Oh, it's a good thing people don't know what I am." Have you ever done that? "It's a good thing they haven't discovered what I did last night, or last week. It's a good thing they don't know all the truth instead of the two percent truth that I told them." Oh, praise God that He says, "I can come and live in your dirty house, because I see the blood." The Holy Spirit dwelleth with you, and shall be in you.

So Jesus says, "I will not leave you comfortless: I will come to you" (John 14:18). The word *comfortless* in the Greek is literally, "I will not leave you orphans." The Lord was going to leave them. He was going back to heaven. He said, "I will come. I will come in the Spirit of truth and I will guide you into all truth."

Shall we close in prayer. Our God and Father we thank Thee for Thyself. We rejoice in Thy great love to us in Christ. Thou knowest our needs and we pray Thee that we may live life in yieldedness to Thee, knowing the joy of the fact that we are well-represented in heaven by Christ; that Thou, O God, art well-represented in our hearts by the Spirit; and that all three of You are together in us and together in heaven. We pray in Jesus' name, Amen.

Troubleshooting Ineffective Prayer

There are always smiles when small children are in the family. Some of the heartiest of these smiles come out of the common everyday occurrences of life. We had spent some time teaching the children that they were not to ask for what they wanted at the table, but were to wait quietly until they were served. Parents often have to tell their children a hundred times over, exactly what is to be done—a hundred times simply because ninety-nine times is not sufficient. Then we have hopes that the lesson is beginning to be learned.

Some months passed and, one day, we were reading the eleventh chapter of Luke at our family worship. We came to the ninth verse, where I read these words of Christ, "And I say unto you, Ask, and it shall be given you; seek and ye shall find; knock, and it shall be opened unto you."

Before I could finish reading the entire verse, our little girl, then aged six, turned wide-eyed toward me, and said, "Oh, no, Daddy. It is not, 'Ask and it shall be given you'; it is, 'Don't ask, and it shall be given you.'" In order to satisfy her I had to explain, carefully, the difference between family discipline and God's orders concerning prayer.

Yet, today, there are many thousands of people who have an entirely wrong idea about prayer. While the little girl may mix her table manners with the thought of approach to God, men of the world mix a thousand false ideas with their concept of what prayer should be.

Once more we are forced to turn to the revelation of God, where we find His thoughts high above ours, even as the heavens are higher than the earth. And we ask a question that draws at our very hearts as hunger gnaws the vitals. Myriads of unsaved people have false ideas about prayer and myriads of Christians are leading prayerless, careless lives. They are missing the marvelous fellowship which God has for those who are willing to recognize the principles of prayer laid down in His Word, clear and plain, for all to see.

God does not hear the prayers of everybody. When unbelievers cry their desires to the heavens, Satan may bring about some response to some of their petitions, but these are moments of great deception. The Almighty seems to turn a deaf ear to their cry. God has said in His Word that He will not hear the prayers of all people.

In fact, if we turn to the words of Christ, we have a statement so definite, so formal, that it is a wonder men have not understood the barrier God has put between Himself and some men. Christ said, "I am the way, the truth and the life; no man cometh unto the Father, but by me" (John 14:6). I repeat it. "No man cometh unto the Father, but by Me."

Now, do not quarrel with the one who brings you this message. That would be as foolish as quarreling with a telegraph messenger who brings bad news in a telegram. If you do not like what I am saying, your quarrel is with the Lord Jesus Christ. It was He who said that no man could ever come to the Father, except through Himself, not I. Men can seek to approach God in two ways. First, they can seek Him in salvation. Here the Word is definite. There is no salvation except through Jesus Christ. This, of course, is the very heart of Christianity.

Or they may seek to approach God in prayer. But Christ says that no man can come unto the Father, except by Himself, Jesus Christ. If your prayer is not made through Jesus Christ, it will not go to God.

Every week men meet in legislative chambers, lodges and other meetings and, for some reason or other, offer a prayer. More often than not, the name of Jesus Christ is left out in order to avoid hurting the feelings of any who might be susceptible. But Jesus Christ says that those prayers do not go to God.

Every day, all over the world, people pray in the midst of their religious form and ceremony. Some pray to one or another of a group of mediators that have been authorized by a church organization.

Christ says that these prayers are not received by God. Think, then, the next time you go to pray. Say to yourself, "Is this prayer I am about to make a prayer that goes to God or to one of Satan's minions? Is this prayer in keeping with the declaration of our Lord, that no man cometh unto the Father, except by Him?"

But now, I want to take Christians into a study of the Word of God that will show us why many prayers, prayers made in the name of Jesus Christ, are hindered, or unanswered.

In the book of Isaiah we have a great principle of prayer stated in one of the later chapters of the prophecy. "Behold, the Lord's hand is not shortened, that it cannot save; neither his ear heavy, that it cannot hear: but your iniquities have separated between you and your God, and your sins have hid his face from you, that he will not hear" (Isa. 59:1,2).

If you pray and do not receive that for which you pray, there are two possible reasons. One is that you are not praying for that which God would consider for your good. The other conclusion is that you are not walking uprightly.

Here, perhaps, lies the chief explanation for the fruitlessness of much Christian praying. In the first flush of a joyful Christian life there has been attraction to the Word of God, zeal for prayer and earnestness in seeking God's will. Then sin has been allowed to enter the life. The prayer life is hindered. The Christian grows cold. His prayers become mere form. He no longer knows the penetrating power that will take him through to the very throne of

God with that piercing insistence, based upon the promises of the Word, that will not let go until the blessing has been received.

The next time that your prayer seems to be unanswered, do not conclude, hastily, that the object of your prayer was not according to God's will, and that, therefore, you are not to receive it. Conclude rather that something is wrong with your heart life. In Psalm 84:11 David said, "The Lord God is a sun and shield: the Lord will give grace and glory: no good thing will He withhold from them that walk uprightly."

Examine yourself in your praying. Has your own prayer life become powerless? Do not put the blame off on God and think that He is unkind and unloving. Do not think that His list of good things is a narrowly restricted list. Think, rather, that you are not walking uprightly. Think that your iniquity has separated you and your God. Think that it is your sins which have hid His face from you.

In one of the old hymns of the church, there is a couplet which expresses this great truth in a forceful way. The hymn writer says, "O may no earthborn cloud arise to hide Thee from Thy servant's eyes." The clouds that hide the sun from our eyes are not our creation; but the clouds which hide our God from us are always clouds of our own making. It is impossible for our Lord to be hidden from us, except by some mist arising from our own hearts.

Let us be more specific. Sin is a short word, but it has many different meanings. What sins arise with such a clamour about the throne of God that He refuses to listen to our cries until we are willing to have these sins covered with the sacrifice of Christ?

One of these is the sin of unbelief. We read in the epistle to James, "If any of you lack wisdom, let him ask of God, that giveth to all men liberally, and upbraideth not; and it shall be given him. But let him ask in faith, nothing wavering: for he that wavereth is like a wave of the sea driven with the wind and tossed. For let not that man think that he shall receive any thing of the Lord" (James 1:5-7). This refers, of course, to the claiming of promises which are made in the Word of God. It does not mean there will never be doubt concerning the will of God in something we are making a matter of prayer. But in all those hundreds of cases where prayer should follow the Word of God, there must not be the sin of unbelief. For to doubt the Word of God is to make God a liar. He has said so Himself. (See 1 John 5:10.)

We have a list of promises where God has told us to pray for certain things in connection with our relationship to Him, our growth in His Word and work, and also, concerning material blessings which He desires to give us. The sin of unbelief in any of these cases can destroy our prayer power and hinder the coming of the answer to us.

A second sin that is mentioned, specifically, as a hindrance to answered prayer, is the sin of the unforgiving spirit. In the Gospel of Mark we read these words of Christ. "When ye stand praying, forgive, if ye have ought against any; that your Father also which is in heaven may forgive you your trespasses. But if ye do not forgive, neither will your

206

Father which is in heaven forgive your trespasses" (Mark 11:25,26).

To those who have not accepted Christ as Saviour we must give warning that this, or any other specification, does not apply in your case. For the unbeliever there is but one hindrance—the lack of new life in Christ through being born again.

But to the Christian, to the one who has been given the right to become a child of God (see John 1:12), this word may reveal the center of your difficulty. Do you hold a grudge against some believer? Have you bitterness in your heart toward some one? Are you unwilling to let God remove that bitterness? That is the reason why the heavens seem as brass above you.

Answered prayer is on the basis of our fellowship with Christ, and there cannot be true fellowship with Him if we have an unforgiving spirit. We have little sympathy with that kind of condescension which promises to forgive, but says that it will not forget. Where there is the true love of Christ there is the fruit of that love. We must not forget that love, "Beareth all things, believeth all things, hopeth all things, endureth all things. Love never faileth" (1 Cor. 13:7,8).

Job received bad treatment from his counselors who called themselves his friends. In the closing chapter of that stupendous epic we find that "the Lord turned the captivity of Job, when he prayed for his friends: also the Lord gave Job twice as much as he had before" (Job 42:10). When Job's heart was cleansed from rancor toward those three killjoys who have become known, ironically, as Job's comforters, God broke through and performed miracles on his behalf.

Still another sin that God says is a cause of unanswered prayer is the sin of family discord. This may surprise some, but God has revealed it to us through the writings of Peter. We read, "Even as Sarah obeyed Abraham, calling him lord: whose daughters ye are, as long as ye do well, and are not afraid with any amazement. Likewise, ye husbands, dwell with them according to knowledge, giving honor unto the wife, as unto the weaker vessel, and as being heirs together of the grace of life; that your prayers be not hindered (1 Pet. 3:6,7). This word is addressed, primarily, to the husbands. The literal teaching of this verse is that husbands' prayers are hindered because they do not have that consideration for their wives which is due them.

Ministers and doctors soon learn to know the real reasons behind the excuses of "incompatibility" which are given to the courts as grounds for divorce. Few people realize, perhaps, the total of bestiality which exists in many marriage relationships that should be fine and heavenly. This cheapness may be understandable in those who make no claim to the spiritual life in Christ. But for those who are Christ's, there is no excuse. The body of the believer becomes the temple of the Holy Spirit and His tenderness must possess us in all of life. If we do not yield to the life of the Spirit within, God tells us, this is a hindrance to our prayers. When God brings warmth and love back into Christian homes where coldness has come, then the prayer power of husbands and wives can be restored to full communion with Him.

The Word of God also tells us that our prayers are hindered when they are offered with selfish motives. We read in the Epistle of James, "Ye ask, and receive not, because ye ask amiss, that ye may consume it upon your lusts" (James 4:3). In the Old Testament there is a verse which seems opposed to this, but which really teaches the same thing. We read in the Psalms, "Delight thyself also in the Lord; and he shall give thee the desires of thine heart" (Psalm 37:4).

Here is the promise of the very desires of our hearts. Yet the New Testament lesson tells us that we do not receive the things which we ask, because we ask from selfish motives, that the answer may be consumed upon our own pleasures. The solution to the difficulty lies in the very nature of God. If people understood God there would be no difficulties at all.

What is the basis of prayer? When God answers prayer is He just handing something to a child to keep the child quiet? Is it a question of divine whim or fantasy? Of course not. God is a God of love and grace, and indeed He desires to give us all blessings. No father and mother ever wanted to give gifts to their own children as much as God desires to bless to overflowing all of His creatures.

Multitudes will not come in by the door which He has opened in Christ Jesus. But the holiness of God will not allow men to come in by any other way. The justice, the holiness, the righteousness of God must be satisfied. Only the death of the Lord

Jesus Christ can perform this work. And among those who have believed in Him there are still multitudes who do not realize that prayer is not merely a nice way to get something for nothing.

Every gift you received cost somebody something. Salvation is a gift, yet it cost God the death of Christ. Every movement of power from God on our behalf is by virtue of what He has accomplished on the cross. All that we have and are comes from God's grace. Whenever we pray and are answered, the answer comes to us purchased by the blood of Jesus Christ. This is the meaning of "in Jesus' name." To use the name of Jesus in a prayer other than this way, is as bad as forging someone's name to a check.

When we delight ourselves in the God of the Lord Jesus Christ we shall receive the desires of our hearts. For when we delight ourselves in Him we shall not have any desires that are apart from His will. If I realize that anything I receive from God comes to me because of the sufferings of my Lord, will I go to Him and ask for something that will not be in accordance with His will? Will I ask for that which is merely a selfish desire? Where there is surrender to the will of God, there is delight in the Person of God. Where there is delight in God, there is understanding of God, and a desire to please Him. Where there is a desire to please Him, there is a harmony with His will that brings us into the fulness of prayer power.

He Himself tells us through John, that "this is the confidence that we have in him, that, if we ask anything according to his will, he heareth us: And if we know that he hear us, whatsoever we ask, we know that we have the petitions that we desired of him" (1 John 5:14,15). This is a major part of the great secret of answered and unanswered prayer. When we really delight ourselves in the Father and ask those things that are well pleasing unto Him, we shall receive exceeding abundantly above all that we ask or think.

But when we are asking amiss, in order that we may consume it upon our own desires, then He will not heed. It is of His kindness and love that He does not give us all we ask for. Happy that Christian who learns that he does not know the proper things for which to pray and seeks the teaching of the Spirit of God who prays within our hearts with the groanings that cannot be uttered! The believer who is taught in the Word of God would never dare to pray for the slightest object without adding, "if it be Thy will." For it would be tragedy if we received all that we desired.

There is one last hindrance which I wish to consider with you. In the book of the prophet Ezekiel we read these words of God to the prophet, "Son of man, these men have taken their idols into their hearts, and set the stumbling block of their iniquity before their faces; should I let myself be inquired of at all by them?" (Ezek. 14:3).

Idols in the heart! This verse may be taken two ways. It may refer to unbelievers who have some idol in their hearts and who refuse to tear it from the throne in order that Christ may enter.

But there is also a sense in which a believer may have idols in his heart. Anything, yes, anything, which is loved more than the will of God can become an idol. And when there are idols in our hearts then the Lordship of Christ is no more a fact within our beings. Then fellowship is destroyed. And anything which destroys fellowship will at the same time destroy the basis of prayer; for every answer to prayer comes on the ground of fellowship between a Father and His child.

"If ye abide in me, and my words abide in you, ye shall ask what ye will, and it shall be done unto you" (John 15:7). If we are abiding in Him we shall not have the throne of our hearts occupied by idols. We shall not ask amiss for our own pleasures. We shall be in the will of God and shall know what it is to have a life of prayer power.

"Holy Spirit, Truth divine,
Dwell within this heart of mine,
Cast down every idol throne,
Reign supreme and reign alone."

A Divine Love Affair

As I read my Bible, I discover more and more that God Almighty never had a thought from eternity to eternity that did not center in Jesus Christ. To God Almighty, Jesus Christ is EVERYTHING, and He loves Him so much that He wants to people the universe with those who are formed in His image. That is why He saved us, as we learn from Romans 8:29: "For those whom he foreknew he also predestined to be conformed to the image of his Son, in order that he might be the first-born among many brethren."[1] God desires that you and I should be like the Lord Jesus Christ. This is the purpose of salvation.

In John 17 we find the Lord Jesus talking to His Father. Here is God Almighty speaking to God; it is a conversation within the Trinity: "Jesus . . . lifted up his eyes to heaven and said, 'Father, the hour has come; glorify thy Son that thy Son may glorify thee.' "

Now the Greek word for glory is very interesting. It is *doxa,* and originally it meant opinion. If you had a straight opinion, you were orthodox; if you differed from others in your opinion, you were heterodox. And if two opinions went alongside each other, they formed a paradox. So orthodoxy (straight opinion) became "my" opinion, while a different opinion was heterodoxy. But little by little the word *doxa* came to be used in connection with one's opinion of God. And since the opinion of God was good, *doxa* finally began to mean glory; so we have doxology, which is the science of glory.

I never come to this chapter without thinking about an incident that happened a good many years ago. When I first came to the Tenth Presbyterian Church I preached on Sunday mornings for three and a half years on the Epistle to the Romans, then for half a year on the Apostles' Creed, one year on the Epistle of Jude, and then I began to preach on the Gospel of John. For twelve years every Sunday morning I preached on the Gospel of John. When I came to this passage, John 17, I preached a sermon on verse 3, "This is life eternal, that they might know thee, the only true God, and Jesus Christ, whom thou hast sent."

This text had a tremendous influence on a man who was then the president of our Board of Trustees, Dr. James Torrance Rue, who was also an orthopedic surgeon at Jefferson Medical School. During the first ten years of my ministry in that pulpit Dr. Rue and his wife came and sat faithfully in the same place every Sunday. But never did I see him respond to anything I ever preached. When the time came for me to preach, he would bow his head, cross his arms, and just sit there. And as soon as the sermon was over, before I had time to get back to shake hands with people, he would be on his way downstairs to go and make his rounds at the hospital while his wife talked with friends. Never—during the first ten years of my preaching did he ever look up—until I came to this text, and it startled me when he finally did.

In referring to John 17:3 I said, "Now notice, 'This is life eternal, that they might know thee.'" I said, "What is it to know Him? Don't ever think that heaven is going to be just sitting on a cloud, playing a harp, and polishing your crown." All of a sudden his head jerked up and he looked at me. I had never seen him like that before. When I said, "Heaven is going to be activity," he began to be more and more interested. "Now for example," I continued, "God is the author of all things. I read in a paper this week that there are 37,000 varieties of wild flowers. Now these are all thoughts of God. God thought up the flowering plants—the red ones, the white ones, the green. He thought up the various leaves, and all the glories of the springtime. If you are botanically minded you can go to God and say, 'I love your flower thoughts. I'd like to classify a million varieties.' And God will say, 'Let there be a million varieties,' and you can go to work on them!"

Well, by this time Dr. Rue had his hand on the back of the seat in front of him, and he was leaning forward with an intensity that I shall not forget. A little while later I went on talking about the activity of heaven. "This is life eternal, that they might know thee—to know the flower thoughts of God, to know the geological thoughts of God, to know the atomic thoughts of God, the electronic thoughts of God, the mathematical thoughts of God; we are going to know everything."

When I went down the aisle at the close of the service he was standing there. He put out his hand and said, "Doctor, I want to thank you for that sermon." He said, "I have always known that I was going to have to go to heaven, but I always looked forward to it with some boredom. I think I can say for the first time in my life that I am eager to go there." He shook my hand and went on his way.

Don't ever think that heaven is going to be sitting on a cloud. There is going to be activity, government, judgment, work. We have no sympathy for that which says, "And now to work, to watch, to war, and then to rest forever." Have you ever had one of those mornings when you came out and said, "Oh, boy, today's the day I can get it done! I could lick my weight in wildcats today. I'm at the peak! This is it!" Well, that's the way you're going to feel forever and ever. And you won't have to have any Benzedrine either. You will have built into you that which will make you perfect in all your eagerness, and perfect in your sense of accomplishment. "This is life eternal, that they might know thee."

It must have been pretty terrible for Christ to have had to leave that life and come down here into the insane asylum of this world, this madhouse, and to live with human beings. I've tried to think of some parallels. We think of the missionary who leaves home to go and live in a civilization where he has a mattress on boards for his bed, and a table eighteen inches away. The baby's bedroom is three feet away from the table, the kitchen is four feet away from the baby's room, and all of the rooms are in one room, ten feet by twelve feet. But leaving an American civilization to live in a mud hut is only one little step down.

I know a worse step. A man who was a member of my congregation many years ago, called me and said, "Dr. Barnhouse, could you take the next train to Trenton? There is terrible tragedy. I'll meet you on the station platform." I was at the station about fifteen minutes later, and an hour later I was in Trenton. When he met me, he said, "Something terrible has happened. Last night at about ten o'clock my wife lost her mind. It was just a violent insane flare-up. We got a doctor in, and he immediately called another doctor, and they signed the papers and committed her to an insane asylum. They took her off late last night, and I have just been over and gotten a private room for her. She's a little quieter this morning."

I went with him to the insane asylum at Trenton, and I walked into that private room, and I saw this woman's haggard and worn face. She said to me, "O Dr. Barnhouse, you will never know. I had a headache, and all of a sudden I felt a great pressure in my head, and the next thing I knew I had come back to consciousness and I was in a room with fifteen other raving maniacs of women. Some of them were naked, some of them were on the floor eating their food with their mouths like beasts. The stink was horrible; and there I was in this pit with all of them. O Dr. Barnhouse, what can I ever do? How can I ever think that it might not happen again?"

It was not more than a month before we were able to get the papers cleared and get her removed from the private room. She never had to go back.

But there's a wonderful illustration in this. For the step from her beautiful home in Princeton, New Jersey, to the madhouse was not as great a step as when Jesus Christ was born into this world and had to live among us. You see we are so accustomed to living with ourselves that we don't know how terrible the human race can be.

Boswell said to Johnson, "Do you think that man is naturally good?" And Johnson said, "Not any more than a wolf." For he knew what was down underneath the veneer that covers much of the civilization of the human race, and how predatory man is, and how eagerly man follows his lusts, his greed, and all of the horrible capacities that came to us when Adam sinned and the race died.

Now in verse 5 Jesus says, "Father, glorify thou me in thy own presence with the glory which I had with thee before the world was made."[1] This was not merely opinion, His being like God. Rather, when we grasp what Christ was saying here, we can understand Philippians 2, that Jesus "being in the form of God, thought it not robbery to be equal with God: but made himself of no reputation, and took upon him the form of a servant"[1] (vv. 6,7).

Thus John 17:5 declares that Jesus Christ was God before his incarnation.

And before the world was, He was God the Son. Do not say that the Trinity is God, Christ and the Holy Spirit. That is a theological error. The Trinity is God, God and God; or God the Father, God the Son, God the Holy Spirit. This is the Godhead, from all eternity.

It was the Lord of Glory Himself who came to redeem us. For thirty years God the Son walked about this earth, and if you had lived at that time you would not have noticed Him in the crowd. I don't know what Jesus looked like, but He certainly was not the effeminate person depicted in art and by Hollywood. Oh, how I hate pictures of Jesus Christ! They are so alien to Him! Why should we have such things when God Almighty tells us, "He had no form or comeliness that we should look at him, and no beauty that we should desire him. He was despised and rejected by men; a man of sorrows, and acquainted with grief; and as one from whom men hide their faces" (Isa. 53:2,3). This is the Lord of Glory.

If you had walked down the street in Jerusalem and had seen Jesus and that tatterdemalion group of ex-fishermen, you would have said, "They certainly come from the wrong side of the Sea of Galilee," and you wouldn't have been attracted to them at all. And the Lord Jesus Christ had to be lifted up and die, in order to draw all men unto Him. But we are not drawn to a physical image, for as Christ said, "God is spirit, and those who worship him must worship in spirit and truth" (John 4:24). The

Lord of Glory doffed His coronation robes and descended to earth to live in the guise of an ordinary man among ordinary men; but now in John 17:5 He is saying, "Father, give Me back all that I had before."

I remember seeing two pictures of George VI of England. One showed him in coronation robes, looking every inch a king, with ermine, and scarlet, crowns, diamonds, scepter and mitre. The other picture showed George VI during World War II at a time when a bomb had fallen in East London, and he visited the spot. Little Union Jacks were mounted on the rubble, and the king and a half dozen other men, wearing derby hats and overcoats, stood among the people sorrowfully viewing the destruction. In order to distinguish George VI from the others, the photographer had superimposed an arrow pointing to "the king." As I looked at that picture of the king in ordinary dress, standing among the ruins with his people and weeping with them, I said, "He is just as much king there as when in his coronation robes."

So, seeing Jesus Christ steadfastly setting His face to go to Jerusalem, I say, "This is the King, the Lord of Glory who so loved me that He was willing to be the Word made flesh."

Did God answer Christ's prayer in John 17:5? Yes, He did, for 1 Peter 1:21 says, "Through him you have confidence in God, who raised him from the dead and gave him glory". In John 17 Christ prays, "O, Father give me glory." And later the Holy Spirit says, "Peter, write it down!" God raised Him from the dead and gave Him glory. Thus on the day of His ascension our Lord returned to heaven and changed His clothes.

I think the best illustration of this that I know is to be found in Revelation 1. I have used this illustration many times because it is one that adapts itself in several ways. Some truths will bear reiteration. I am not afraid to teach certain truths again and again and again, because God says that it is line upon line, precept upon precept, here a little, and there a little. In Revelation 1 we have a little picture of what happened when God took Jesus Christ back into heaven. The story is told to us in the form of a vision which John had of Jesus Christ. It's a strange vision; in fact, if you try to think of it as something to be seen with the eyes, it becomes as horrible as a Ripley "Believe It or Not" cartoon.

John says, in verse 12, "I turned to see the voice. . . ." That, already, you see, is something strange, "to see a voice." A physicist might do it if he had proper electronic instruments. But he said, "I turned to see the voice that spake with me. And being turned, I saw seven golden candlesticks; and in the midst of the seven candlesticks one like unto the Son of man, clothed with a garment down to the foot, and girt about the paps with a golden girdle. His head and his hairs were white like wool, as white as snow; and his eyes were as a flame of fire; and his feet like unto fine brass, as if they burned in a furnace; and his voice as the sound of many waters. And he had in his right hand seven stars: and out of his mouth went a sharp two-edged sword: and his countenance was as the sun shineth in his strength" (Rev. 1:12-16).

So far as I know, only one artist has ever been fool enough to try to put this on canvas. I saw the original of a painting in Kassel, Germany, done by an artist who lived two or three hundred years ago. It was ridiculous! Here was a man in a long garment; peeping out from the bottom were shoes made of fine brass; around his middle was a tight girdle; out of his mouth came a sharp sword that looked like a serpent's tongue; "His eyes as a flame of fire" looked like automobile headlights coming out of the tunnel in the darkness. The whole thing was absurd.

Someone says, "Doesn't it say it right there?" But you see this picture in Revelation is an index. If you take a good concordance and start to study the Word of God you will soon discover that every line in this vision is an index to a vision in the Old Testament. For instance, "His head and his hairs were white like wool, as white as snow." If you look up in a concordance "white wool," "white hair," "white as snow," it takes you back to Daniel 7. There Daniel had a vision and said, "I beheld . . . the Ancient of days . . . whose garment was white as snow, and the hair of his head like the pure wool" (Dan. 7:9).

After Jesus rose from the dead and ascended into heaven, John said, "Who is Jesus?" and God said, "Look, He is the Ancient of days of Daniel." Who else has feet like fine brass? If you turn back on Jeremiah it describes Jehovah of Hosts coming in judgment, and His feet are as fine brass, to tread the wrath of God. Who has eyes as a flame of fire? If you turn to Ezekiel you find that this is an index to the vision of Ezekiel. You have seven lines here that take you to seven great visions in the Old Testament, each one of which was a vision of the Lord God Almighty. So God says, "Do you want to know who Jesus is? He is the Jehovah of Isaiah; He is the Ancient of days of Daniel; He is the Lord God of Hosts of Jeremiah; He is the Son of man; He is everything that God was to the prophets of the Old Testament." Jesus now is exalted at the right hand of the Father. He is our God.

And when He got to heaven, He heard His Father say, "Sit at my right hand till (and that word *till* is very important) I make your enemies your footstool."

One day Christ will come forth from heaven in a manner described in the Old Testament, *so terrible* that I dare not originate the language. Isaiah says that Jesus Christ is going to squash our civilization like a bunch of grapes.

I have been in Mediterranean countries at the time of making wine and have seen the men roll their trousers up to their knees and go into the winepress to tread out the grapes with their bare feet. The men trample the grapes till the juice splashes on them.

When He comes again, the Lord Jesus Christ will crush beneath His feet our American way of life, for never before have so many sinned against so much. University life, Wall Street, Broadway and Hollywood, the arts, literature, and ecclesiasticism will be stepped on and crushed by Jesus Christ at His Second Coming. This is the teaching of the Word of God. "Sit at my right hand *till* I make your enemies your footstool" (Heb. 1:13). The day will come when He will rise from the throne of God, lay aside the robes of His meditation, gird upon Him the sword of Justice, and come to rule the nations with a rod of iron and dash his enemies to pieces as a potter's vessel.

In that future day, we who belong to Christ will join in the great chorus of Revelation 11:15: "The kingdom of the world has become the kingdom of our Lord and of his Christ, and he shall reign for ever and ever."[1] Yes, the Father "raised him from the dead and gave him glory."

Just as Proverbs 11:10 says, "When the wicked perish there are shouts of gladness."[1] I cannot tell you how glad I was to see the picture of Mussolini hanging head down, dead, and to know that this vicious monster had been removed from the earth.

Oh, if you know Jesus Christ, you will hate sin. Don't ever say, "God is love," without balancing it with, "God is hate." God is love of the sinner, but God is hate of sin. Unless you make this balance, you have a lame God, a false concept of God. Hebrews 1:9 gives one of the marks of the deity of Christ: "Thou [Jesus] hast loved righteousness, and hated iniquity; therefore God, even thy God, hath anointed thee with the oil of gladness above thy fellows."

Jesus Christ hated sin. He told the Pharisees that they would depart into the lake of fire. I love Him for this. Oh, that we might learn to follow our Lord Jesus Christ in His hatred of sin, and understand that He is Lord!

Now we are ready for our last text, and we go back to John 17. We find out what Jesus did with the glory the Father gave to Him. Let me give you these two texts and then add the third. First, He prayed, "Father, give Me glory, the glory that I had with Thee before the world was." Then Peter says, God raised Him from the dead and gave Him glory. Now back in John 17:22 we read, "And the glory which thou gavest me I have given them." This is none other than the Bridegroom's present to the Bride. This is a wonderful thing.

For many years it has been my custom, whenever I married anybody, that when the bridegroom hands me an envelope, I go and say to the bride, "Here is my wedding present to you. If he has been very generous to the preacher, you've got a good sum." If he has given me five dollars, that's what she gets; if he gives me twenty dollars, that's what she gets. I just give it back to the bride. The Bridegroom's present to the Bride, which doesn't pass through any intermediary, is this: "The glory which thou gavest me I have given them." The Lord Jesus Christ says, "I have chosen you." Oh, do you understand your place in the plan of God? Do you understand that God loves you because of Christ, and God is determined to make you like Christ? He will whittle you, He will cut away, He will rub you with sandpaper X-fine, and ultimately He will accomplish that for which you were predestined.

Oh, how many people glibly recite Romans 8:28 without knowing Romans 8:29! They say, "Yes, we know that all things work together for good to them that love God, to them who are the called according to his purpose." But what is His purpose? It is this: "For whom he did foreknow, he also did predestinate to be conformed to the image of his Son, that he might be the firstborn among many brethren" (Rom. 8:29).

God will never stop working on you until you become like Christ. "It does not yet appear what we shall be, but we know that when he appears we shall be like him" (1 John 3:2). The Bible also says that the believer in the Lord Jesus Christ is to be "the fulness of him that filleth all in all," and that the last shall be first, and the first shall be last.

I have no doubt whatsoever that some cook on Main Street is going to have a much bigger place in heaven than some of the people she's worked for. And I have no doubt whatsoever about some obscure little preacher who has been pastor of a little church of fifty or sixty people out in the sticks writing eternal truths on a few dull hearts, but pouring out his heart to the Lord. At the time that the rewards are given he may have a much greater award than the preacher who was able to fill a church and have a radio program and all the rest of it. This is a thing which should cause everyone of us to tremble, every day, as we read, "Beware, lest anyone take thy reward; beware, lest anyone take thy crown." In other words, beware lest we turn our lives inward, and begin to live for *ourselves* instead of turning our lives outward to live for Jesus Christ, and to allow Him to flow over to others.

What do you think God left us here for? Stop and think now. Why does God leave us here on this earth? I am presuming that you are a believer in Jesus Christ. If you are not *yet* a believer in Jesus Christ, this of course cannot be for you. I must in all fairness, in faithfulness to God, tell you, if you are not a believer in Jesus Christ as your Saviour, that you are on your way to a Christless eternity, without hope, and without God. Call it hell, call it the lake of fire, call it what you will, it is separation from God, it is eternal doom, it is eternal wrath, it is eternal judgment. For God has but one will for you, that you should repent, and should come to the knowledge of Jesus Christ.

But if you are a believer in Christ, why do you think God leaves Christians here? You can't say He leaves us here to get us ready for heaven. I was just as ready for heaven when I had been saved two seconds, as when I was saved fifty years. My readiness for heaven is Jesus Christ. Why are we left here then?

You are left here as witnesses for Christ, by the way you live. If you walk into a room full of people that are not Christians, immediately they should think, "I can't tell any dirty stories while he's here; there's something about him that's just going to make it fall flat." You won't have to say anything. You don't have to go and say, "Oh, brethren, your language is not. . . ." You see, the Christian is not like that at all. It's just the way you live, the way you are, the way you act, the way you speak, the tone of voice; it's the fact that they know you won't lie, won't chisel, won't cheat, that you won't enter into any little double-dealing, that you won't report gossip, that you're not a buzzard, that you won't be a scandalmonger. It's the very fact that people see you have a heart overflowing with the love of Jesus Christ.

Then why has He left us here? He has left us here, not to get us ready for heaven, but that we may be His witnesses. He said, "When I am through with you here, I am going to take you to heaven, and in *proportion*, in proportion to your surrender, I will reward you in heaven." You see, getting into heaven is Jesus Christ, but what you are in heaven depends entirely on how you have lived right where you are now.

"Isn't everybody going to be alike?" Oh, no! No, no, no, no! The Lord, in a parable, said that He will give to one to rule over one city, another over five cities, another over ten cities. This is a parable, but it shows gradations in the judgment of God. Now nobody is going to be jealous, and nobody is going to be proud.

We are all to be *like* the Lord Jesus Christ.

If we liken human beings to containers, here is a thousand-gallon container, and a five hundred, and a hundred, and a fifty, and a ten, and a five, and a two, and a one gallon, two quarts, and pints, and gills. God has made many more quarts and pints and gills than He has great containers. You come to St. Paul with his ten thousand gallons; then you come on down to Luther and Calvin, and you see these vast containers; and the Wesleys, and Moody of other ages and Billy Graham of our age; you come on down through various sizes of Christians, to the little humble person in the African bush that the world doesn't know anything about.

This person may be not only a quart, or a pint, but maybe a gill, and God says, "In heaven, I am not going to reward them on the basis of how big a splash they made in the earth. I am not run by Madison Avenue or Hollywood methods of doing things." God says, "I am going to reward them by a *percentage* basis," and a one gill totally yielded to God in heaven is going to be far greater even than a ten-thousand-gallon container partially yielded. Thus we must understand that everything is on the basis of our surrender. What *fools* men are to live for the world, and suck on the life of that which is on this earth. We are here for only a moment, and then forever, *forever*, we are to be there. *What* we are there depends on *how* we live now.

I'll close with a story. It's a story I saw in *Time* magazine a few years ago. I don't know the end of it, but the beginning makes such a wonderful story that it suffices. Down in Bolivia, the major industry is tin; and back in the old days, Patino was the family that was better known in South America than the Rockefellers in North America. The Patinos were the tin kings. As a family they were worth a billion dollars.

The young son of the family was appointed ambassador to France. He was only twenty-nine years of age, but if you have a billion dollars in Bolivia, you are liable to get appointed ambassador to wherever you want to be. So he was on his way to be ambassador to France from Bolivia, but he stopped by the United States, and *Time* magazine said it was rumored that he wanted to marry an American girl and that he would be looking. Naturally there would have been no dearth of candidates, because he had bought a house on the Avenue du Bois, just off the Champs Elysees in Paris, and undoubtedly his home was to be the center of the social season in Paris. The girl he married would have been number one hostess in Paris as well as in South America. That's where the story ended.

Now I don't know whether he married a Bolivian or a French woman or what, but just let's suppose that he comes to Philadelphia and he falls in love with somebody. What's going to be the difference in that girl's life? She's engaged to be married to a man who has a billion dollars, whose mother tongue is Spanish, and she's going to live in Paris as the number one hostess. So she's sitting in her house, and the telephone rings, and the girls say, "Come on over and play canasta."

And she says, "Haven't you heard? I'm going to be married, and I have an appointment with my couturiere this afternoon."

The next day when the telephone rings, a boy calls her up and says, "I just got in from Korea. How about a date for tonight? Remember the wonderful dates we used to have?"

She says, "Maybe you haven't heard the news. I'm engaged to be married, and I can't have any dates anymore."

Then the phone rings and some other girls call her up. "Come on over and talk about the girls that aren't here tonight."

She says, "I'm sorry, but you see I'm engaged to be married and I have my French teacher coming in for a French lesson."

Immediately all her interests in the little circles where she had lived, the little twittering life before, all fall away, and her interests now begin to be centered on one fact, "I'm going to be married to a man of responsibility, authority and position, and I must begin to get ready for it."

Listen to me. Patino, the billionaire, ambassador to France, is a poverty-stricken hobo in comparison with Jesus Christ!

Can you ever be the same again when you realize that Jesus Christ loves you? Can you be the same when you know that you have been joined to Him, that your dowry is nothing less than the glory of the Godhead? We are not lifted to the level of angels, principalities, powers or even the archangel; we are sons of God, to be seated upon the throne of the Lord Jesus, joined with Him in the administration of the universe. This is our One Lord.

The Lord's Prayer

Jesus never prayed with His disciples. He always prayed alone. When you and I pray—and I've had great times of fellowship with other believers in prayer—we take the place as sinners together before the grace of God. But Jesus couldn't have done that. He couldn't have said to the disciples, "Come on. Let's get down on our knees and cry out to God," because He was God and they were men.

The prayer in John 17 is written down by John but John was not there when it was prayed. I believe that the Holy Spirit, later on, by dictation inspiration, word for word, gave to John the words spoken here. This is the true Lord's Prayer.

My early spiritual life was formed in no small measure by certain experiences with God in prayer meetings. I can remember, when I was sixteen or seventeen, going with a half dozen young men in our late teens to the top of Mt. Wilson in California and spending the entire night on the mountain praying and waiting for the sunrise. I worked for a summer helping to build the Church of the Open Door in Los Angeles. I thank God for that summer where, for eight hours every day, I carried ninety pounds of cement and God built up the constitution of a horse which enabled me to do the work of a horse for all the years since.

One night several of us decided that we wanted to have a prayer meeting. The church building was up to about twelve stories at that time, a rein-forced-concrete affair, and it had a little elevator powered by a "dunky" engine. We told the elevator operator that we wanted to go up to the top and spend the night in prayer. So, just at closing time we went up and the elevator with its "dunky" engine, went back down and the operator went home. There were no stairs or ladders or any other way down. We spent all night in prayer. And the seven men who were on that rooftop, without exception, have gone on in the work of the Lord. For instance, Van Eddings later founded the Orinoco River Mission in Venezuela. Oscar Zimmerman started the Emmanuel Mission to Seamen and Albert Siegle went on to spend his life in Thailand and Bangkok as a missionary.

When we prayed together, in those times of laying hold of God and surrender of self, and asking Him to deal with the innermost being of our sin, we were together in a fellowship that recognized our sinfulness. This is why Jesus never prayed with the disciples. He wouldn't have gotten down and said, "O Lord, we come miserable sinners." You discover that He always prayed alone—when He went alone in the mountain, to pray, or He departed by the lake and prayed, or He rose a great while before day and prayed.

Now He taught the disciples how to pray. He said, "Pray then like this: Our Father who art in heaven" (Matt. 6:9). And people have come to call that "The Lord's Prayer," but that's not "The Lord's Prayer," that's "The Disciples' Prayer." This prayer in John 17 is The Lord's Prayer. This is a conversation inside the Trinity. When I was a young Bible student, I began to think of God talking with God, and on a page in my notebook, I wrote "Conversations Inside the Trinity." As I read the Bible, every time I came to one of these conversations I would just turn to that page and write the message. And, so you have references such as Psalm 110:1, "Jehovah said to My Lord, 'Sit at My right hand till I make your enemies your footstool.'" Or, Hebrews 10:5-7, "when Christ came into the world, He said to God the Father . . . 'Lo, I have come to do Thy will, O God.'" Or such verses as Genesis 1:26; 11:7; Isaiah 6:8, all indicate conversations within the Trinity. This was God conversing with God.

Now note, I want you to see the last line in John 14. They had been in the upper room and the last line of chapter 14 says, "Arise, let us go hence" (John 14:31). Then the first line of chapter 15 says, "I am the true vine." I believe that this was spoken in full moonlight because there is always a full moon at Passover. You never had an Easter week without a full moon because the whole of the Passover is centered around the time of the full moon. As Jesus and the disciples went out toward the Mount of Olives, they passed a wall with a great vine climbing along it. Jesus looked at the vine in the bright light of the full moon and said, "I am the true vine." And through chapters 15 and 16, Jesus spoke to the disciples. Then, if we go to the other Gospels (see Matt. 26:30-46; Mark 14:32-42) we discover the disciples continually falling asleep while Jesus was praying. In John 17 He began to pray to the Father, and I believe God put this chapter here in order to show us what Jesus is praying today.

We have seen that as the Holy Spirit prays for us "with groanings that cannot be uttered," so Christ is praying in heaven for us. You have two Beings who are praying for you. The Holy Spirit within you is interceding for you with groanings that cannot be uttered (see Rom. 8:26,27), and there is never a moment that Jesus is not praying. He ever liveth to make intercession for us. (See Heb. 7:25.) And the things that He prays for us are the things set forth in this passage.

In verse 13, Jesus says, "And now come I to thee." I don't think that means: "Now come I to thee in prayer." Earlier in this chapter He had already been praying. In saying "And now come I to thee" Jesus means, "I'm going to arise from the dead and ascend into heaven. The Ascension is about to take place." "And," He continues, "these things I speak in the world." Notice again the great importance of the word *world* in the Gospel of John. The word *world* in Greek is *kosmos.* You know it in the word *cosmopolitan.* A cosmopolitan is a citizen of the world, a man with a worldwide outlook. Now the word *kosmos* means the world that crucified Christ. And the Lord is talking about the Church and the world.

And by the *Church,* I mean all believers—what Calvin called "the invisible Church" and what Lutherans call "the hidden Church." For the hidden Church is the invisible Church. There are undoubtedly born-again believers in the Greek Orthodox Church, in the Roman Catholic Church. I knew at least one born-again believer who remained in the Mormon church—he never moved away from it and was tremendously unsettled, but nevertheless had been born again beyond any shadow of doubt. I once baptized and took into our church a person who, two weeks before, had been a reader in one of the Christian Science Churches of Philadelphia and had gotten saved.

God knows where His Church is hidden. That's why you are never to draw a sharp line and say, "All these are damned," or "There may be a few in that church who are saved, but if they really were saved, they would belong to our little group." No, friends, you make no lines to separate believers. This is known to God alone.

Now the Lord says, "I come to thee, and these things I speak in the world"—here He is in the midst of the world—"that they"—the Church, the born-again believers, the hidden people—"might have my joy fulfilled in themselves." "My joy!" Now this is what God wants in human beings. He wants us to be filled with joy. Oh, if you aren't joyful, I mean radiantly, abundantly joyful, you do not understand what God has available for you.

If someone says, "Dr. Barnhouse, you don't know. Here I am thirty and I'm not married. Life is passing me by and I'm . . ." Look, if you say that, you have not understood the sovereignty of God. He wants you to be filled with joy no matter what your circumstances. "But God has given me a weak constitution and I go and I'm not able to . . ." God almighty planned for you to have that weak constitution. He has His purpose for you, and if you go and say, "Lord, there is the stream. I'm going to stop trying to buck it. I'm going to float with Thee and Thy will and Thy way," then you will begin to have His joy.

Now what was His joy? What was the joy of Jesus Christ? He says here in verse 13 that His purpose was for us, the born-again believers, to have His joy. Jesus had joy about the future. In Hebrews 12:2 it says, "Who for the joy that was set before him, endured the cross. . . ." That was the joy of redeeming us. But that was not the joy that sustained Him in His daily living. The joy that sustained Him˙ was His moment-by-moment contact with the Father, that absolute oneness and fellowship that binds them together and makes them absolutely one.

Listen to Jesus in Psalm 5. Verse 10 proves that this is Jesus Christ talking. For on the Day of Pentecost Peter quoted this verse in reference to Christ, "Thou wilt not leave my soul in hell, nor wilt thou suffer thine Holy One to see corruption." So let's listen to Jesus in verse 5. "Jehovah is the portion of mine inheritance and of my cup: thou maintainest my lot. The lines are fallen unto me in pleasant places; yea, I have a goodly heritage"—you and I are the goodly heritage—"I will bless Jehovah, who hath given me counsel: My reins also instruct me in the night seasons. I have set Jehovah always before me: because he is at my right hand, I shall not be moved. Therefore my heart is glad, and my glory rejoiceth: my flesh also shall rest in hope." (See Psalm 16:5-9.)

Now, you see, we are accustomed to hearing so often the phrase, "Jesus was a man of sorrows and acquainted with grief." And I would not detract in the slightest from the fact that He was a man of sorrows and acquainted with grief. But let us also say that He was a man of joy and acquainted with fellowship! He was a man of joy who lived in the Trinity with God the Father and God the Holy Spirit. The Lord Jesus Christ wants us to have joy and He wants us to have it the same way He had it—by constant fellowship with the Father.

What we're learning in this verse is that right now we have the same fellowship with the Father that Jesus Christ had, and that as we accept that relationship and enter into it, His joy is fulfilled in us. It was Jesus who taught that in the new birth we become His children. In Galatians 4:6, we read, "And because ye are sons, God hath sent forth the Spirit of his Son into your hearts, crying, Abba, Father" *(abba pater)*, which means Daddy Father. *Abba* means Daddy in Greece and Turkey and Syria. Every child in the streets calls his parents

"Mamma" and "Abba." *Pater* is the big word for "Father," but *Abba* is the intimate word "Daddy." This is one thing for which I could shake the old graybeards who translated the King James Version. They were so solidly Puritanical, even though they hated the Puritans, that they were scared to death of realizing they could run up to God as I could run up to my father when I was a child.

One time I was greeting my wife at the airport when our daughter was only about three. I greeted her last. And when I came to greet her she had her arms wrapped tightly around my knee. She was down there hugging my knee, and she put her feet up on top of mine and I lifted my feet right up in the air, and she came with it.

I have no objection whatsoever in your approaching God this way. Just go as a child and hurl yourself at Him and say "Daddy Father." You see, God doesn't expect in our prayers that we say "Poor worm of the dust that I am." Jesus says, "I'm teaching you that you have the same relationship with the Father as I do." And thus it is that we cry, "Abba, Father."

Look at 1 John 1:3,4. There we read, "That which we have seen and heard declare we unto you, that ye also may have fellowship with us: and truly our fellowship is with the Father, and with his Son Jesus Christ." Then what does it say? "These things write we unto you, that your joy might be full." So we go right back to John 17, where Jesus says, "These things I speak in the world, that they might have my joy fulfilled in themselves." Oh, how eager Jesus Christ is for you to have His joy. And let me tell you, if you are frustrated, it is not His fault. If you are not living in the fulness of joy you do not have what God wants you to have.

Let me prove this to you. John 15:11 says "These things have I spoken unto you, that my joy might remain in you, and that your joy might be full." Now look at John 16:24. "Hitherto have ye asked nothing in my name: ask, and ye shall receive, that your joy may be full." And now in our text, John 17:13, "That they might have my joy fulfilled in themselves." This is what God wants you to be, no matter what your circumstances—sorrowful, yet always rejoicing; as poor, and yet always making many rich.

When I was only fourteen, a man who led me in the development of my spiritual life, said, "Every life is a sermon and every sermon should have a text." He said, "Choose a text. Ask God to give you a verse for your life." And I chose Philippians 3:10, "That I may know him, and the power of his resurrection, and the fellowship of his sufferings, being made conformable unto his death." That man also taught me that in Bible study you should read "wholesale and retail." "Read it through from cover to cover with great sweeps, not stopping to look at details. Then take one book and make it your own."

And I chose Philippians. I read Philippians hundreds of times in every possible version and translation, and I memorized it. It only has a hundred and four verses. But you know, the word *joy* and *rejoice, joy* and *rejoice, joy* and *rejoice* are found eighteen times in the little book of Philippians. Yet, in the first chapter, Paul says, "I am about to come up for trial before Nero and my bonds in Christ are manifested every place. I'm in chains. People go around the block to avoid speaking to me." (See Phil. 1:13-18.) And later he says to Timothy, "God bless the house of Onesiphorus, for he was not ashamed of my chains" (see 2 Tim. 1:16), which proves that some people were ashamed of them. Yet in the midst of this you find *joy* and *rejoicing,* eighteen times. Fifteen percent of all the verses in the whole epistle tell of joy and gladness in the midst of difficulty.

Sometimes we sing a hymn with the chorus, "When we all get to heaven, what a day of rejoicing that will be!" Well, let's sing a new verse and put in today's date. For instance, "When May 1 comes, what a day of rejoicing that will be!" and the next day, change the verse to, "When May 2 comes, what a day of rejoicing that will be!" And if you are planning to teach a Sunday School lesson next February 20th, include in the lesson, "When February 20th comes, what a day of rejoicing that will be!" April 15—that's tax day—"What a day of rejoicing that will be!" "Well," someone says, "I'm having final examinations." "What a day of rejoicing that will be!" You see, God says it doesn't make any difference about the circumstance. He said "I am inside." *Circum* means around. *Stance* refers to the things that are standing, like a man's stance when he's playing golf. *Circumstances* are the things that are all around you. Well, what difference do the things around you make if Christ is in you? You see, that's joy. That's the utter absolute joy that we may have day by day and moment by moment.

Now He's talking about joy, and He says, "I have given them thy word, and the world hath hated them" (v. 14). Look back in verse 8 "I have given unto them the *words*"—plural, but here in verse 14, "I have given them thy *word*." Day by day He had given them the words, but now He has given them the Word, the great truth that which we have in Scripture. And this, He says, is the channel of the Father's love. If it's the channel of the Father's love, then it's the source of joy. Our source of joy is to be found in this Book. It's the cup from which we drink, the invisible eternal Word.

Now get the word *and*. That's important. "I have given them thy word *and* the world hath hated them." Now as I said before, the word *world* is found seventy-nine times in the Gospel of John. What is the world? Oh, the world is, "Get your name in the paper." "Be seen with prominent people." The world is the name dropper.

I read in the *New Yorker* once a story of someone who had just come back from Hollywood. He became insufferable because in every conversation, when people said to him, "Oh, you've been out in Hollywood?" he would say, "Oh, yes, and Clark said this to me, or Gary said this, or Marilyn said this and Lana said that." And the person was pompous out of all proportion because of his name dropping. That's what the world wants—to be seen, to be heard. That's why they're so definite about being at the theater and the opera on opening night. That's when it really counts to know the right people.

And believe me, this exists in the Christian world

too. A lot of two-by-four Christians want to prove they are from this Bible institute or that, and they let everybody know it. You see, this is the fad. This is the world, and this worldliness is in the church.

Now Jesus says that the world hates—hates—hates the true believer. The world is never going to hate a believer who is a pompous, boastful, proud person. If you're just out shooting off your mouth about Christianity playing the world's game, why the world will say you're just a religious nut. But if, all of a sudden, you come to Christ, and you don't care what the world thinks about you, and you'd rather be found talking to someone who is born again, whom the world never heard of and never will hear of, then the world will hate you.

Let's see some of the things that the Father says about the world. 1 John 2:16 reads, "For all that is in the world (Philadelphia, Los Angeles, New York), the lust of the flesh, the lust of the eyes, and the pride of life, is not of the Father, but is of the world." And if you want to know the course of this world, Ephesians 2:2,3 says you were "children of disobedience, children of wrath." We had our life in the course of this world. And in Romans 12:2, "Be not conformed to this world." Don't be shaped by Kansas City or Anytown, U.S.A. Then Galatians 1:4 says that Jesus died and shed His blood that He might deliver us from Philadelphia, Pennsylvania. It says "this present evil world" and "this present evil world" is any place where you happen to be living.

Someone says, "You haven't been in the suburbs and seen the dogwoods and the daffodils." No, but

I've been to the academy of music and I've been to Wanamakers and I've been inside the union league. I've seen all of these things. And let me tell you that the world is the world, is the world, is the world! The Bible says that Jesus died in order to deliver us from this whole idea of being, of having, of getting and scheming.

Now, I want you to note three very important words in verse 14, "Even as I." Oh, isn't that wonderful! He says—and I want you to note this—"The world hates them because they are not of the world, even as I am not of the world." Of course He wasn't of the world. "The first man is of the earth, earthy: the second man is the Lord from heaven" (1 Cor. 15:47). In Hebrews 7:26 it says He was "separate from sinners." And in John 8:23 He said, "Ye are from beneath; I am from above: ye are of this world; I am not of this world."

"Now then," the Lord says, "the fact that I've put you in this world is going to make the world hate you, because I have given you My words and My Word and I'm making of you a people of joy, and your joy is going to accuse the others." For instance, say you are a nurse in the hospital, and you are filled with the joy of Christ in the midst of a bunch of girls who would simply die if they didn't have a date on Saturday night. If you say, "Oh, it's quite all right. The Lord knows my life and He can take care of all of my problems," then they will know your attitude.

"Oh, why aren't you out trying?"

"Well, I'm in trusting." This will raise their animosity more than anything else.

"Why aren't you like other people?"

"Well, I don't want to be like other people."

"You think we're not good enough?"

"Oh, that's not it. I want to be like Jesus Christ."
Then hatred comes.

Nobody will hate you if you say, "I'm going to form a league for temperance" or "I'm going to form a league to stop gambling" or "I'm going to form a league to do away with prostitution or with liquor or with dope." The world doesn't object to "these reformers."

But when you say, "I'm going to be like Jesus Christ, and that means I can be happy in Him," then God gives you the privilege of catching up with joy. The Constitution of the United States gives to every man the "right of liberty and the pursuit of"—the chasing of—"happiness." But it never gives him the right to catch up with it. But in Christ, we have joy. We have *already* caught up with happiness.

I remember the time in my own life as I developed when I had had just enough of this joy to be miserable in the night club, but not quite enough of it to be happy in a prayer meeting. Have you gone through that state yet, when you haven't learned what it is to rejoice in Christ and let Him be the fulness of all things?

Maybe it will help you to know what we are as Christians and why we are not of the world. In 2 Corinthians 5:17 it says, "If any man be in Christ he is a white-washed Adam." Oh no! I beg your pardon. I made a mistake. "If any man be in Christ he is a new creature." In Hebrews 3:1, it says we are "partakers of the heavenly calling." And in Philippians 3:20 it says, "Our [citizenship] is in heaven." In 1 Peter 1:4 it says we have an inheritance that is "incorruptible, and undefiled, and that fadeth not away, reserved in heaven" for us. This is the reason why we are pilgrims and strangers in the world. And this allows us to see why we can be joyful.

Now Jesus is praying for us. He's praying for us because He knows our peril. There's a peril in being in the world. There's great danger in being in the midst of Philadelphia. I'm not talking about going down the streets where the hoodlums are. I'm talking about the danger in some churches of just having everybody say, "It's all nice, it's all nice," and you have just enough inoculation to keep you from catching reality. It's possible to be inoculated with religion that keeps you from catching reality. But what we must do is have that inoculation which makes us resistant to all of the viruses that would destroy our spiritual life. We must realize that in being joined with Christ, we are in a perilous position, because the world hates Him.

So in verse 15 He says, "I pray not that thou shouldst take them out of the world." Now it might seem logical, if this world is such a terrible place to say, "Lord, why don't You take us home to heaven?" In the Old Testament two men asked God to let them die, and God didn't answer the prayer of either one of them. Elijah said, "Here I am under the juniper tree and I alone am left. I want to die." (See 1 Kings 19:4.) And Jonah, when he had preached and come out of Nineveh said, "It will be a whole lot better for me to die." (See Jonah 4:3.) God didn't answer the prayers of either of them. What God does say is, "I pray not that thou shouldst take them out of the world, but that thou shouldst keep them from the evil," that is, from Satan. In other words, God is saying, "It's a whole lot better for you to live in Philadelphia and have the victory over evil than it is for you to go to heaven."

As a pastor, I've had occasion to visit in homes where someone in the prime of life says, "Grandmother is in here. Come and see. Oh, Pastor, please pray that the Lord will take her home to heaven." No! No! No! The Lord Jesus prays, "I pray not that thou shouldst take them home to heaven."

"Oh, but it makes things so difficult for us." That's just what you need, Grandmother living with you as an invalid for ten years. It could be just the sandpaper needed to cut you down to size.

"Oh, but it is such a block on all our desire." That's right. This is the reason why God is allowing these things to happen. "Oh, but it would be such a deliverance. Grandfather's mind is failing. He comes and says, 'Did I ever tell you about the story when I was a boy?'" Yes, he's told it 7,324 times. That's the way old people are. And you middle-aged people, as your parents grow older, don't forget that you're going to face this fact. And when this happens, it gives you the responsibility of caring for them in the midst of a world that says, "Put them away," "Get them out of sight," "We'll make every sacrifice to put them away where they won't be under our feet." But the Lord says, "I pray not that thou shouldst take them out of the world, but that thou shouldst deliver them from the evil one."

God is saying that victory over the world is better than separation from the world, because when He leaves us right here and allows us to triumph over all circumstances and keeps us in joy, this is triumph.

You'll notice that He asks God to keep us. He doesn't say, "Give them the power to keep themselves." I can't keep myself. In 1 Peter 1:5 you read this great fact about this keeping. "Who are kept by the power of God through faith unto salvation ready to be revealed in the last time." Now let's go a little further.

In John 17:16 Jesus repeats what He said in verse 14, but He means a different thing this time. In verse 16 He says, "They are not of the world, even as I am not of the world." And back in verse 14 He said, "They are not of the world, even as I am not of the world." Why did He repeat it? In verse 14 He is telling why the world hates the believer. In verse 16 He is using this phrase in order to ask the Father to keep us from evil. Since we are not of the world, we must be kept by Him.

Now whenever you look in the Scriptures, you discover this tremendous contrast between the world and us. The world's standing is in Adam, our standing is in Christ. The world is under condemnation. We have been accepted in the beloved. The world is born of the flesh. We are born of the Spirit. They are evil and we are holy. The world has a different father—"Ye are of your father the devil." We are children of God by faith in Christ Jesus. The aim of the world is self, and the aim of the believer is to please Christ. The citizenship of the worldling is on earth and our citizenship is in heaven. And they have a different way of life from ours. They have a different destiny. Their destiny is the lake of fire. And our destiny is the Father's house, where there are many mansions.

So in verse 17 Jesus prays, "Sanctify them through thy truth," which means to set them apart. And in verse 19 He says, "For their sakes I sanctify myself." *Sanctify* has several different meanings. It comes from the Latin *sanctus*, which means holy. Depending on the usage of the word, it can mean to set apart for a spiritual purpose, or to make one holy. ("This is the will of God, even your sanctification.") Here it refers to being set apart. Certain things are set apart for God. Jesus Himself is sanctified, set apart. So He is saying, "Set apart My Church. Set apart My true believers by Thy truth. Thy Word is truth." Thus, the Bible becomes the standard by which we judge everything else.

And then in verse 18 He says, "As thou hast sent me into the world, even so have I also sent them into the world." This is what God wants you to do. Are you an elevator operator? Well, then you are to be the Word made flesh going up and down. And when for the seventeen thousandth time somebody comes in and says, "You have a rather up-and-down life" (I understand that this is told at least three times a day to elevator operators. They get so tired of it they don't know what to do.), if you are in Christ, you can be the Word made flesh instead of getting angry at them. You can simply answer, "Well you know, I set my affections on things above and not on things beneath, for Christ is my life."

And if you answer that every time, some of them will look at you and soon they will stop making the same wisecrack. And if you are a student you can understand that God made you the Word made flesh on that campus. And you are to be the Word made flesh if you are a clerk in a store. And no matter what you are doing, you can be the Word made flesh dwelling there.

There was once an advertisement that said, "Bibles that are bound in hard cover; Bibles that are bound in soft leather." And someone said, "The greatest Word of God that there is, is the Bible bound in shoe leather." You are to be the Word made flesh in your circumstances, in your school, your office, your store, your factory, your shop, your hospital. You are to be Jesus Christ there. Jesus is saying, "I'm going to the cross and die so that they also might be set apart by the truth. As the Father hath sent Me, so send I you." Jesus did not die merely in order that you might have a free insurance policy against the flames of hell. Some people look upon Christianity as nothing more than cheap fire insurance. But believe me dear friends, Christianity is you becoming Jesus Christ in the world.

You are to be Jesus Christ today. You are to be Jesus Christ at the breakfast table. You are to be Jesus Christ when you walk into the office. You are to be Jesus Christ when the boss's back is turned. You are to be Jesus Christ when the off-color wisecracks are heard. You are to be Jesus Christ in every act of kindness. If somebody takes advantage of you, instead of snapping "That's your job! Do it yourself!" just quietly do it in Jesus' name and for

His sake. We allow ourselves to be put upon. We are reviled and we revile not again. We are persecuted and we bless. This is the reason you're left here, to be Jesus Christ today, tomorrow and until He returns.

I close with verse 20. He says "Neither pray I for the twelve disciples alone, but also for those in the twentieth century who will believe on me through their word." Isn't this wonderful? Here is a prayer of Jesus specifically praying for you and for me. He says, "I'm not only praying for these twelve, but I'm praying for Donald Barnhouse, who will believe because of Paul's word. I'm praying for those in Philadelphia in the twentieth century who have come to Christ because of the word of Matthew, Mark, Luke, and John." Here is the true apostolic succession. You and I are the vicars of Christ. We are here instead of Christ, the Word made flesh by the power of the Holy Spirit to go forth and live for Him. May God make us to understand what our place is in Christ.

The Christmas Story Before Pilate

In John 18:37 we have, "To this end was I born, and for this cause came I into the world." This is Christ's announcement of the purpose of Christmas—Christmas as announced in Pilate's Judgment Hall, approximately six or eight hours before He was crucified. He tells why He came. Let's go back and look at the circumstances. Earlier in the chapter we read that Pilate said to Jesus, " 'Are you the King of the Jews?' Jesus answered, 'Do you say this of your own accord, or did others say this to you about me?' Pilate answered, 'Am I a Jew? Your own nation and the chief priests have handed you over to me; what have you done?' Jesus answered, 'My kingship is not of this world; if my kingship were of this world, my servants would fight, that I might not be handed over to the Jews; but my kingship is not from the world.' Pilate said to him, 'So you are a king.' Jesus answered, 'You say that I am

253

a king. For this was I born, and for this I have come into the world, to bear witness to the truth. Everyone who is of the truth hears my voice'" (John 18:33-37).

It's very interesting to note that in one of the greatest moments of tension in the life of the Lord Jesus, He answered with the Christmas story. He knew He was going to die. He had steadfastly set His face to go to Jerusalem, and had said, "My hour is come." The night before, He had prayed in the garden of Gethsemane, and had sweat, as it were, great drops of blood. Then He had been arrested. When darkness came, Peter had followed afar off and denied Him with oaths and cursings. Jesus has looked at Peter and Peter has gone away weeping. Now daylight comes. The judge is out in his Praetorium. And Jesus explains the Christmas story.

"Why were you born, little baby?" Oh, the world does not know the Christmas story. The Christmas story of Christ in a manger, with Mary the big personage in the picture, is a satanic deformation if we do not understand that this baby grew up. The Christ who remains a baby will not be the Lord over the life of any being. And if you are to understand Christ—well, picture in your mind a Christmas card that is higher than it is wide, and in the front page a hole shaped like a cross. And through the cross you can see the little baby on the other side. If you do not see Baby Jesus through the cross, you have not seen Baby Jesus! You have not seen why He came. You have not understood what He meant when He said, "To this end was I born, and for this cause came I forth."

Now the little baby has grown up, and in a few hours He is to die. He stands accused before Pilate, and Pilate says, "Are you the King of the Jews?" A Roman governor would, of course, be extremely interested in those of royalty in the province he governed.

When the British arrived in Africa, one of their first points was to find out who the chiefs were, to pamper them and give them special gifts. Many an African chief was knighted by the king or queen and given the title, "Sir," in front of his long, unpronounceable name. Many of these paramount chiefs were looked at very carefully. Their sons were sent to Oxford and Cambridge, and they went back to take their positions in Africa. At times Britain tried to exile them from their homes by keeping them in England and not letting them go back where they could make trouble.

If an empire is going to have trouble it is often going to have trouble with the local princes. So a well-trained Pilate, a Roman out "in the sticks" of Jerusalem, exercising his sovereignty, would naturally be extremely interested in anybody who might pretend to be a king. For here could be a seedbed of revolution; here could be rebellion.

"Are you the King?" And the Lord Christ, in order to set Pilate right, simply said to him, "Did you think of this by yourself? Or did someone put you up to asking this question?"

And right away, of course, Pilate can begin to adjust, and not think of Jesus as a potential threat against the Roman Empire. Jesus' question naturally revealed the cabal that was against Him. It showed that there was a group of men who wanted His life and who had yielded Him over for their own sinister purposes.

So Jesus set Pilate at ease. He said, "My kingship"—and this is the true meaning of the word. *Kingdom* is a much weaker word than *Kingship,* for *dom* on the end of a word, like *dukedom* or *Christendom,* is a suffix that indicates territorial sway, domination, dominion. But the Lord is saying, "I'm not talking about how many geographical miles might come under My sway or be in My realm. I'm talking about My *kingship.*" Now, *ship* is a quality of being, and if a man is a king, his kingship and his authority centers in himself, and not in what land he might hold.

The Lord Jesus Christ says, "My kingship is not of this world." Let us never forget that the authority, the dominion, the sovereignty, of Christ is entirely a question of WHO HE IS. Who is He? Well, He claims Kingship. He says, "I am the King. My kingship is not of this world." If His kingship is not of this world, it's either from hell or from heaven. There is no third place where it might be from.

Now there is a kingship that rises out of the sinister ideas and rebellion of Satan. Jesus said that Satan's kingdom is divided against itself, thus teaching that Satan does have a kingdom. Some of the angels that originally followed Lucifer in his fall rebelled against him. Wars in this world are caused by conflicts between Satan's generals of lesser rank who are trying to make it on their own. This is the essence of history, as seen from the point of view of the Bible. The Pharisees claimed that Jesus' kingship was from hell, for they said, "This man casts out demons by Beelzebub the prince of demons." (See Mark 3:22.) And the Lord Jesus announced, "Anyone who thinks that has committed the unpardonable sin." For to say that the working of Jesus is the working of Satan shows that a man is in complete rebellion against God. Not only has he rebelled in his own right against God, but he has taken up his place with God's greatest. defiant enemy, and says, "I'll follow Satan. I'll go with him." And God says, "When a man gets that far, there is no repentance for him. There is no pardon."

So, by the sheer logic of the facts, we are forced to show Jesus Christ's kingdom is not from hell, but from heaven, and therefore, from God. Many years ago I drew a little outline that showed what Jesus is. Put at the top of a page the words "Christ claimed to be God." Under that statement draw two vertical lines and label one "True," and the other "False." Now if His claim to be God is true, then it is true that He is God. But if His claim is false, then draw two more lines to show either that He knew the claim was false, or He did not know the claim was false. If Jesus Christ said, "I am God" and did not know that it was a false claim, then He was insane. If someone comes to you and says, "I am Napoleon Bonaparte," you know very well where he belongs. And if he says, "I am God Almighty," this is the same thing. Now if the claim is false and a man ignores the fact that he is making a false claim, then this is crookedness.

Again you are forced by sheer logic to say that Jesus Christ was a crook, or insane, or that He is

God. And this is the dilemma that Jesus Christ puts before all the universe in Pilate's Hall when He stands and says, "My kingship is not of this world." Ruling out this planet and seeing the authority of Jesus, what is your answer? Is He from hell or from heaven? And if you say, "Well, of course, He is from heaven," then I say to you, in the name of God, you are His subject. If you are His subject, then get down in front of Him and bow before Him, and accept His allegiance, and say, "Lord Jesus Christ, I worship Thee."

When He said, "My kingship is not of this world," Pilate answered, "So you are a king." Jesus answered in Greek a phrase that means, "You say it," which was a very good Greek expression that was in constant use among the Rabbis in the rabbinical writings. It means "this is true." In our day we have the slang expression, "You said it," but in Jesus' day it was distinguished language. "You said it, Pilate." And thus it was that the Lord Jesus Christ announces in no uncertain terms, "I am King." Dean Alfred, in his *Greek New Testament Commentary* points out that the punctuation should be in the middle of the sentence here. It should be, "You say it. I am a king."

Then Jesus says, "To this end was I born." O little baby of Christmas, now we can begin to understand. A few hours before you die you say, "To this end was I born."

"Where did you come from, baby dear?
'Out of the everywhere into here.'
"Where did you get those eyes so blue?
'Out of the sky as I passed through.'

"Where did you get that pearly ear?
'God spoke and it came out to hear.'"

Back in the old days, no mother ever had a little child that didn't sometime or another run up against this little bit of doggerel that is so filled with the sweetness of mother love, and yet, of course, we know that the baby did not get its blue eyes from passing through the sky, and so on. But what is inherent in this poem is certainly true with the Lord Jesus Christ. "Where did you come from, baby dear?" No other baby did come "out of the everywhere" but the Lord Jesus Christ did! He came from eternity.

"My kingdom is not of this world. . . . To this end was I born. I came to bear witness of the truth." Here Jesus was speaking to Pilate, and Pilate asked a question that has been echoed by cynics through the centuries. "What is truth?" said jesting Pilate. But despite his jesting, the Lord Jesus gave a straight answer. For when He said, "I came to bear witness unto the truth," first of all, Jesus Christ is declaring that truth is an entity. Truth is not in fragments. Truth holds together. There is no phase of truth that is not related to every other phase of truth. The inspiration of the Bible is related to the structure of the atom. The virgin birth is related to the multiplication table. All things that are truth are a part of the Truth.

And a Christian is never afraid of truth. This is why a true Christian can go into a biological laboratory and become a great biologist. He may work on the creation of the protein molecule. He may even be the one who shall put the amino acids together in such a form that the newspaper will announce, "Scientists have created life in the laboratory!" Now, there may be little, insecure people who jump and say, "Oh, no, no, no! Leave that to God. Don't let a scientist do that." But, I tell you this. A true Christian need never be afraid of truth.

They tell me that in college some of the most difficult cases of psychological tensions come from young people who are brought up in ultrafundamentalist homes, and who have been taught that God Almighty created the earth in six twenty-four-hour days, and that Adam and Eve were created on the fourth of November at three p.m. in 4004 B.C., according to Ussher's chronology. When they come to college and learn that this isn't true—and certainly it is not true—they say, "Well, then . . . we have to throw away the whole Bible." What happened was that they took the Bible and a line of interpretation, and little by little they confused the two, and began to think that the line of interpretation was inspired instead of the Bible being inspired.

We are not afraid of truth today. I do not think that there is any intelligent Christian who does not know beyond any question that the earth is tens of millions of years old, and that man has existed in this earth for tens of thousands of years. This does not destroy the Bible in any way.

Christ said, "I came to bear witness of the truth," and the truth is an entity. It is one, whether it is biological truth, geological truth or theological truth. You have no idea how confused people were four hundred years ago when men first began to say that the earth turned around the sun. People said, "It can't be true!" But it is true. The earth turns around the sun, and as it turns on its own axis, what appears to be the rising of the sun is merely in illusion. "Why this can't be true," they said. "The Bible says, 'From the rising of the sun to the going down of the same.' Therefore, the sun must rise." And they were as much in a dither about the rising and setting sun as some Fundamentalists are today about the language of creation.

There are people in the United States who say, "The Lord God formed man out of the dust of the ground." And they have God doing it in a "cookie-cutter" fashion. They say He made a mud pie and when He leaned over and breathed into a sculptured being, part of the mud became hair, and part of the mud became toe nails, and part became epidermis, and so on. Well, this idea has to go, just as the idea of the actual rising and setting of the sun had to go. The truth about the earth and the sun did not destroy the Word of God. And the truth about the age of the earth is most certainly not going to destroy the Word of God. We face these things and we understand that what has to give is the nature of our comprehension of the language of the phenomena. As we go on we will discover many new things about the Word of God. Ultimately, the physicist may even recognize that Colossians is correct, as he studies the structure of the atom and says, "What keeps the whirling electrons from going out by centrifugal force? What is it that keeps them together?" We read in Colossians, "By him (Christ) all things consist" (Col. 1:17). We can understand what He means—that His Kingship is over all truth, and the truth that holds all things together.

Not only does He point out the unity of truth, but He also points out the objectivity of truth. The truth is there. It is fact. It is coldly objective. And when we can discuss it without prejudice, without any self-consciousness, then it becomes the most personal. Even as a biologist might look through a microscope, so we look through the microscope of the Word of God. We bring ourselves under the scrutiny of the eye of God, and we say, "Look! There am I, a lost sinner. I need Christ." In the microscope of God, we see ourselves objectively.

There am I. I'm a sinner. What can I do about it? Nothing. What can be done? *God will do it for me!* In my sin there is objective truth. In the cross of Jesus Christ, there is objective truth. What He did on the cross for me is immediately relevant, and I find that my problems are met, and my frustrations are gone, and the Lord of mercy has come to bear witness to the truth.

Now, this brings us to the point that truth must come from above. "My kingship is not of this world." "I have come to bear witness of truth"; therefore, truth is not of this world. Truth is of God. James 1:5 says, "If any of you lack wisdom, let him ask of God." Samuel Morse was once seen bowing his head over his desk as he worked. When someone said, "What are you doing?" He said, "I'm asking God for help. Every time I go into my laboratory," he explained, "I say, 'O God, I am nothing. Give me wisdom, give me clarity of mind.'" Is it any wonder that the first telegram ever sent was, "What hath God wrought?" For Morse knew that God had done it. Truth must come from above.

And then we also see here that truth must come from a person sent from God. "To this end was I born, and for this cause came I into the world. . . ." (John 18:37). And so, when the Lord Jesus Christ announced that He had come in relationship to truth, He declared that this truth must come through a person sent from God, and that He Himself was that person. He said, "I am the truth." I think we can trace what began to frighten Pilate at this point. He was scared to death. He did everything he could to get out of this situation. Not wanting to judge Jesus, he said, "I find no fault in this man." What set the governor to being afraid? It was Jesus' words, "To this end was I born, to this cause *came* I."

Now you and I can't say, "I came into this world." I didn't come into this world. I was brought into this world. Every time a baby comes into this world, the doctor or midwife takes hold of the first part of the body that comes from the mother's womb and pulls. Sometimes some of us had to have extra assistance. But we are always dragged into this world. And certainly our spirits did not exist beforehand. We have no memory of the past; but this baby, this Christmas baby could remember the past. He had a memory of Abraham, Moses, and even of the throne of God. "For this cause came I into this world." And this was the sentence that set Pilate to thinking.

And it won't be long before the people will add

263

this tremendous verse, "By our law he ought to die because *he made himself the Son of God.*" (See John 19:7.) When Pilate relates those words to what Jesus has already said to him, he will try even harder to get out of pronouncing the death sentence on this innocent man.

If we look back over Jesus' ministry, we see that Jesus' statement, "For this cause came I into the world," is the same thing He has been saying all along. Look at these words from earlier in His ministry, "The Son of man is come to seek and to save that which was lost" (Luke 19:10). "I am not come to call the righteous, but sinners to repentance" (Mark 2:17). "For even the Son of man came not to be ministered unto, but to minister, and to give his life a ransom for many" (Mark 10:45).

So we put all these things together, and we find the Lord Jesus, calmly, dispassionately testifying to a governor who represented the world's greatest empire, before He went to the cross to die, "I, the Christmas baby, came into this world for a purpose. I didn't come to give sickly sentimentality or to cause advanced commercial sales in the month of December. I came to bear witness to the truth."

Now look at the last phase of verse 37, "Every one that is of the truth heareth my voice." This is the tremendous thing. Pilate heard His voice in his eardrums, but he didn't hear His voice in his heart. He dismissed it with a philosophical retort, "What is truth?" and went back off the scene for a while, rather annoyed at what he had heard.

What is your response? Are you going to shrug off what you've read and say, like Pilate, "Well, what is truth?" And then others say, "Well, let's go back and drown our thoughts in Christmas spirits." Some do that. It is not at all surprising that the liquor corporations report more liquor is sold in the month of December than in any two-month period at other times of the year. Why? Well, with all this joy, and with all this gladness, and with all this, even indirect, preaching of Christ, men have to be faced with the reality of truth or insulate themselves from it. And they insulate themselves with that which deadens their senses.

Each one of us is brought face to face with this man who stands there so quietly, this man who is about to die. As He looks us in the face He says, "Do you want to know the meaning of Christmas? The meaning of Christmas is truth. The meaning of Christmas is God. The meaning of Christmas is redemption. The meaning of Christmas is the finality of the Kingship that is not of this world. The meaning of Christmas is the sovereignty of God!"

He Died That Day

"Then delivered he him therefore unto them to be crucified. And they took Jesus, and led him away. And he bearing his cross went forth into a place called the place of a skull, which is called in the Hebrew Golgotha"—and in Latin Calvarius. It means the skull. It means a bone in the head without the flesh, a bone with two eyeholes and a hole for the nose and a grinning jaw. That was somewhat the way this hill was. The people said it looked like a skull, and so they called it Skull Peak —Calvary—Golgotha: "where they crucified him, and two others with him, on either side one, and Jesus in the midst" (John 19:16-18).

Now here is the most wonderful picture of your salvation and mine, for there in the center is the cross where Christ is and on two sides the crosses of the two thieves. Many years ago I published in a book, *Teaching the Word of Truth,* a little outline in which I pointed out the difference between the two thieves. And I tell it to you in the story of an incident that took place during the third or fourth year of our radio broadcast.

I was working in my office at the church one morning when the janitor came and said, "There's a gentleman out here who wants to see you." He gave me the man's card and I saw that he was the British sea captain of the Mauritania, which was at that time the largest ocean liner crossing the Atlantic. I came out with his card in my hand and found him standing inside the door of the church.

As I came up to him, he said, "Beautiful church you have here."

And I said, "Yes it is. I'm very thankful for the people who built it a hundred years ago."

"It's a great deal like the Basilica at Ravenna in Italy."

"Well, as a matter of fact," I said, "it's an architectural copy and the people that built this room brought workmen from Italy. These marble colums and this tessellated ceiling and the mosaic were all done by Italian workmen."

We talked about this for a moment, and then I said, "You didn't come here to talk with me about church architecture did you?"

"No," he said, "as a matter of fact I didn't." As we walked back toward my office, he told me why he had come. "As you see," he explained, "I'm captian of the Mauritania and I go back and forth across the Atlantic about twenty-three times a year." He said, "Every other Sunday on the way down the coast of Newfoundland I get your radio broadcast out of Boston. And last Sunday, when I listened to you, I said to myself, 'I've got twenty-four hours when I land in New York. I'm going over to Philadelphia to see that preacher.' So I took the train this morning from New York and I just came down on the off-chance that I might see you."

"Sir," I said, "have you been born again?"

He said, "That's why I came down to see you."

By this time we had reached the prayer meeting room, where there was a chalkboard. I took up a piece of chalk and I said, "Sir, let me put it very simply for you," and I drew three crosses. I said, "Now you know that when Jesus Christ died on the cross there was a thief on either side?"

"Yes."

Under the first cross I wrote the word *in*. Then I said, "This man had sin *in* him. He was a guilty sinner. This man here," and I pointed to the third cross, "also had sin *in* him." I wrote the word *in* under each of the two crosses. Then under the cross in the middle I wrote the words *not in*. "This man *did not* have sin in Him. Christ was the sinless spotless Lamb of God. Now," I said, pointing to the first and third crosses, "in addition, these men had sin *on* them." And I wrote *on* under both crosses.

His brow puckered for a moment, and I said, "Do you want to know the difference between sin *on* you and sin *in* you? Do you drive a car?"

He said, "Yes, I do."

"Did you ever go through a red light?"

He said, "Yes, I did."

"You were guilty, weren't you?"

269

"Yes."

I said, "Did the police catch you?"

He said, "Well no, they didn't."

"But, you had it *in* you, didn't you?" I said, "and if the police had come and given you a ticket, then you would have had that 'sin' *on* you. That's the difference between having sin *in* you and having sin *on* you. Now all of us have sin *in* us. We are all guilty. And all of us also have sin *on* us. This first thief had sin *in* him and sin *on* him; this second thief had sin *in* him and sin *on* him. They were exactly alike."

Then I wrote the word *on* over the cross of Christ. I said, "Christ also had sin *on* Him. But He did not have it *in* Him. The sin that He had *on* Him was my sin." I turned my chalk sideways and I rubbed it through the word *on* under the first cross and drew a big arrow pointing to the cross of Christ. I said, "God justified this thief and put all the guilt of his sin over here *on* Jesus Christ. Now, sir," I said, "Christianity is simply this," and I pointed to the center cross, "there is the perfect Christ who came and died for you and me. Here are two types of people," I said, pointing to the other two crosses. "We both are alike, we all have sin *in* us. And all of us have had sin *on* us. But now my sin is *on* Christ. Now, sir, you are either like this first thief or like this second thief. Sin is *in* you, *in* me, and it is *on* yourself or it is *on* Christ. God says that Christ took your sins. Which are you like?"

He was a tall, cultured man of distinction and didn't have to carry on his briefcase the stickers that showed he had traveled more once or twice.

His weather-beaten face seemed to have the map of the world on it. His face worked for a moment and you could see that his British calm was greatly moved, and he was intensely trying to keep back tears. Suddenly he put his hand out and said, "By the grace of God, I am like this thief!"

I said, "Your sin is *on* Christ. God says so."

He said, "God says so."

Then he shot out his hand and took mine and said, "That's all I want. I can go back now."

I said, "No, come in and sit down." We sat down and talked for an hour about what to do next in the Christian life. Then we had lunch together and he went on his way back to New York.

Now here is a great picture of what happened when the Lord Jesus Christ died. Every person is like one of these two thieves. I tell you in the name of God that your sin is *in* you. You know that. You know you're a sinner. You know the dirty things you've done, the runaway things you've done. You know what is in you, just as well as I know what is in me. I know how God has forgiven me. I know that my sins have been put upon Christ. When Christ takes our sin, then lives are transformed. This is that which can take a woman who is a tramp and make of her a saint. This is that which can take a man who is vile and can make of him a man of God. Your sin is still *in* you, but when you become a Christian, your sin in *on* Christ. And now He can make it possible for the sin that is *in* you to be kept down by the inward life of the Lord Jesus Christ.

So they crucified Him with a thief on either side and Jesus in between them. And Pilate wrote a title with the words *Jesus of Nazareth, King of the Jews* and he put it on the cross. Now atheists, skeptics, and agnostics have taken references to the wording of this title in Matthew, Mark, Luke and John and said, "Oh, they contradict each other. They are worded differently." Well, how silly can people get in their attacks on the Bible? The reason there is a different wording is because this sign was written in three languages. John 19:20 says, "It was written in Hebrew, and Greek, and Latin." It was written in Hebrew, the language of religion; in Greek, the language of culture and science and in Latin, the language of law and government. Matthew, who wrote to the Jews, translated the Jewish title and wrote down what was there in Hebrew. Mark, who wrote to the Romans, probably translated the Latin. Luke who wrote to the Greeks, probably translated the Greek. Thus we have it recorded in these three different ways. You can find contradictions if you are looking for them, but you can find agreements if you are willing to accept the teaching of the Holy Spirit. The minute I show you the possibility of a simple explanation, the arguments against Scripture or against the inspiration of Scripture fall apart.

Now I want you to note this amazing thing. Then the Jews came to Pilate, mad as could be because everyone at the Crucifixion could see written on the sign that Jesus of Nazareth was the King of the Jews. They hated this! Here was a crowd of fantastic God-murderers, who were willing to do anything to strike against Christ. They had said, "We will not have this man to reign over us!" So when the Roman governor put a label on the cross, "Jesus of Nazareth, King of the Jews," they came back and said, "Oh, please write, 'He said He was the King of the Jews.'" Well, a Roman knew how to be a Roman. He said, "What I've written, I've written! Get out of here! I'm through with this!"

Look back for a moment, if you will, to John 11:47. The chief priests and the Pharisees were in a council and they said, "What are we going to do? This man is doing so many miracles that if we let Him alone, all men will believe on Him and the Romans will come and take *our* place—and we'll lose our meal ticket. If there is a difficulty of any kind, we will be put out as leaders!" And one of them, named Caiaphas, being the high priest that same year, said unto them, "Ye know nothing at all, nor consider that it is expedient for us, that one man should die for the people, and that the whole nation perish not" (John 11:49,50).

Now here he was hating Christ and here he was in the office of high priest, yet God Almighty, in spite of the man's unbelief, honored the office which He had created in the time of Aaron. And He put in the vocal cords of that man—He forced that man—to make a confession that Jesus Christ was the Saviour. We see this in John 11:51 where it says that Caiaphas did not speak this of his own accord, "but being high priest that year, he prophesied that Jesus should die for that nation." So you have the religious leader of the people saying, "Christ is the Saviour."

Then in John 19 you have the political leader saying that Christ is the King. And you may be sure that God Almighty caught hold of Pilate just as He caught hold of Caiaphas. And Pilate said, "What I have written, I have written." So God has the high priest say, "This is the Saviour," and God has the political leader say, "This is the King." This unconscious testimony is declared before the religious leaders and before all of the people. Jesus Christ is God. He is the King, He is the Saviour.

"Then the soldiers, when they had crucified Jesus, took his garments, and made four parts, to every soldier a part; and also his coat: now the coat was without seam, woven from the top throughout" (John 19:23). In other words, it was the coat of the poor. You see, if you just had a big blanket-like thing that you could just throw over your shoulder, it would be simple to weave. But to tailor a garment that has coat sleeves in it, you've got to cut the sleeves.

And by the way, the *Revised Standard Version*, in the book of Genesis, says that Joseph had a coat "with sleeves" (see Gen. 37:3), and the old King James Version says a coat "of many colours." I'm sorry to dissipate the childhood thought that Joseph had a nice little rainbow-red-orange-yellow-green-blue-and-violet coat. He didn't. His older brothers had the simple throw-over garment and Jacob had given Joseph a tailored coat. The Hebrew word here refers to the breadth of the palm of your hand—"a coat of *breadths*."

Somehow the translations in the sixteenth century didn't know much Hebrew and when they reached this passage, they translated it "a coat of many colours," but it does not mean that at all. What Joseph's brothers wore, and what Jesus wore, were the simple cloaks of the poor. You can see the garment of the poor, like the poncho or the serape, throughout the world, even today. To get a tailored coat costs more money. Jesus wore this single garment of the poor, a coat without seam woven from the top throughout.

"They said therefore among themselves, Let us not rend it, but cast lots for it, whose it shall be: that the Scripture might be fulfilled which saith, They parted my raiment among them, and for my vesture they did cast lots. These things therefore the soldiers did" (John 19:24). Oh, how God took care of the fulfillment of all the things that had been inspired in the Scriptures. Tucked into the Old Testament here and there, from Genesis all the way through Malachi, are those little phrases that were fulfilled in Christ. And here we have this great fulfillment that they gambled for His garments.

Now someone has written a novel called *The Robe* and they've made a movie out of it based on a proposition that the "robe" had miracle power. In churches all over Europe, there are supposedly pieces of Christ's garment, made out of about nine different kinds of cloth. It's been estimated that pieces of the "true cross" are made out of eleven different kinds of wood, at least. So that cross must have been fearfully and wonderfully made! If you go into the Escorial in the north side of Madrid in Spain, there is a bronze tablet on the wall which catalogs the relics in its church. I copied the inscription and translated it from the Spanish and put it in our magazine once. The bronze plaque says that they have the following relics: complete skeletons of saints—17 (my figures are not exact but the idea is here); bones as big as the tibia—76; skulls—115; bones as small as the carpals, metacarpals, and phalanges—2,785; hairs from the beard of Christ—4; 5 drops of milk from the Virgin Mary's breast; 2 pieces of the seamless robe; 11 pieces of the true cross—and it goes down all this list, this folderol, that they have there for the gullible people to come in and worship, and to which they're supposed to bow in veneration.

Oh, thank God, that we know these things are false! But how do we know? Well, in the first place, let's stop and think about a comparison. How far away are we from George Washington? About two hundred years—two hundred years in a land where there is printing and where it is possible to keep accurate records. If someone came and said to you, "I've got a button that was on George Washington's coat," you would think about as much of that as if someone said, "Here's a string from Nero's fiddle when he burned Rome." This is total folly!

The era of relics came at the time of the Crusades. There were practically no relics before that time. But when the Crusades caught interest in Europe and a town raised the money to send their knight and his retainer to join the Crusades for releasing Jerusalem from the hands of the Moslems, their last words were, "Bring us a piece of the true cross." The hometown wanted a relic. Well, when these people got out of Palestine and looked around, they said to the local populace, "Have you got any relics? We want to buy relics."

Some fellow said, "Yes, here's John the Baptist's

head over here." So they sold it to the relic hunters. And in Italy today, you've got John the Baptist's head in one place and you've got it in another place. When you ask the guide about it, he'll say, "Well, that's the head of John the Baptist as a boy and this is the head of John the Baptist as a man." And that's the calibre of relics that were brought home.

I'm reminded of *Time* magazine's story of the boy who went to Guadalcanal after the Marines had landed and defeated the Japanese on the island. When everything was quiet, the merchant marine landed with goods and supplies and some of the crew immediately wanted to buy relics. One of them came up to a tough old sergeant and said, "Can I get a Japanese battle flag?"

The sergeant shifted his quid from one cheek to the other and said, "Well it all depends. I can get you one for fifty dollars." The boy bargained a bit and then the sergeant said, "Okay, I'll get it for you for forty dollars—but I can't get it for about three days."

Then the sergeant took a piece of old parachute made out of nylon in Scranton, Pennsylvania. He cut it out and took some red paint to put the Japanese sun on this "flag." Then he got some old cans with Japanese labels on them, and copied all these markings on the flag even though he didn't know what they meant. Next, he took a bit of something that looked like blood, smeared it on, knocked the "flag" on the ground to get it dirty as could be and sold it to the boy for forty dollars. This "authentic" flag was taken home to Wisconsin and the sailor showed it to the Rotary Club where they gave him a welcome dinner as a hero, and he spoke of this Japanese battle flag. But somebody there, who knew Japanese, knew right away that this was not an authentic relic. So he read inscriptions like, "Do not store next to the engines," "Keep in a cool dry place," and so on.

Well, this is the quality of the relics in many churches. Let's not forget it. They are monstrous deceptions! And yet in the United States thousands of people go every year to Quebec to make a pilgrimage to the "Shinbone of St. Anne." The time between the death of Christ and the supposed relics is hundreds of years. And the Lord arranged that there be no relics by giving us the record that the soldiers gambled for His garment, as a fulfillment of prophecy. The power of Christ is in the Person of Christ, not in pieces of cloth or pieces of wood or bones or anything else that sinful man can think up.

Now in verse 28 we read, "Jesus knowing that all things were now accomplished, that the Scripture might be fulfilled, saith, I thirst." As early as the second century Irenaeus said there was a tradition in the church that Jesus Christ quoted Scripture out loud, beginning with Psalm 22 and continuing with Psalm 23 and Psalm 24. Scripture does give us the fact that He did quote Psalm 22:1, "My God, my God, why hast thou forsaken me?" But I think there is evidence that the Lord spent all of His time on the cross, those six hours, with the Scriptures. Following the order of the Law, the Prophets, and the Psalms, I believe that Jesus systematically checked through the Scriptures by saying, "Is there anything in the Law that hath yet to be fulfilled—anything in Genesis? No, check. All is fulfilled. Exodus? Check, all is fulfilled. Leviticus? Numbers? Deuteronomy? The Prophets—Isaiah? Jeremiah? All is fulfilled in all the Prophets. The Psalms?" He came down in the Psalms to a verse that says, "In my thirst they gave me vinegar to drink" (Psalm 69:21). Then He said, "This is the one thing not fulfilled, of all that is written in the Old Testament." And so in a loud voice, He cried, "I thirst." And they brought Him vinegar and lifted it up to Him, and as soon as this happened, He said, "It is finished."

Now I am quite well aware of the application of the death of Christ for sin, but let me point out that there is also a great application with reference to the Old Testament Scripture. When the Lord had checked, rechecked and double-checked the Law— everything was accomplished, the Prophets—everything was accomplished, the Writings—everything was accomplished, the Psalms—the last thing that had to be accomplished was, "They gave me vinegar to drink." And Jesus, it says, in order "that the Scripture might be fulfilled, saith, I thirst. Now there was set a vessel full of vinegar: and they filled a sponge with vinegar, and put it upon hyssop, and put it to his mouth. When Jesus therefore had received the vinegar, he said, It is finished" (John 19:28,29).

"The Old Testament is accomplished! Everything is fulfilled! All that is written of Me has now been established."

Oh, yes! other things are finished too. We sing in one of our hymns, "It is finished, all the signs and

279

shadows of the ceremonial law; It is finished, it is finished." Many things were finished. My sins were finished. The guilt was put upon Him and it's no longer on me. He was wounded for my transgressions, and bruised for my iniquities and the chastisement of my peace was on Him and by His stripes I am healed. And when Satan accuses me, I say, "It is finished!"

Oh, let me plead with you if you have unconfessed sin, if you have a lie on your lips. (And I know that there are people who have lies on their lips.) You can come to the Lord and say, "Jesus Christ, You died for this and I know what I am. 'Amazing grace, how sweet the sound that saved a wretch like *me!*'" If you come to the Lord and confess this, let the Lord begin to work in your life. Then the Lord can do for you what you cannot do for yourself. And the Lord God Almighty can restore you to fellowship, to power, to joy. He can mend broken homes. He can do all these things—but you've got to let Him have it His way.

"He said, It is finished: and he bowed his head, and gave up the ghost" (v. 30). Oh, what wonderful truths we have here, of Christ and the Scripture, the written Word and the living Word! How He meets our needs! I don't care what your need is, He can meet it.

You know, I believe that it is impossible to shock me anymore. I go out all over the country preaching in churches and when I go to a town, elders, deacons, and ministers sometimes, who can't go to someone in their own town come and talk to me. An elder doesn't want to go to his own preacher and say, "Preacher, I've been your elder and I've been doing this-and-that and I need to talk to someone about it." He doesn't want to go to his own preacher, but he will come to the visiting preacher. And I've had three murders confessed to me, and innumerable adulteries and thefts; and men who came and said, "I'm seven thousand dollars short in the bank and they are going to find that my account is out of order. What can I do? What can I do?" I'd say it's impossible to shock me anymore.

I know what the human heart is, first of all, because I know the Word of God. Secondly, I know my own heart. A verse says, "There hath no temptation taken you but such as is common to man" (1 Cor. 10:13). Now if you want to know psychology, you go look in the mirror and watch yourself, and look at yourself, and say, "God Almighty, is the whole human race as bad as that?" And God says, "Yes, it is." We sing it:

"Guilty, vile and helpless we; Spotless
    Lamb of God was He;
'Full atonement' can it be? Hallelujah!
    what a Saviour!
Lifted up was He to die, 'It is finished,'
    was His cry;
Now in heaven exalted high; Hallelujah!
    what a Saviour!"

Now this is your Saviour. This is the one that died there. He looks out over you, over your sin, over your life. "He knoweth our frame; he remembereth that we are dust" (Psalm 103:14). He took the vinegar. He said, "It is finished." And He died.

281

This is your Saviour. This is my Saviour. Let Him be our Lord.

Shall we pray. O God our Father, we thank Thee for Thyself. We praise Thee for Thy great faithfulness—there is none like unto Thee. How we rejoice in what Christ Jesus did for us in dying upon the cross and we pray Thee, O Lord, that whoever has a special need of Thee—and that means each one of us—that we can come resting, resting in the joy of what Thou art, that we can begin to find out the greatness of Thy loving heart. Thou hast bid us gaze upon Thee, and Thy beauty fills our souls, for by Thy transforming power Thou hast made us whole. May we rest in Thee. We ask it in Jesus' name, Amen.

God Put You Here "On Purpose"

When the Lord Jesus Christ died, the disciples were frightened. They thought that they themselves might be crucified. And as rapidly as possible, they took flight. Their refuge was an upper room in somebody's house, where they had gone up and closed the door, and were huddled there in fear. And suddenly the Lord Jesus Christ came through walls and was standing there in the midst of them. "When the doors were shut . . . Jesus [came] and stood in the midst, and saith unto them, Peace be unto you. And when he had so said, he showed unto them his hands and his side. Then were the disciples glad, when they saw the Lord" (John 20:19,20). And the Lord began to speak in a great way, giving the purpose which He had in His heart for these disciples. He said, "As my Father hath sent me, even so send I you" (v. 21).

Now this is nothing less than the statement of the fact that God has bound us up with Jesus Christ in His purposes. "As my Father hath sent me, even so send I you." God had an eternal purpose for Jesus Christ, and we shall see from the Bible that that eternal purpose includes us. We read, "In whom we have redemption through his blood, the forgiveness of sins, according to the riches of his grace; wherein he hath abounded toward us in all wisdom and prudence; having made known unto us the mystery of his will, according to his good pleasure which he hath purposed in himself: that . . . he might gather together in one all things in Christ" (Eph. 1:7-11). The center of God's purpose is to gather all things together in Christ.

God has no thought in His creation that is apart from Jesus Christ, and the love that He has towards His Son, and the glory that He purposes to show through Jesus Christ. Now, our union with Christ is within the framework of this eternal purpose. The Bible has a dozen references, perhaps, that give us details of what God purposes to do with us eternally, what He has already begun in us now, and what He wishes to be through us while we are living and working and waiting here.

In the first place, then, let us look at some of the things that God proposes to do with us in the future. We read in Titus 3:7, "That being justified by his grace, we should be made heirs according to the hope of eternal life." So one of God's purposes is that we might be made heirs, heirs of God, and joint heirs of Jesus Christ. God intends to govern the universe by Christ, plus those who have believed in Him in this age. It is nothing more nor less than God's statement that you and I are to be the colonial administrators of the universe. God is not going to govern the universe through angels. And we are not going to *be* angels. The angels will be our domestic servants as we read in Hebrews 1:14, "Are they [the angels] not all ministering spirits [domestic servants], sent forth to minister for them who shall be heirs of salvation?" We are the heirs of salvation. And God proposes to use us in the government and administration of the universe.

I believe that most people walking about the earth, most Christians, haven't the foggiest notion of the grandeur of their destiny in eternity. Many years ago, A.B. Simpson said, "As I see the Word of God, I do not put it beyond Him, that some day He shall say to some of us, go there to that place in space, create a world by the power that I give to thee. Develop it and govern it for Me."

The Bible does not teach that being in heaven means you are to sit on a cloud polishing your crown and strumming your harp. Those are figures of speech. The music of the harp is the symbol of eternal ecstasy and the crown is the symbol of government that all have to do with our association with the Lord Jesus Christ. You'll be working in heaven. You'll be at the height of all of your powers forever, with no thought of fatigue and with an infinite variety of work to do. It will call for everything that is within you in the perfection and happiness of your union with the Lord Jesus Christ. We are heirs, and we are joint heirs.

In Ephesians 2:7 we read, "That in the ages to

come he might shew the exceeding riches of his grace in his kindness towards us through Christ Jesus." God proposes to do things because He wants to show the exceeding riches of His grace. Anyone who has become a parent knows that in the heart of the parent is the desire to do something for the child. And if years pass and you become a grandparent, there comes the thought, "I would like to do something for my grandchildren." The Bible teaches that God is doing everything for Jesus Christ and that, through Jesus Christ, God proposes to do as much for us as He does for Jesus Christ. The Scripture can give us something no less than this, that we are "fellow heirs," and that we are "accepted in the beloved," indeed, according to Ephesians 1:23, we are "the fulness of him that filleth all in all." This is God's eternal purpose.

In the second place, let us look at some of the things that God proposes to do in us now. God is beginning to work in us who are believers, rooting and preparing the purposes that He plans to work out now and in eternity.

In Romans 9:23 it says He saved us in order "that he might make known the riches of his glory on the vessels of mercy, which he had afore prepared unto glory." We were vessels of mercy. We had been vessels of wrath, and then we became vessels of mercy. Now a vessel is a vase, it is a container. And He says that we are vessels of mercy, prepared to glory. We are, if you will, candles that God intends to light up with a fire that burns and is not consumed as we blaze forth His glory. The angels in eternity, when they see us, will know that the Lord Jesus

Christ came from heaven to save us from the pit, lifted us up, and gave us eternal life.

They will know that Jesus was made lower than the angels and stooped to the cross in order to bring us from the depths of the depravity of sin; that everyone of us who is thus lifted, and made like Christ, shall call forth from the full and angelic world the thought of "How great is the grace of God! Look at that flashing saint! Look at that child of God! Look at that human being become an heir with Christ! How great is the grace of God that dust has been taken to heaven and has been fashioned to show forth the glory of Christ!"

But God has done that already. In the midst of a world that knows not Jesus Christ we can already witness to the fact that our vessels of wrath have become vessels of mercy. And such were some of you: but you were washed. You were by nature children of wrath and children of disobedience. "But God, who is rich in mercy, for his great love wherewith he loved us, even when we were dead in sins, hath quickened us together with Christ" (Eph. 2:4,5). God chooses to use us as torch lights that shall flame His glory through eternity. And He wants that process to begin right now so that anyone coming in contact with you shall say, "That is a redeemed one."

One of the tragedies of Christians in America today is that so many fundamental Christians get together with each other. They have their parties together, they have their fellowship together, their socials together, their picnics together, and all of their friendships together. Many of them are not aware of the light they could cause outside. Oh, some of you run up against it in business life. But even business life is organized in such a way that it's rather possible for nice people to have their lives bounded on one side by their home, and the other side by their office, with occasional side trips to this amusement or that amusement, or to this church or that church. But you do not know the horror of what life is outside of Christ. And yet, God has meant that we be in the midst of this world as shining lights, holding forth the Word of Life.

Not only does God want us to be vessels of mercy, but it tells us in Ephesians 3:10,11 that another purpose in saving us is "that through the church the manifold wisdom of God might now be made known to the principalities and powers in the heavenly places. This was according to the eternal purpose which he has realized in Christ Jesus our Lord."[1] In other words, God is saying, "The reason that I have saved you, the true church, is that I wanted to exhibit you in the invisible realm. I wanted to let all the angels of heaven that followed the devil to look on the earth and see you. I want them to realize that the principles I established in the beginning are true, that I don't take men to the highest heaven by their own climbing. I take men who deserve to go to hell, who go down to the cross, and by virtue of the death of Jesus Christ, pass out of death and into life. I lift them up through Jesus Christ. The moment I do so, I have proclaimed the eternal law," says God, "that power does not come from grasping, that power does not come through climbing, but power, true power comes through descending, through surrender, through yielding. The way to climb up is down. 'For whosoever exalteth himself shall be abased'" (Luke 14:11). Each believer is a witness before the forces of Satan that God's way of doing things is the only way that works. And that's why we must learn to say in response to Him, "Make me a captive, Lord. Then I shall be free. Force me to render up my sword, and I shall conqueror be."

Another purpose of God that has already begun now, and will be carried on forever, is defined in Romans 8:29 where it says, "He also did predestinate [us] to be conformed to the image of his Son, that he might be the firstborn among many brethren." The reason God saved us is that out of this world and out of the mud of the fall, He might reach down and grasp in sovereign grace countless multitudes from Adam's race and then transform them and shape them into the image of Jesus Christ. And just as a butterfly flying around your garden probably can't tell the difference between a man of seventy and a boy who is twenty, or the difference between a man and a woman, so in the future, in heaven, an angel looking up to God will have trouble telling the difference between you and Jesus Christ.

Now it's tremendous as we understand what is being taught here—that we might be shaped to the image of His Son, that we might be the "firstborn among many brethren" in God's family. Now you can readily see that, if He has begun this in us, He desires greatly that this work be continued.

In Ephesians 1:4, God gives another purpose for

saving us. It tells us He saved us in order "that we should be holy and without blame before him in love." He wants to begin this in us NOW. He has given us the holiness that is in Christ. He had made us without blemish in His sight. Because we are already saved, we are seen in the perfection and glory of Jesus Christ.

He wants us to be holy, without blemish, in our practical life and living. The moment we understand God's eternal purpose in saving us, that eternal purpose becomes a divine imperative to call us to yield ourselves to Him, and to walk worthy of the calling wherewith we have been called.

Still another purpose is set forth in Ephesians 1:12 where it states, "That we should be to the praise of his glory." Anyone—men, angels, or demons—seeing us should say, and we should say of one another, "How wonderful is the grace of God that He should be able to touch me without dirtying His finger! How wonderful the grace of God that He was able to take hold of us and that we are the monuments of His love and His grace."

Then there is a third category of purposes. For we have seen purposes that have their whole issue with us in eternity, and we have seen others that begin in us now. There is still a third set of purposes, the practical purposes that God is working through our lives. And while, of course, some of these may carry over into eternity, God has specific purposes for working through us while we live this life in the flesh. Never forget that God tells us we live this life in two different places. He says that we are in the world, in the world that crucified

Christ. Paul puts it, "The life that I now live *in the flesh . . .*" When anything wonderful appears in the life of a Christian, when we find anyone who has been touched by Jesus Christ, when we see something that sublimely shows Christ has been working in the life, someone from the heavenly realm looking at it seems a stark contrast between the beauty of Christ and the ugliness of the world. It would be like seeing a magnificent lily growing in a manure pile. God has reached into the mud and has saved us out of darkness into light and is working things in us at the present time.

Let's look at some of them: Philippians 1:6 says, "Being confident of this very thing, that he which hath begun a good work in you will perform it until the day of Jesus Christ." God gladly states that His purpose in saving you is to take you where you were when He saved you, and then to begin to work on you. He's never going to let you go.

I once spent some time working with three adolescents who had been committed to the Lord by their godly Christian parents. These teen-agers were tugging against everything they had been taught. They wanted to have their names flashing in neon lights. They were hoping for the world's glamour, not knowing that they were doomed to disappointment. God's purpose in the life of a Christian is to cut us away from the things of the world and make them a disappointment to us. God always wants to curtail anything that you take from the world. If you are grasping at anything for personal ambition or trying to exalt or to aggrandize yourself, then God wants that to sour on you.

God is going to take you on *His* way, and *your* way will have to be conformed to that if you are going to have true joy. Any way that is apart from His way must be broken. "There is a way which seemeth right unto a man, but the end thereof are the ways of death" (Prov. 14:12). We must learn that any human way must always lead to disappointment. Then the quicker you come to the place of surrender, the quicker He is able to move in, and give you the best that He had for you in the first place; the best that you refused because it didn't fit your specifications of what you thought the best should have been.

The second purpose He's working right now we find in 1 Peter 2:9, "That you may declare the wonderful deeds of him who called you out of darkness into his marvelous light."[1] One of the reasons why He saved us is that we might declare these wonderful deeds. In the midst of this world, what are we to be talking about? Who is to be the theme of our conversation? What is to be the center of our life and living? What is to be the purpose of all that we're doing? To exalt Christ! Our purpose is that in every way possible as we walk and move among men, Christ should have all the glory. He should have all the praise. Everyone that we come in contact with should know, if there is the slightest difference between us and the ordinary man of the world, that Christ is the One who makes the difference.

Say there is a businessman in a position where it's the accepted thing to take graft, and everyone knows that he doesn't. So they say to him, "You're a fool to pass this up." And he says, "That's all right. You see, the Lord called me out of darkness into light and I'll have my money when He wants to give it to me, but I'll have it in His way." They may call him a fool, but he has witnessed for Christ. And they know that he can't be reached.

And that principle may be applied in a thousand ways of life. We are to declare the wonderful deeds of Him who called us out of darkness and into His marvelous light. We are to declare "how wonderful God is! How loving and kind He is! What steadfast love He has toward us!"

And then in 1 Peter 2:5 He says that He has saved us so that we might "offer spiritual sacrifices acceptable to God through Jesus Christ."[1] He has saved us for this purpose so that as we live there might come from our hearts a well-pleasing surrender to Him. In the midst of this world that crucified Christ, in the midst of this world whose motto is "Take care of yourself, nobody else is going to do it," God delights in that we can say, "Lord, I offer you myself. You can do with me whatever seems good to You." No matter what happens, we take it as coming from the hand of our Father. Even though we fall into tragedies as great as those that beset Job, we see that they are not tragedies when they are given to us by our Father. They really give evidence that we have a loving God, and that we are quite willing for Him to light any kind of a fire in us that He wishes to light.

Then in Ephesians 2:10 it says, "For we are his workmanship, created in Christ Jesus unto good works, which God hath before ordained that we should walk in them." This is the reason He saved you. He put you where you are in order that you might walk in a pattern of good works which He has prepared for you in advance. God has a plan for your life. And that plan includes the development of your character and the plowing of your whole being in order that the Seed of Life might be planted in well-worked ground and bring forth fruit that is well-pleasing to Him. We are "created . . . unto good works, which God hath before ordained that we should walk in them."

Every once in a while, I come up against somebody that says, "If you are once saved you're always saved, aren't you? Isn't that what the Bible teaches? Then that means that as long as you believe, you can do as you please, right?" It doesn't mean anything of the kind. It means just the opposite. If I am once saved it is because He has begun a good work and He will keep on perfecting it until the day of Jesus Christ. And when He saved me, He put me in a road and said, "I have created these good works that you should walk in them." There's no question whatsoever of the Christian saying, "Well, I'm saved. I can now take the bit in my teeth and go any way I wish." True, there are moments when the flesh rises and seeks to have its own way. But, nevertheless, the general trend and tendency of the life that is in Christ must be in the path that He prepared for us, "created in Christ Jesus unto good works, which God hath before ordained that we should walk in them."

Well, what are these good works that were created before I was born? Where are they? Why, they are in Christ. God wants Christ to be in me. Every good work that we see in Christ was prepared in order that we might work the same works. So then, if you want to know what God saved you for—whatever the pattern of your life may be at your work or at your rest or whatever it might be—you are to live Christ. And what does that involve? Love, joy, peace, longsuffering, gentleness, goodness, faithfulness, self-control. This is the path God has for us. Christ lived and exhibited these fruits of the Spirit. These are the works that God "hath before ordained that we should walk in them."

God has a plan for you. This must go into every part of the being of the Christian. It must affect every phase of his life. The plan includes steadfast love, which is going to show courtesy.

If a Christian man has power steering, he will not steal the parking space of someone that doesn't have it, even though he could get in quicker. He will not be a menace to anyone else's driving along the way. Love will be manifested in the way he speaks to those who are less fortunate in life. We seek to be Christ in the place where God has put us, seeking to touch men and women with the hand of Christ. For God has no other way of touching men and women today, except by your hand. God does not work from heaven on the cases of misery that are in the world. If anybody is going to be touched by Jesus Christ, they are going to be touched by your hands.

It is interesting, and very relevant to this issue, that at the time of the judgment of the nations Jesus says to men, "Inasmuch as ye have done it unto the least of these my brethren, ye have done it unto me."

"When did this ever happen?"

"I was hungry and you fed Me, I was naked and you clothed Me. I was sick and you visited Me. I was in prison and you came unto Me—when you did it unto the least of one of my brothers." (See Matt. 25:35-40.)

I can remember an incident that took place several years ago. In England I met a man who was an officer in the Cold Stream Guards. He was the handsomest man you'd ever want to meet, every inch an English nobleman, officer and gentleman. Major William Bach was house officer in Buckingham Palace, probably chosen because you couldn't find any human being that would look better when he was wearing the big bearskin hat and the scarlet coat on parade.

Bill was coming to the United States for a visit. I had made all the arrangements for him to be entertained in different homes, and for him to speak to some people in the business and social centers of our country that needed someone to come with a profound word. When I met him in New York at the airport, I took a couple of hours to show him New York City. First we stopped down at Wall Street in order that I might take him to the skyscraper office of a friend of mine, whose windows commanded a beautiful view over New York Bay. There was traffic congestion and we had to wait for a place to park. Eventually we drove into a service station and I said, "Can I have the car oiled and greased?" It was the only way that we could get a place to park—anyway, the car would be needing to be oiled pretty soon, so we were killing two birds with one stone.

And as we got out of the car, there came up to us one of the most miserable human beings that I have ever seen. The man looked as though he had slept in a coal bin for weeks. Filth and dirt and coal grime were in the pores of his skin. His hair was matted. There were sores on every visible part of his body, as though his body were being eaten away by an advanced case of syphilis, or some disease of that kind. He was one of the most formidable looking creatures of despair that I had ever seen.

He came up to us and put out his hand and said, "Will you help me?"

This English nobleman, who didn't have any American money yet, put his hand in his pocket and said, "Oh, I don't have anything."

I put my hand in my pocket and I said, "We give you this in the name of the Lord Jesus Christ."

Then the man began to cry. Tears ran down his face and he said, "I know, I was brought up in this." And as we spoke to him there about his soul, he said, "You know, I have gone down to the docks at least ten times and said, 'O God, I'm going to throw myself in and drown myself,' but," he said, "there's always something that keeps me from doing it."

We talked there for fifteen or twenty minutes, gave the man a little money, told him not to use it for drink, and gave him the name of a mission where he could be taken care of. And the man said, "Oh, thank you, thank you."

297

We said, "You know we give you this in Jesus' name."

"God bless you," he said.

Now, I don't know that man, but when I think of Christ on the earth, I think of that man. For Christ said, "Inasmuch as you have done it unto the least of one of these, you have done it unto Me." Furthermore, the Bible says, "He who is kind to the poor lends to the Lord"[1] (Prov. 19:17).

Sometimes I wonder about those in the gutters; yes, the Blacks in the cities; the tens of thousands that now filter in from Puerto Rico, all in such need. The world says to them, "Get out of the way! Get out of the way!" But I wonder if God has not put them round about us and that we should take the opportunity to say, "I want to touch you and minister to you in the name of the Lord Jesus Christ." And when you do that, God says; "I've put you on earth in order that you might see straight, that you may not see with the eyes of a world that idolizes and honors success."

Someone once said that a banker was a person who would lend money to those who could prove they did not need it, but would not lend to those who really need it. Perhaps that's a cynical commentary on banks; but believe me, there is a truth here to which the whole world's philosophy is geared: Our kindness and generosity are for those who do not need it. That's why Jesus is needfully saying, "When you invite somebody to dinner, invite somebody that will not be able to invite you back." When you do something for somebody in the name of Christ, do it for somebody that will not be able to return the favor. "This," says the Lord, "pleases Me." For it shows that the life of Christ is in you, and it shows you recognize that He who has begun a good work in you is taking you out of the world which says, "Every man for himself, and the devil take the hindmost," and is putting in you the Spirit of Christ which says, "I have sent you here. As the Father hath sent Me, so send I you."

Go right now and be Jesus Christ to those around you. That is God's purpose in saving you.

The Post-Resurrection Ministry of Jesus

We come now to the post-resurrection ministry of our Lord. You remember that when Jesus arose from the dead He said to Mary, "Touch me not; for I am not yet ascended to my Father" (John 20:17). And a little while later He said to Thomas, "Touch me." (See John 20:27.) This proves, of course, that by then He had ascended into heaven. Christ probably ascended into heaven many times between His resurrection and what we call the Ascension. The Ascension as we know it was only the making visible of the last ascension. He did not live down behind a rock in the valley of the Jordan after He arose from the dead. He lived in heaven. And He came back and presented Himself from time to time to the disciples in the dozen appearances that took place. And all of this teaches us how close heaven is to us.

301

Then, if a physicist comes to you and says, "But, now wait. We know the distances of the stars and the speed of light," we simply answer that the Lord Jesus Christ in His resurrection body which was a material body, which ate broiled fish and honey—was nevertheless a body that passed through the walls of the tomb and the walls of the room. That that body was not governed by physical laws, but by spiritual laws. And He could travel with the speed of thought. He is infinite and He has revealed to us only a tiny segment of all of the laws that He knows and all of the truth that He is.

Verse 1—"After these things"—that is to say, after the resurrection day appearances—"Jesus shewed himself again to the disciples at the sea of Tiberias; and on this wise shewed he himself. There were together Simon Peter, and Thomas called Didymus"—that is the twin—"and Nathanael of Cana in Galilee, and the sons of Zebedee, and two other of his disciples. Simon Peter saith unto them, I go a fishing" (John 21:1-3).

The Lord had told them to go back north and they had gone back north. And the old urge had come upon Peter, "We can't sit around and do nothing. Let's go back to our old trade. I am going fishing." And the others said, "We'll go with you."

Verse 3—"They went forth, and entered into a ship immediately: and that night they caught nothing. But when the morning was now come, Jesus stood on the shore: but the disciples knew not that it was Jesus. Then Jesus saith unto them, Children, have ye any meat?"—any food—"They answered him, No. And he said unto them, cast the net on the right side of the ship, and ye shall find" (John 21:3-6).

This word must have struck them with tremendous force. We remember that three years before, Jesus had come to them and said, "Launch out into the deep, and let down your nets." And they had said, "We have toiled all night, and have taken nothing." And He had said, "Cast your nets on the other side." And when they did, they had pulled in so many fish that the nets broke. (See Luke 5:4-6.)

And here now, He that had come to them three years before, comes to them with the exact same command. And yet they had seen Him and had known Him to be dead. And then there had been these appearances in the upper room; but then He had disappeared. But now there He is.

Verse 6—"They cast therefore, and now they were not able to draw it for the multitude of fishes. Therefore that disciple whom Jesus loved"—John that is, the young John—"saith unto Peter, It is the Lord. Now when Simon Peter heard that it was the Lord, he girt his fisher's coat unto him, (for he was naked,) and did cast himself into the sea. And the other disciples came in a little ship; (for they were not far from land, but as it were two hundred cubits,)"—or about four hundred feet—"dragging the net with fishes" (John 20:6-8).

Verse 9—"As soon as they were come to land, they saw a fire of coals there, and fish laid thereon, and bread. Jesus saith unto them, Bring of the fish which ye have now caught. Simon Peter went up, and drew the net to land full of great fishes, an hundred and fifty three: and for all there were so many, yet was not the net broken," (John 20:9-11). What a beautiful little touch! Three years before, when Jesus had started with them in this way, the net had broken and they had lost everything. So now you can imagine these men. They hardly dared to speak. They knew it was Christ, and yet they knew that He had died. And the fact of the Resurrection was still a strange and a tremendous thing.

We have lived with the Resurrection all of our lives. From babyhood you have known what Easter was. You may have celebrated it from childhood. Jesus was here, He died and rose again, and is in heaven. But when it first hit them, it came as something new and frightening. If we find atomic power new and the world comes at it cautiously, you can imagine what it was to discover the resurrection of Jesus Christ.

Verse 12—"Jesus saith unto them, Come and dine. And none of the disciples durst ask him, Who art Thou? knowing that it was the Lord. Jesus then cometh, and taketh bread, and giveth them, and fish likewise. This is now the third time that Jesus shewed himself to his disciples, after that he was risen from the dead," (John 21:12-14).

Verse 15—"So when they had dined, Jesus saith to Simon Peter, Simon, son of Jonas, lovest thou me more than these?" Now in order to understand this we must realize three things. The night before the Crucifixion, Simon had said, "You can count on me though all men forsake Thee, you can count on me. I've been out and bought a sword and I'll be ready to take care of You." But Christ had said to him, "Before the cock crows, thou shalt deny Me thrice."

And Peter had boasted of his love. (See Matt. 26:33,34.)

Now in Greek there are two words for love. In order to explain it, let's call it "a hundred-percent love," and "sixty-percent affection." *Agapao* is the great word, and *fileo* is the word for "sixty-percent affection." Now the first time He came to Peter and said, "Simon Peter, do you love Me with the great one-hundred-percent love more than these?" Peter said, "Yea, Lord, Thou knowest that I have a sixty-percent affection for Thee."

Brother, that's a whittled-down Simon Peter. There is no boasting now, no bragging. You see, this is a man that has been transformed. Then Jesus said to him, "Feed my lambs." Jesus said again to him the second time, "Simon, son of Jonas, do you have this great one-hundred-percent love that you were boasting about before?" And Peter said, "Yea, Lord, thou knowest that I have a sixty-percent affection for Thee." And He said unto him, "Feed my sheep." He said unto him again the third time, "Simon Peter, son of Jonas, do you have this sixty-percent affection?" And Peter was grieved because He said unto him the third time, "Do you have this sixty-percent affection?" (See vv. 15-17.)

Now some of the commentators have tried to say that Peter was grieved because Jesus asked him three times to parallel the three times that Peter had denied Him. But I think that is foolish when we understand the difference between the two verbs. What is happening here is that Peter is getting a real look at himself. Where he had before seen Christ through his own eyes, he now sees himself through Christ's own eyes. And that's where we must go always. We must always begin to see ourselves as God sees us, and then at utter nothingness we are at the place where we can go on with God.

"Peter was grieved." Now what did he do? Did he say, "Look here, I, I, I . . ."? That's the way he would have answered before. But to my mind, this is one of the most beautiful lines in the Bible. Peter saith unto Him, "Lord, thou knowest all things. Thou knowest that I have the sixty-percent affection for Thee." (See v. 17.) How wonderful that is! Isn't it true that many of us have betrayed Him and followed afar off, have denied Him with oaths and cursings, and have denied Him with indifference, and have denied Him by being too busy about the unimportant things of this life?

Somebody might come to you and say, "Do you call yourself a Christian?" And when you look at Christ, you don't have to say, "Well, Lord, add up the balance sheet." You'd be afraid to do that. I'd be afraid to do that. We know what we are. What we can say is, "Lord, it is in your heart and in your mind. There's the evidence, not in me." The proof that I love Jesus Christ is in the heart and mind of Christ. And that's where our strength comes from. "Thou knowest that I love thee." And Jesus saith unto Peter, "Feed my sheep." Isn't it wonderful!

In the beginning three years before, just after the miraculous draught of fishes, Jesus had said, "Follow Me and I will make you fishers of men." Now He says, "Follow Me, and I will make you feeders of lambs, and feeders of sheep." How wonderful this is! And this is our function as Christians. We are to be fishers of men and feeders of lambs. That's evangelism and that's edification. That's justification and sanctification. We are to see men saved and we're to see men grow.

Verse 18—"Verily, verily, I say unto thee, When thou wast young, thou girdest thyself, and walkedst where thou wouldest: but when thou shalt be old, thou shalt stretch forth thy hands, and another shall gird thee, and carry thee whither thou wouldest not. This spake he, signifying by what death he [Peter] should glorify God." Peter was martyred. He was chained, he was taken and he was killed. We do not believe that it was in Rome. That's a fiction that was added centuries later. But Peter did suffer for the sake of the Lord Jesus Christ. And when Jesus had spoken this, He said unto Peter, "Follow me" (see v. 19).

Now, you still see the natural man in Peter, because Peter says, "Isn't that interesting. So I'm not going to grow old but I'm going to die a martyr's death. Well, isn't that interesting? Lord, what's going to happen to John?" "Then Peter, turning about, seeth the disciple [John] whom Jesus loved following; which also leaned on his breast at supper, and said, Lord, which is he that betrayeth thee?"—this is an identification of John—"Peter seeing him saith to Jesus, Lord, and what shall this man do?" (v. 21). Now, if we translated Jesus' answer into modern American language, it would be, "That's none of your business." "If I will that he tarry till I come, what is that to thee? follow thou me" (v. 22).

There are some questions where we are not to in-

307

terfere. The spiritual life of another person does not regard you. If you see someone and you have some thought about them, pray for them. But you have no control over their lives. You are not God for them. They're not to be God for you. You do not judge them. You live your life with God.

Because of what Jesus said, "Then went this saying abroad among the brethren, that that disciple should not die: yet Jesus said not unto him, He shall not die; but, If I will that he tarry till I come, what is that to thee?" (v. 23).

And now, John ends his Gospel, "This is the disciple which testifieth of these things, and wrote these things: and we know that his testimony is true. And there were also many other things which Jesus did, the which, if they should be written every one, I suppose that even the world itself could not contain the books that should be written. Amen" (vv. 24, 25).

The Four Comes

I want you to look at the word *come* in four different contexts. I want you to see it first of all in John 1:39. This was the *come* of salvation, the *come* of invitation to meet the Lord Jesus Christ. It was at a time when one of the disciples had been chosen. John the Baptist and two of his disciples had just seen Jesus, and in verse 36, John said, "Behold, the Lamb of God! And the two disciples heard him speak, and they followed Jesus. . . . They said unto him, Rabbi, (Master,) where dwellest thou?" And Jesus said, "Come and see." (See John 1:36-39.) This invitation is offered to "the whole world," to every individual that ever lived. *Come*. God so loved the world, the world of sinners, not merely the world of the elect, but the world of sinners. God loved them. God is not engaged in a fantastic mockery. He is calling men to believe. It's true that there are men who are dead in trespasses and sins; their will is turned away from Christ. When Jesus said, "Ye *will* not come to me, that ye might have life" (John 5:40). He was telling the truth.

It's interesting, as we note the context of that first chapter of John, that He uses different methods in inviting different people. He does not violate human personality. God does not go to a man who is a great mathematician and speak to him in a way that is contrary to science. He does not go to a humble person who has no education and talk to him in words of five syllables. He accommodates Himself to the mind and the heart of each.

Here were two disciples. They followed Jesus. Jesus said, "Come and see." One of these men then went and found his brother and said, "We've found the Messiah." He brought his brother to Jesus and Jesus walked up to this man and said, "Your name is Wishy-Washy." (That's the real meaning of Simon.) "Your name is Wishy-Washy and it's about to become Rock. You're going to be petrified— Peter-fied." Instead of that gelatin down his spine, he was going to get a ramrod. Now this was going to be by the nature of Christ, but you'll notice how different the approach. He walks up to a man and changes his name by announcing a change of nature.

A little farther down in John 1 Jesus meets Philip and says, "Follow Me." And Philip then finds Nathanael and says, "We've found the Messiah, Jesus of Nazareth." Nathanael replies, "Can any good thing come out of Nazareth?" And then Philip repeats the words that Jesus had said, "Come and see." How does the Lord meet him? By a miracle. He says, "I saw you when you were there under the fig tree." And when Nathanael suddenly realizes that he is in front of Somebody who can reveal his heart and his thoughts and his mind, he says, "Thou art the Son of God. Thou art the King of Israel." (See John 1:43-49.)

In the same way, if you turn to the end of John, you'll notice that after the Resurrection, Jesus reveals Himself to different people in different ways. He does not violate human personalities. Here is Mary and He walks up to her. Blinded with her tears and fatigue, she thinks He is the gardener. And then He says, "Mary." When she hears that tone of voice, right away she knew Him.

I suppose you have had the same experience with the telephone as I have. When the telephone rings, I say "Hello," and there are some people that start to talk right away. They recognize my voice, and after they say "Hello," they just go right on talking. I never have to say, "This is D-G-B talking," and they don't have to say, "This is So-and-So talking." We can walk right into a conversation, so well do we know each other's tone of voice. And this was so when the Lord Jesus rose from the dead. "Mary," He said. Thus He revealed Himself to her by the mere pronouncing of her name.

He comes to the disciples in the upper room and suddenly, with the door shut, He appears in front of them. They recognize Him immediately, by this astounding thing He has just done. But Thomas, the doubter, says, "I won't believe unless I see." And the Lord comes right to him and says, "That's all right, Thomas, I can get along with men who have this desire to see before they believe. I wasn't timid when I started salvation. I'm not touchy," says God. Oh, you see, if God had been touchy, He never would have come to this earth. If God had taken offense at the way people do things to Him, He never would have come. But the Lord Jesus came. He never was offended by anybody, He never took offense, He was moved by compassion. So when He talks to Thomas, He says, "Oh, you're the one that wanted to see. Come, put your fingers right here in My hand, and in My side. Be not faithless but believing."

The Lord does not violate human personality. I tell you, whoever you are, that God will meet you on your own ground. He will make Himself so clear that if you say no to Him, you will be a hypocrite when you are saying it. And forever after, you will never be able to look yourself in the eye again and call yourself an honest man. For the Lord Jesus Christ will meet you on your level.

Now I want you to turn to Matthew 11 and see the *come* of security. "Come unto me, all ye that labour and are heavy laden, and I will give you rest" (Matt. 11:28). *Come.* I believe that this goes much further than salvation. "Come unto me, all ye that labour and are heavy laden, and I will give you rest. Take my yoke upon you, and learn of me; for I am meek and lowly in heart: and ye shall find rest unto your souls. For my yoke is easy, and my burden is light" (Matt. 11:28-30). It's well to note that the word *rest* is found twice here. Two centuries ago, Charles Wesley wrote the hymn, "Let us all in thee inherit, Let us find the second rest. Take away our love of sinning. Alpha and Omega be." This was a declaration of the two kinds of rest. And what Wesley was singing was, "Let us find the *second* rest." Jesus said, "Come . . . and I will *give* you rest. Take my yoke . . . and ye shall *find* rest." They are quite different. The one is peace *with* God; the other is the peace of God. One is a rest that is given; the other is a rest that is found. "Come unto me . . . and I will give you rest" is the *rest* of security and the "take my yoke" is the rest of surrender. The first is a sign that the war is over and you can enter into peace, the second lets you enjoy the peace.

So many Christians are like the man in the old story in England, back in the days of coaching. There was a man riding along with his horse and carriage, and there was a peddler walking along with his pack on his back. The man on the carriage stopped and said to the peddler, "Would you like a lift?"

And the peddler said, "Oh, thank you, you're very kind.

After he had climbed on and sat down and the horses were moving ahead, the man said, "Why don't you take off your bundles?"

"Well," the peddler said, "you're being so kind as to carry me, I just didn't want to put you to further trouble."

And yet that's the way a lot of Christians live their lives. They say, "God, You saved me, but oh, what a burden I have." Well, brother, let your burden go too. You're not only saved but you're safe.

God didn't give you six-months' life. He gave you eternal life. God didn't give you ten-year life. He gave you eternal life. And it's a present possession. You shall never perish but *have* everlasting life.

There's another point I want to make here. "Come and see," is the *come* of invitation and salvation. "Come and rest," is the *come* of security. The third point is in Mark 6:31, where the Lord invited the disciples to come apart and rest. "And he said unto them, Come ye yourselves apart into a desert place, and rest a while: for there were many coming and going, and they had no leisure so much as to eat." And this is talking to Christians and telling them that they had better take it easy from time to time. Every once in a while you come to somebody in Christian life and work that thinks he has to do the whole thing—he works himself into a nervous breakdown, saying, "There's so much to be done. I've got this and this and this to do." No, you don't!

Someone says, "Dr. Barnhouse, you work awfully hard." Yes, I do. But you know, I'm much more tired before I begin a sermon than when I finish one. You have no idea how preaching the gospel rests me. I am delivered. That word *delivery* is a very beautiful word. Deliver comes from *delier* in French, which means to untie. And it came into English with William the Conqueror, and was first used in reference to obstetrics—the "delivery" room, where a woman was *delivered* of her child. The cord is severed and she is set free from that which she had carried.

When I get to heaven I hope God's going to let me meet the preacher who first applied this idea to preaching. He probably said something like, "O God, I've got to preach to these people. They are coming and woe is me if I preach not the gospel." And when he had finished, perhaps he came home and said, "I am delivered!" After preaching a sermon he felt like the woman who has carried a ten-pound child for nine months and knows how every step is uncomfortable until, all of a sudden, she's free from that sweet burden. How different everything is in a day or two.

How wonderful this great fact is that we are not to do it all! The Lord says, "Come and rest." I've had people so foolish as to think that if they didn't work hard someone else might be lost. "Oh, yes," someone says, "I do that all the time." Well, it's just not true. Someone says, "If I don't go out to that island in the mission field—you mean that I don't have the power of taking someone to heaven and hell?" Of course you don't. "Well, if I'm just a little more faithful, won't one more be saved." You can't find that in the Bible. Salvation depends upon His faithfulness, not yours. "Well, now, Doctor, aren't you going to make it easy for people to be lazy?" God's plan is to work through people. But if you decide to be lazy, He'll send someone else—and *you* will be the loser. I've found that people who believe what I believe are the most active. They are the ones who "preach the word; . . . instant in season, out of season; reprove, rebuke, exhort with all longsuffering and doctrine" (2 Tim. 4:2). When our part is finished, we say, "Lord, from now on it's up to You."

One night I was preaching in a seminary in Chicago, and when I finished, the president said, "Now

315

we are going to cancel the next hour's classes and Dr. Barnhouse is going to answer questions. He has raised so many that it will keep the faculty busy for two or three months, so let's get the worst of them out of the way." I love to do that! That's my particular forte—dropping buttonhooks in your mind so you'll want to see. If I can get you to looking for the answer to one question, you may find the answer to some other question that God wants you to know.

Well, the first question they asked me at the seminary was: "If you say that God is everything in salvation when you preach, what do you preach to?" I had just said that the carnal mind is enmity against God (see Rom. 8:7), and that the heart is deceitful above all things and incurably wicked (see Jer. 17:9), and that salvation "is not of him that willeth, nor of him that runneth, but of God that sheweth mercy" (Rom. 9:16). So they said, "What do you preach to?"

I said, "I preach to a cubic foot of air in front of my mouth and from then on it's up to the Holy Spirit." This question of preaching the gospel is exactly the same thing as radio and electronics. If someone turned the current off on the microphone when I was doing a broadcast, I might with my best voice say "K-a-a-nsas C-i-i-i-ty," but nobody would listen to it. It wouldn't get to Kansas City. I can't yell loud enough for someone in Kansas City to hear me. But as long as the electricity is on, I can say, "Kansas City," and they hear me. Now in the same way I can preach to you and I can say, "O-o-o-oh, Soul!" The words just go ringing around in

316

the porches of your ears. If it's going to go the long distance to the heart, God has to take it there."

Now it's a tremendous thing to come into a recognition of this fact. Then you can do your work and when you've finished you say, "Lord, it's up to You." When you know that, you see, you don't have to go fussing and say, "Well, now could I have done it better? Where could I improve?" The real question is: Were you yielded to the Lord? Did you ask the Holy Spirit to use you? Was there any part of your being that was not surrendered? If there wasn't, then you simply say, "Lord, I am a pipe. I can carry the water. You're responsible for the pressure. You're responsible for the flow."

And so the Lord said to His disciples, "Come apart and rest." They were so nervous. They had just come back from preaching and healing. "Lord," they said, "the demons are subject to us!" He said, "You need a vacation." And that's why a lot of Christians need a lot of time. It's a wonderful thing, I know sometimes, when I have been hours and hours at my desk, and I just want to get up and walk out into the garden. Then when I get back inside, I discover that not only has the wind blown through my mind, but the Holy Spirit has blown through my heart, and I'm ready to sit down and go to work again.

The Reader's Digest, a few years ago, told about the bishop who said, "I have the burdens of the world upon me!" And one night at midnight, the Lord said to him, "Bishop, you go to bed, I'll carry it till morning." He says to you, "Come ye yourselves apart . . . and rest a while."

And then, lastly, I turn with you to John 21:12. The Lord had been raised from the dead. When He met the disciples by the Sea of Galilee after the Resurrection, He said to them, "Come and dine." Now this is satisfaction. Oh, the joy of dining with the Lord! You know, whenever the Bible speaks of eating, you'll discover that it means fellowship. That's why we talk about the fellowship of this table. Did you know that the Greek word *koinonia* is translated by two English words? One is *communion* and the other is *fellowship*. *Communion* and *fellowship* are exactly the same thing, as when we say, "I'm going to take communion." I wish we didn't use that Latin-French word. I wish we used the old Anglo-Saxon word, "We're going to take fellowship." We're going to come together and be with the Lord, and we're going to be good fellows together. Truly our fellowship is with the Father, and our fellowship is with one another.

You know as well as I do that there are Christians who are going to heaven miserably. And there are other Christians who are going to heaven with all the joy of God. Jesus says, "Come and dine." You see in the Song of Solomon the kind of fellowship He seeks. Don't be afraid of the Song of Solomon! Yes, it talks about the sex act. The union of the bride and the bridegroom, so beautifully portrayed in the poetry of the Song of Solomon, is a God-given picture of the union of Christ with the Church. It says, "He brought me to the banqueting house, and his banner over me was love" (Song of Sol. 2:4).

Surely this is what the Lord wants us to have. He wants us to have fellowship with Him. He wants us to know that oneness that will help us understand how God feels inside of the Trinity. You know, it is possible. How does He feel? The Father and the Holy Spirit are all together with Himself. They are one in perfect love. God says, "I want you inside of this. Come and dine. Sit down at My table with Me." Learn what it is to fellowship.

Oh, to know the Lord! "I am His and His forever; He has won me by His grace." How true these hymns are.

"Heaven above is softer blue,
Earth around is sweeter green!
Something lives in every hue
Christless eyes have never seen:
Birds with gladder song o'erflow,
Flow'rs with sweeter beauty shine,
Since I know, as now I know,
I am His, and He is mine."

"Yes," says someone, "how do you get that way?"

"Come and dine." It's the Lord who says it to you. "Come and dine." Take time. Turn off the television. Turn off your radio. Sit down with the Word. Some evening, instead of watching a worthless show, spend time with Jesus, the priceless treasure. "Come and dine." Just turn and say, "Lord, to Thine honor and glory, I'm turning that thing off tonight, and I want You to speak to me. Show me, Lord." Brother, He'll come through. He'll do it. You'll learn answers you never knew were there. He's able.

So just let me conclude.

"*Come* and see."

"*Come* and rest."

"*Come* apart and vacation awhile."

"*Come* and dine."

This is the Lord's concern for you. He brings you all the way from a lost condition, through the security of knowing that you're in Christ, into the place where He trains you and teaches you to know that you can't do it all, that He's doing it through you; to the place where He says, "My child, this is your place at the table—next to Me."

Shall we bow in prayer. "O God our Father, we pray Thee that Thou shall do what we can't do. We have spoken words to men's ears. Wilt Thou take these words to our hearts. We ask it in Jesus' name, Amen."